Adobe® Premiere®
Elements 10

CLASSROOM IN A BOOK®

The official training workbook from Adobe Systems

-2:29

www.adobepress.com

Adobe® Premiere® Elements 10 Classroom in a Book®

Adobe Press books are published by Peachpit, a division of Pearson Education located in Berkeley, California. For the latest on Adobe Press books, go to www.adobepress.com. To report errors, please send a note to errata@peachpit.com. For information on getting permission for reprints and excerpts, contact permissions@peachpit.com.

Writer: Jan Ozer
Editor: Connie Jeung-Mills
Development Editor: Stephen Nathans-Kelly
Production Editor: Tracey Croom
Copyeditor: Anne Marie Walker
Keystroker: Megan Tytler
Compositor: Danielle Foster
Indexer: Karin Arrigoni
Cover design: Eddie Yuen
Interior design: Mimi Heft

Printed and bound in the United States of America

ISBN-13:   978-0-321-81101-1

ISBN-10:   0-321-81101-1

9 8 7 6 5 4 3 2 1

WHAT'S ON THE DISC

Here is an overview of the contents of the Classroom in a Book disc.

The *Adobe® Premiere® Elements 10 Classroom in a Book®* disc includes the lesson files that you'll need to complete the exercises in this book, as well as other content to help you learn more about Adobe Premiere Elements 10 and use it with greater efficiency and ease.

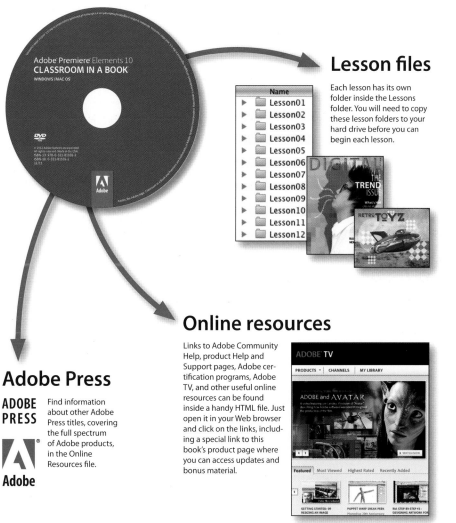

Lesson files

Each lesson has its own folder inside the Lessons folder. You will need to copy these lesson folders to your hard drive before you can begin each lesson.

Online resources

Links to Adobe Community Help, product Help and Support pages, Adobe certification programs, Adobe TV, and other useful online resources can be found inside a handy HTML file. Just open it in your Web browser and click on the links, including a special link to this book's product page where you can access updates and bonus material.

Adobe Press

ADOBE PRESS

Find information about other Adobe Press titles, covering the full spectrum of Adobe products, in the Online Resources file.

Adobe

CONTENTS

GETTING STARTED

Adobe Premiere Elements 10 delivers video-editing tools that balance power and versatility with ease of use. Premiere Elements 10 is ideal for home users, hobbyists, business users, and professional videographers—anyone who wants to produce high-quality movies and DVDs.

If you've used earlier versions of Premiere Elements, you'll find that this Classroom in a Book covers the many new advanced skills and innovative features that Adobe Systems introduces in this version. If you're new to Premiere Elements, you'll learn the fundamental concepts and techniques that will help you master this application.

About Classroom in a Book

Adobe Premiere Elements 10 Classroom in a Book is part of the official training series for Adobe graphics and publishing software developed by Adobe product experts. Most lessons in this book include self-paced projects that give you hands-on experience using Premiere Elements 10.

The *Adobe Premiere Elements 10 Classroom in a Book* includes a DVD attached to the inside back cover. On the DVD, you'll find all the files used for the lessons in this book. As an overview, in the first two lessons, you'll learn your way around Premiere Elements' interface, how to set up a project, and how to customize critical preferences.

In Lesson 3, you'll learn how to capture and otherwise import video into Premiere Elements. Starting with Lesson 4 and continuing through Lesson 13, you'll open projects on the DVD or create your own from contents on the disc, and learn how to convert your raw, captured clips into a polished movie.

Prerequisites

Before you begin working on the lessons in this book, make sure that you and your computer are ready.

Requirements for Your Computer

You'll need about 4.3 gigabytes (GB) of free space on your hard drive for the lesson files and the work files you'll create. For some lessons, you will need to have 2 GB of RAM installed on your computer. Note that the lessons assume that you have installed all templates and associated content available with the DVD version of Premiere Elements 10. If you see a template that's not installed on your computer, you should be able to simply choose another template and continue with the lesson.

Required Skills

The lessons in this *Adobe Premiere Elements 10 Classroom in a Book* assume that you have a working knowledge of your computer and its operating system. This book does not teach the most basic and generic computer skills. If you can answer *yes* to the following questions, you're probably well qualified to start working on the projects in these lessons. You will almost certainly get the most benefit from working on the lessons in the order in which they occur in the book.

- Do you know how to use the Microsoft Windows Start button and the Windows task bar? On the Mac, do you know how to run applications from the Dock or in the Applications folder? In both operating systems, can you open menus and submenus, and choose items from those menus?

- Do you know how to use My Computer, Windows Explorer, Finder, and/or a browser such as Internet Explorer or Safari to find items stored in folders on your computer, or to browse the Internet?

- Are you comfortable using the mouse to move the pointer, select items, drag, and deselect? Have you used context menus, which open when you right-click items in Windows or Control-click items on the Mac if you're working with a single-button mouse?

- When you have two or more open applications, do you know how to switch from one to another? Do you know how to switch to the Windows or Macintosh desktop?

- Do you know how to open, close, and minimize individual windows? Can you move them to different locations on your screen? Can you resize a window by dragging?

- Can you scroll (vertically and horizontally) within a window to see contents that may not be visible in the displayed area?

- Are you familiar with the menus across the top of an application and how to use those menus?

- Have you used dialogs (special windows in the interface that display information), such as the Print dialog? Do you know how to click arrow icons to open a menu within a dialog?

- Can you open, save, and close a file? Are you familiar with word-processing tasks, such as typing, selecting words, backspacing, deleting, copying, pasting, and changing text?

- Do you know how to open and find information in Microsoft Windows or Apple Macintosh Help?

If there are gaps in your mastery of these skills, see the documentation for your operating system. Or, ask a computer-savvy friend or instructor for help.

Installing Premiere Elements 10

Premiere Elements 10 software (sold separately) is intended for installation on a computer running Windows XP, Vista, or Windows 7, or Mac OS 10.5x or later. For system requirements and complete instructions on installing the software, see the Premiere Elements 10 application DVD and documentation. To get the most from the projects in this book, you should install all the templates included with the software. Otherwise, you may notice "missing file" error messages.

Copying the Classroom in a Book Files

The DVD attached to the inside back cover of this book includes a Lesson Files folder containing all the electronic files for the lessons in this book. Follow the instructions to copy the files from the DVD, and then keep all the lesson files on your computer until after you have finished all the lessons.

Copying the Lessons Files from the DVD

1 Insert the *Adobe Premiere Elements 10 Classroom in a Book* DVD into your DVD-ROM drive. Open the DVD in My Computer or Windows Explorer (Windows), or in the Finder (Mac OS).

2 Locate the Lesson Files folder in the Premiere Elements 10 folder on the DVD, and copy it to any convenient folder on your computer. Just remember where you copied it, because you'll be opening the lesson files frequently throughout the book. In the Lesson Files folder, you will find individual folders containing project files needed for the completion of each lesson.

3 When your computer finishes copying the Lesson Files folder (which could take several minutes), remove the DVD from your DVD-ROM drive, and store it in a safe place for future use.

Additional Resources

Adobe Premiere Elements 10 Classroom in a Book is not meant to replace documentation that comes with the program, nor is it designed to be a comprehensive reference for every feature in Premiere Elements 10. Only the commands and options used in the lessons are explained in this book. For comprehensive information and tutorials about program features, please refer to the following resources.

Adobe Community Help: Community Help brings together active Adobe product users, Adobe product team members, authors, and experts to give you the most useful, relevant, and up-to-date information about Adobe products. Whether you're looking for an answer to a problem, have a question about the software, or want to share a useful tip or technique, you'll benefit from Community Help. Search results will show you not only content from Adobe, but also from the community. With Adobe Community Help you can:

- Access up-to-date definitive reference content online and offline
- Find the most relevant content contributed by experts from the Adobe community, on and off Adobe.com
- Comment on, rate, and contribute to content in the Adobe community
- Download Help content directly to your desktop for offline use
- Find related content with dynamic search and navigation tools

To access Community Help: The Community Help application downloads when you first install Premiere Elements 10. To invoke Help, press F1 or choose Help > Premiere Elements Help.

To ensure that you have the latest version of the Community Help application, download it from www.adobe.com/support/chc/index.html.

Adobe content is updated based on community feedback and contributions. You can contribute in several ways: You can add comments to both content and forums—including links to web content, or publish your own content using the Community Publishing AIR app. You'll find more information about how to contribute at www.adobe.com/community/publishing/download.html.

See http://community.adobe.com/help/profile/faq.html for answers to frequently asked questions about Community Help.

Adobe Premiere Elements 10 Help and Support: Point your browser to www.adobe.com/support/premiereelements where you can find and browse Help and Support content on adobe.com.

Adobe TV: At http://tv.adobe.com, you'll find an online video resource for expert instruction and inspiration about Adobe products, including a How To channel to get you started with your product.

Resources for educators: The website www.adobe.com/education includes three free curriculums that use an integrated approach to teaching Adobe software and can be used to prepare for the Adobe Certified Associate exams.

Check out these useful links as well:

Adobe Forums: The website http://forums.adobe.com lets you tap into peer-to-peer discussions, as well as questions and answers on Adobe products.

Adobe Premiere Elements 10 product home page: You can find even more information at www.adobe.com/products/premiereel.

Free trial versions of Adobe Photoshop Elements 10 and Adobe Premiere Elements 10: The trial version of the software is fully functional and offers every feature of the product for you to test-drive (does not include Plus membership). To download your free trial version: http://www.adobe.com/cfusion/tdrc/index.cfm?product=photoshop_elements&loc=en_us

1 THE WORLD OF DIGITAL VIDEO

Lesson overview

This lesson describes how you'll use Adobe Premiere Elements 10 to produce movies and introduces you to the key panels, workspaces, and views within the application. You'll also learn the benefits of subscribing to Adobe Photoshop.com.

In this lesson, you'll learn to do the following:

• Navigate the Adobe Premiere Elements workspaces

• Import and tag media

• Upload and share content with Photoshop.com

This lesson will take approximately 45 minutes.

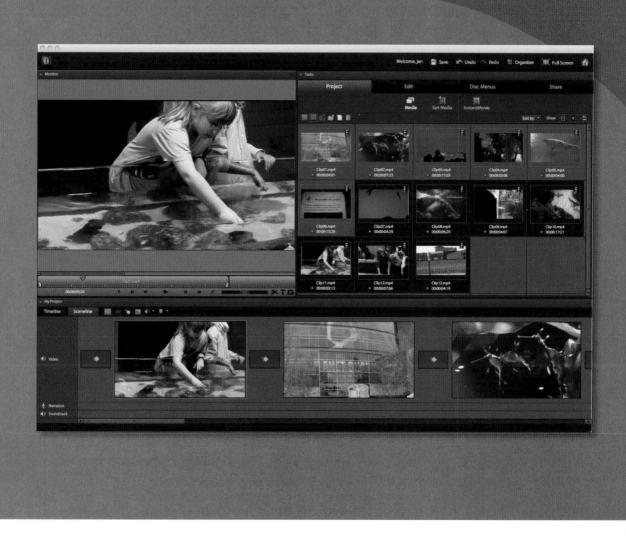

The Adobe Premiere Elements workspace.

How Adobe Premiere Elements Fits into Video Production

Video producers are a diverse group, and each producer uses Adobe Premiere Elements differently. At a high level, however, all producers will use Premiere Elements to import and organize footage (video, stills, and audio)—whether from a camcorder, digital camera, or other source—and then edit the clips into a cohesive movie. If you have Premiere Elements and Adobe Photoshop Elements, you have an extraordinarily flexible and well-featured platform for projects that combine still images and video on the Mac and Windows operating systems.

From a video perspective, such editing will include trimming away unwanted sections of your source clips, correcting exposure, and adjusting color as needed, and then applying transitions and special effects as well as adding titles. On the audio front, perhaps you'll add narration to your productions or a background music track. When your movie is complete, you might create menus for recording to DVD and/or Blu-ray Discs, and then output the movie for sharing with others via disc (such as DVD or Blu-ray), the web, or file-based output.

Premiere Elements facilitates this workflow using a simple three-panel interface with custom workspaces for each of the four production steps: clip acquisition and organization, editing, disc menu creation, and sharing. This chapter introduces you to the Premiere Elements interface and these four workspaces.

You undoubtedly purchased Premiere Elements to start producing movies as soon as possible. Taking a few moments now to read through this overview will not only get you up and running in Premiere Elements more quickly, but it will also help you understand how this book is organized and where to find the content that details the operations you'll be performing in future projects.

The Adobe Premiere Elements Workspace

● **Note:** Sometimes when you run Premiere Elements, you will be asked to log in to Photoshop.com. If you have an account and want to log in, you can do so. Otherwise, click Skip this step to avoid logging in.

When you launch Adobe Premiere Elements, a Welcome screen appears. If you're already running the program, you can make the Welcome screen appear by clicking the Premiere Elements Welcome Stream button on the extreme upper right of the program. From here, you can open the Organizer, start a new project, or open a project. The bottom of the Welcome screen displays the status of your Photoshop.com membership and provides access to your Account Details, your Shared Gallery, and Adobe Premiere Elements Tutorials. After you make some selections the first time you run Premiere Elements, the large center screen will also contain information about tutorials available to Plus members on Photoshop.com.

WELCOME TO
ADOBE® PREMIERE® ELEMENTS 10

ORGANIZE

NEW PROJECT

OPEN PROJECT

You've got Plus, and that means MORE!

With Plus, you can do so much more with your videos and photos.

Your Plus benefits include:
- Automatic online backup
- 20GB of online video and photo storage
- Exclusive access to rich libraries of how-tos, movie themes, effects, and more
- Ongoing deliveries of creative moviemaking extras
- And more

Learn more

Welcome back, Jan!

Your Personal URL : http://janleeozer.photoshop.com

Manage My Adobe ID...

Your Adobe Online Storage :

20.0GB

Used : 474.5MB   Free : 19.5GB

Manage My Backup...

Tips and Tricks...

Benefits of an Adobe ID...

Help and Support...

Note: The screen that you see may be slightly different than this if you haven't run Premiere Elements before, but the major buttons and operations will be identical.

Note that Adobe now includes a complete version of the Elements Organizer on the Mac and Windows platforms. The Organizer is a great place to start many projects. It offers excellent tagging and search tools, the ability to view all your media in one place irrespective of its actual location on your hard drive, and the ability to easily share and archive your collections of video and still images. If you also own Photoshop Elements, you'll share the same Organizer, so you can access all your content from either Premiere Elements or Photoshop Elements, and you can launch a range of activities and workflows from either application from within one common content database.

Let's load some video files to see how starting projects in the Organizer works. Specifically, let's load only the video files from the Lesson04 folder that you copied to your hard drive from the DVD.

1   Start Adobe Premiere Elements and click the Organize button in the Welcome screen. The Organizer opens. If this is the first time you've worked with Adobe Premiere Elements or the Organizer, it will be empty and may ask you to identify folders where your media is located. If you've worked with it previously, it will contain other content that you've used before.

2   In the Organizer, choose File > Get Photos and Videos > From Files and Folders. The Get Photos and Videos from Files and Folders dialog opens.

3   Navigate to your Lesson01 folder.

● **Note:** The Organizer can input video footage directly from all camcorders except for tape-based camcorders, like DV and HDV, and analog camcorders. Footage from these devices must be captured before importing the video into the Organizer. For this reason, if your project involves video from DV, HDV, or analog camcorders that you previously haven't captured to a hard drive, you should start your projects by clicking New Projects in the Welcome screen. (See the section "Setting Up a New Project" in Chapter 2.) Otherwise, if you're working with footage from any camcorder or digital camera that stores video on a hard drive, DVD, SD media, or similar nontape-based storage, you can input that footage directly from the Organizer.

4 Select all video files (those with a .mp4 extension).

5 On the bottom right of the Get Photos and Videos from Files and Folders dialog, click Get Media. The Organizer loads the video into the Browser pane. If this is the first time you've used the Organizer, you may get a status message stating that the only items in the main window are those you just imported. Click OK to close the message; do not click Show All, which displays the entire Catalog.

Working in the Organizer

In the Organizer workspace, the main Work Area is the Browser pane where you can find, sort, and organize your video, audio, photos, and other media files. On the right is the Task pane, which includes four tabs that open the Organize, Fix, Create, and Share panels. You'll learn the operation of all four panels in Chapter 4; for now, here are a couple of highlights.

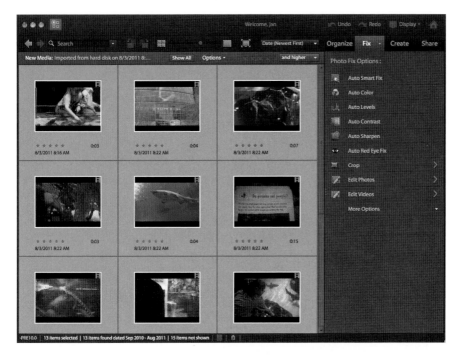

In the Organize panel, shown on the right, you can apply tags to your videos to help organize them or run the Auto Analyzer, which applies Smart Tags to the clips. Smart Tags assist in multiple activities, including creating InstantMovies (Chapter 4) and directing Smart Trimming (Chapter 5) and SmartFix (Chapter 6). To run the Auto Analyzer function, select a clip or clips, right-click, and choose Run Auto-Analyzer. Don't do this now, though; you'll explore this option further in Lesson 4.

In addition, in the Create panel, you can start a number of projects, including InstantMovies and DVDs with menus, as well as a host of photo-related projects. In the Share panel, you can launch Premiere Elements to upload video to YouTube or to a mobile phone. And in the Fix panel, you can send all selected videos to Premiere Elements for editing. Let's do that to start your tour of the Premiere Elements workspace.

1   In the Organizer, click the Fix tab to open the Fix panel.

2   Press Ctrl+A (Windows) or Command+A (Mac OS) to select all videos currently in the Organizer (only those videos that you just imported should be displayed).

3 In the Fix panel, click the down triangle on the top right of the Fix tab, and choose Edit Videos.

4 If this is the first time you've used this function, you'll see the status message shown in the next figure. Click OK to close the message.

5 The New Project panel opens. Type *Lesson01* in the Name field (Premiere Elements will add the necessary extension), and click the Browse button to change the location of the project, if desired.

6 Check the Project Settings in the lower-left corner of the New Project panel. If the Project Settings field shows AVCHD LITE720p30, proceed to step 9. If not, click the Change Settings button to open the Setup screen.

7 In the Change Settings window, in the Available Presets box, click the triangle next to AVCHD, and choose the AVCHD LITE 720p30 preset.

8 Click OK to close the Setup dialog.

9 In the New Project panel, click OK to save the new project file. The newly created project opens. Click Yes if the SmartFix dialog asks if you want to Fix quality problems in clips.

10 In the Premiere Elements menu, choose Window > Show Docking Headers to display the panel headers shown in some of the following screen shots. If you've used Premiere Elements previously, choose Window > Restore Workspace to restore the program to its default configuration. If you want your image to match that in the figure, click the first scene in the Sceneline and move the current-time indicator about 20 frames to the right.

A. Monitor panel. **B.** Tasks panel (The Project workspace is selected. Note that your Project workspace may contain different items. **C.** My Project panel (Sceneline selected). **D.** Current-time indicator.

The Premiere Elements workspace is arranged in three main panels: the Monitor panel, the My Project panel, and the Tasks panel. The following sections provide an overview of these panels and the role they play when you are working on a movie project.

Monitor Panel

The Monitor panel serves multiple purposes. It enables you to edit as well as to view your movie in one convenient place. You can navigate to any position in the movie and preview a section or the entire movie. In this role, the Monitor panel previews the movie that you are building in the My Project panel using the VCR-like controls beneath the playback window. Other chapters will detail the Monitor panel's controls and operation; here you can experiment with the playback controls to get a feel for how to use them.

In other roles, the Monitor panel also offers tools to trim unwanted footage and split clips. You can drag one scene onto another to create picture-in-picture effects and add titles and other text directly in the Monitor panel. The Monitor panel adjusts its appearance for some editing tasks. When creating menus, the Monitor panel switches to become the Disk Layout panel; in title-editing mode, the Monitor panel displays additional tools to create and edit text.

My Project Panel

The My Project panel lets you assemble your media into the desired order and edit clips. This panel has two different views:

- **Sceneline:** In the My Project panel's Sceneline, the initial frame represents each clip. This display makes it easy to arrange clips into a coherent series without regard to clip length. This technique is referred to as *storyboard-style editing*. The Sceneline is useful when you first start editing a movie because it allows you to quickly arrange your media into the desired order; to trim unwanted frames from the beginning and ends of each clip; and to add titles, transitions, and effects.

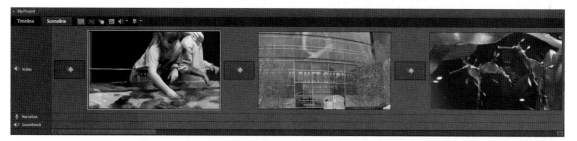

- **Timeline:** In the upper left of the My Project panel, click Timeline to change to the Timeline view; then click the Backslash key to spread the project content over the Timeline. The My Project panel's Timeline presents all movie components in separate horizontal tracks beneath a timescale. Clips earlier in time appear to the left, and clips later in time appear to the right. Clip length on the Timeline represents a clip's duration. The Timeline is useful later in the project and for more advanced editing, because it lets you better visualize content on different tracks, such as picture-in-picture effects and titles or narration and background music.

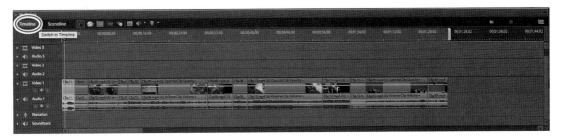

Tasks Panel

The Tasks panel is the central location for adding and organizing media; finding, applying, and adjusting effects and transitions; creating DVD and Blu-ray Disc menus; and sharing your finished projects. It's organized into four main task workspaces: Organize, Edit, Disc Menus, and Share. Within each workspace are all the tools you need to accomplish your tasks.

Project workspace

The Project workspace is divided into three views to view the content included in your project (Media), input media (Get Media), and create an InstantMovie (InstantMovie). If you don't start your projects in the Organizer, you'll typically start by clicking Get Media in the Project workspace to find and load content into the project.

Tip: In older versions of Adobe Premiere Elements, you could open the Elements Organizer by clicking Organizer in the Project workspace. In this version, you can open the Organizer in all workspaces by clicking the Organizer button on the top toolbar.

- **Media:** In this view you can view, sort, and select media you have captured or imported into your project. Media can be presented in List view or Icon view, which you can select by using the buttons at the upper-left corner of Project view.

- **Get Media:** This view shows buttons to access all the different methods for acquiring media for your movie. These include getting videos from the Elements Organizer, a DV Camcorder, HDV Camcorder, DVD Camcorder or PC DVD Drive, a Flip, AVCHD, Cameras and Phones or Removable Drive, and a Webcam; getting photos from a Digital Still Camera, Phones or Removable Drive; and getting videos, photos, and audio from Files and Folders, which you'll use to retrieve files that already exist on your hard drive.

- **InstantMovie:** This view automatically and quickly steps you through the selection and editing portion of movie creation, as well as adding theme-based effects, title, transitions, and audio. If you click InstantMovie, click Cancel on the lower right of the Organize panel to return to that workspace.

Edit workspace

If you were working on a real project, after importing and tagging your media, you'd be ready to edit. Click Edit to enter the Edit workspace, which is divided into five views for accessing effects and transitions, creating movie titles from templates, selecting and applying movie themes, and choosing from available clip art libraries.

- **Effects:** This view shows video and audio effects and presets you can use in your movie. You can search for effects by typing all or part of the name into the search box, browse through all available effects, or filter the view by type and category. You can apply video effects to adjust exposure or color problems, apply perspective or pixelate, or add other special effects. Audio effects help you improve the sound quality, add special effects like delay and reverb, and alter volume or balance.

- **Transitions:** This view shows video and audio transitions you can use in your movie. You can search for transitions by typing all or part of the name into the search box, browse through all available transitions, or filter the view by type and category. Transitions between clips can be as subtle as a cross-dissolve or quite emphatic, such as a page turn or spinning pinwheel.

- **Titles:** This view shows groups of preformatted title templates you can use in your movie. You can browse all available templates or filter the view by categories such as Entertainment, Travel, and Wedding. Title templates include graphic images and placeholder text that you can modify freely, delete from, or add to without affecting the actual templates.

- **Themes:** This view displays movie themes that you can use to instantly and dramatically enhance your movies. Using Themes enables you to create professional-looking movies quickly and easily. Themes come preconfigured with effects, transitions, overlays, title and closing credit sequences, intros, sound effects, and more. You can choose to simply apply all the available options in a theme or select just the options you want.

- **Clip Art:** This view displays clip art libraries that you can drag and drop into your projects. Clip art libraries include Animated Objects, Costumes, Baby-oriented clip art, and the thought bubbles and similar text-oriented clip art shown in the next figure, which were selected by clicking the Filter By list box and choosing Thoughts and Speech Bubbles.

Disc Menus workspace

Use the Disc Menus workspace to add menus to your movies before burning them onto DVDs or Blu-ray Discs, or creating web DVDs. The Disc Menus workspace lets you preview and choose preformatted menu templates you can use for your movie. You can browse the available templates by categories such as Entertainment, Happy Birthday, Kid's Corner, and New Baby.

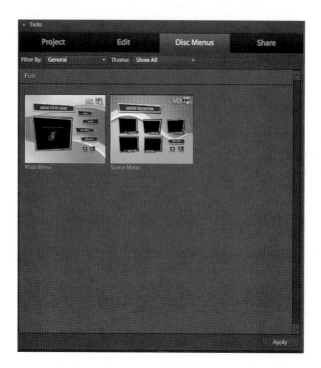

Share workspace

After you've finished editing your movie and you're ready to create a web DVD, burn a disc, or save your movie for viewing online or on a mobile phone, PC, tape, or other device, click Share. The Share workspace shows buttons for accessing all the different methods for exporting and sharing your movie: web DVD, Disc, Online, Computer, Mobile Phones and Players, and Tape.

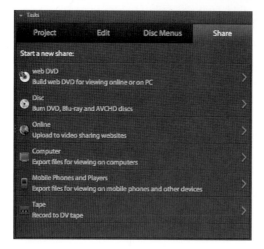

Properties View

Often during editing or when producing disc menus, you'll need to customize effect parameters or menu components after applying or selecting them. Properties view (Window > Properties) lets you view and adjust parameters of items—such as video or audio clips, transitions, effects, or menus—when an item is selected in the Monitor or My Project panel.

Info and History Panels

The Info panel displays information about a selected clip in the My Project panel. Among other things, the Info panel can be helpful in identifying the duration of a clip.

1 To open the Info panel, choose Window > Info. You can then drag the Info panel by its title bar to reposition it on the screen, if necessary.

2 Click to select a clip in Project view or the My Project panel. The Info panel displays the clip's name, type, start and end points, duration, video and audio attributes, the location in the Timeline/Sceneline, and the position of the cursor.

● **Note:** You may have to grab an edge and expand the window to see all the properties.

The History panel (Window > History) keeps a running list of every step you take during a project and adds each action to the bottom of its list. To undo an editing step, click it in the History panel. To undo multiple steps, click the earliest step that you'd like to undo, and Premiere Elements will also undo all editing steps after that point.

These are the most prominent panels and workspaces within Premiere Elements. Now let's take a brief look at Photoshop.com, which is where you'll back up and share your photos and movies.

Working with Photoshop.com

Photoshop.com is an online photo and video hosting, editing, and sharing site. If you're using Premiere Elements in the United States, you can register for a free Basic Membership or opt for the Plus Membership (check www.photoshop.com for pricing). All members can back up images and movies on the site. Basic members are allocated 2 gigabytes (GB) of storage space, and Plus members have access to 20 GB of storage, or about four hours of DVD-quality video, with the option to purchase more online storage.

If you're already a member of Photoshop.com, you can log in from Premiere Elements by clicking Sign In on the toolbar on the upper right. If not, you can click Create New Adobe ID to register for the service.

All members control the content that is uploaded to their Photoshop.com accounts with this Preferences panel, which you access in the Elements Organizer by choosing Edit > Preferences > Backup/Synchronization (Windows) Adobe Premiere Elements 10 > Preferences > Backup/Synchronization (Mac OS).

Photoshop.com Plus members also receive free access to online moviemaking ideas and tutorials. If you have a Plus Membership, Premiere Elements will display these tutorials in the Welcome screen that opens when you first run the program and from time to time on the lower right of the My Project panel.

● **Note:** If you're working with a trial version of Adobe Premiere Elements, you may not see all of these options.

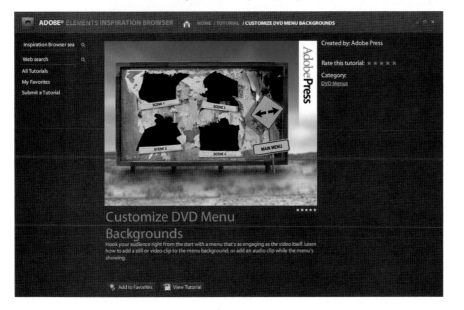

Click the tutorial title to launch the tutorial in the Adobe Elements Inspiration Browser.

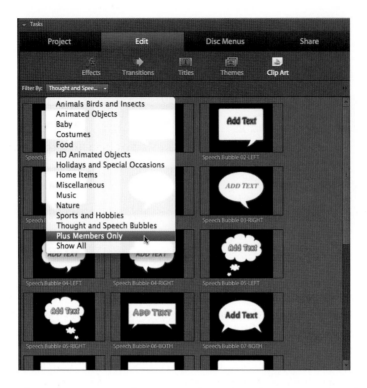

Plus members receive free content from Photoshop.com, such as the titles shown in the previous figure. Note that Adobe Premiere Elements will download these files automatically once they're available and will display them in the Photoshop.com folder.

Review Questions

1 What are the three main panels in Premiere Elements, and what function does each serve?

2 What types of projects should you consider starting from the Organizer, and why?

3 What are the two views of the My Project panel, and what are their respective strengths?

4 What are the three major benefits of Photoshop.com's Plus Membership?

Review Answers

1 The three main panels are the Monitor, Tasks, and My Project panels. You build your movies by adding clips to the My Project panel. The Monitor panel serves multiple roles, allowing you to preview your movies and create titles and other effects. The Tasks panel has four workspaces that allow you to organize your clips, create InstantMovies, and render your movies for sharing with others. It also contains content such as effects, transitions, themes, titles, and disc menus.

2 Any project that doesn't involve capture from tape should start from the Organizer. Starting work in the Organizer provides faster access to tagging and sort tools, and direct access to production activities like creating an InstantMovie or uploading a video to Photoshop.com.

3 Premiere Elements offers two views in the My Project panel: Sceneline and Timeline. The Sceneline shows only the first frame of the clip and is ideal for quickly arranging the order of your clips and performing basic edits. The Timeline displays clips on separate tracks and is superior for advanced edits like picture-in-picture and other overlay effects, and for adding background music or narration to your productions.

4 Plus members receive up to 20 GB of storage space (compared to 2 GB for the Basic Membership), access to tutorials, and additional content when released by Adobe.

2 GETTING READY TO EDIT

Lesson overview

Now that you're familiar with the Adobe Premiere Elements interface, you'll learn how to create a project, set relevant user preferences, and configure the interface to your liking. For those tempted to skip this chapter, understand that although Premiere Elements is a wonderfully flexible and customizable program, once you choose a project setting and start editing, you can't change the setting.

Although you can often work around this issue, in some instances you may have to abandon the initial project and start again using a different setting to achieve the desired results. Invest a little time now to understand how Premiere Elements works with project settings so you can get your project done right the first time.

In this lesson, you'll learn to do the following:

- Create a new project

- Choose the optimal setting for your project

- Set preferences for Auto Save, Scratch Disks, and the user interface

- Customize window sizes and locations in the workspace

- Restore the workspace to its default configuration

This lesson will take approximately one hour.

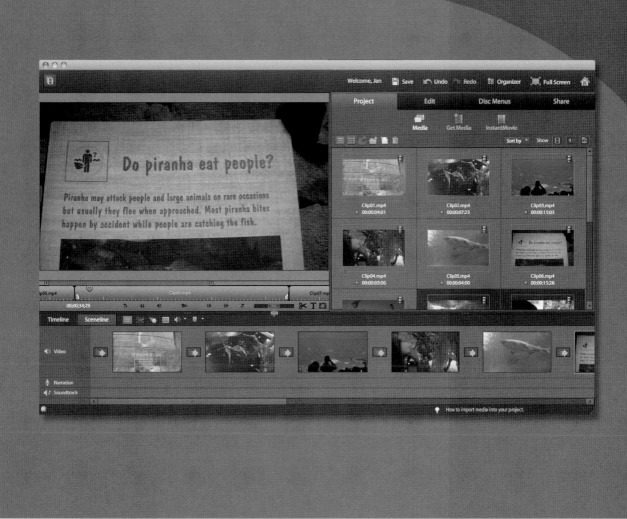

Customizing Premiere Elements' interface
in Storyboard mode.

Setting Up a New Project

Premiere Elements can work with video from any source, from DV camcorders shooting 4:3 or 16:9 (widescreen) standard-definition (SD) video to the latest HD camcorders. For the best results, you should choose a project setting that matches your source footage by following the procedure described here.

After you choose a setting, Premiere Elements automatically uses the same setting for all future projects, which should work well if you use the same source video format for all subsequent projects. Should you change the format, however—for example, from DV to HDV—remember to change your project setting as well.

1 Launch Premiere Elements and click the New Project button in the Welcome screen. If Premiere Elements is already open, choose File > New > Project.

2 Click the Browse button and save the project in the Lesson02 subfolder in the Lesson Files folder, which should have been created when you copied the DVD contents to your hard drive.

Note: For more information on a preset, click the setting, and Premiere Elements will display technical details in the Description field.

3 Check the Project Settings in the lower-left corner of the New Project screen. If the Project Settings match those shown in the figure (or your actual source footage when creating your own projects), proceed to step 4. If not, click the Change Settings button to open the Setup screen.

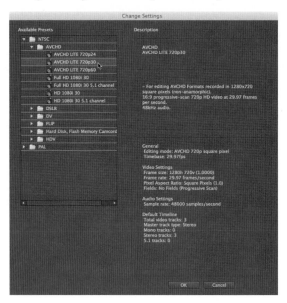

4 For this project, click the AVCHD LITE 720p30 preset in the NTSC > AVCHD folder. For your own projects, click the preset that matches your source footage.

5 After choosing a preset, click OK to close the Setup screen.

6 In the New Project panel, name the project *My Project* and store it in the previously selected Lesson02 folder. Then click OK to save the new project file.

Diagnosing Settings-related Issues

As mentioned, choosing the right preset is critical to a successful editing experience. To help ensure that you choose the right preset, Premiere Elements alerts you with the Mismatched Project Settings Preset dialog when the first video clip that you add to the project doesn't match the preset.

Typically, you should click Yes and change the project settings to match the clip. Exceptions might be when the first clip that you add to the project comes from a source other than the main footage you'll be using for the project. Unless you have a reason to choose otherwise, click Yes when you see the Mismatched Project Settings Preset dialog.

If you've chosen the wrong project setting, the most common problem you'll encounter is differences in the aspect ratio of your video. This is evidenced by black bars across the sides or top and bottom of the video in the Monitor panel, which is a display technique called *letterboxing*. Premiere Elements will letterbox a 16:9 video displayed in a 4:3 window, producing the black bars on the top and bottom of the video in the Monitor panel, as shown in the next figure.

● **Note:** In some projects, particularly those that include both 16:9 and 4:3 footage, letterboxing is inevitable, at least when you initially insert the file into the My Project panel. Note that you can use Motion controls to eliminate the letterboxing as detailed in "Reframing a Clip Using Motion Controls" in Lesson 6.

● **Note:** This is a descriptive section— don't try to follow along in Premiere Elements; just learn through the screens shown in the book.

1 Letterboxing typically means a mismatch between your project settings and source video. To view the current project setting, choose Edit > Project Settings > General. As you can see on the Project Settings screen for this project (shown on the next page), letterboxing occurs because the Editing Mode is QuickTime DV NTSC (rather than AVCHD) and the Pixel Aspect Ratio is D1/DV NTSC (0.9091), which is 4:3 video.

2 Because you're editing HD video footage, your project Pixel Aspect Ratio should be Square Pixel (1.0). Both fields are grayed out and inactive, indicating that you can't change their values. Click OK to close the Project Settings screen.

In addition to these two issues, the Project Settings have the wrong timebase, which should be 30, not 29.97. Also, the source video on the DVD is progressive, not interlaced, so the Fields box should display No Fields (Progressive Scan). These latter two discrepancies could cause problems down the line, but the most obvious issue is the letterboxing, which is caused by the difference between the 4:3 preset and 16:9 source footage.

3 To view aspect ratio-related information about clips in the My Project panel, choose Window > Info. If you don't have any clips in the My Project panel, drag one down from the Media view into the Sceneline or Timeline in the My Project panel.

4 Click any clip in the Timeline or Sceneline. In the Video description line in the Info panel, you can see that the video has a frame rate of 30 frames per second (fps) and a resolution of 1280x720, which is widescreen 16:9, with a pixel aspect ratio of (1.0). Note that you may have to make the Info dialog on the right wider to see the complete description.

To display the 16:9 video in a 4:3 project, Premiere Elements inserts letterboxes on the top and bottom of the 16:9 video, as you can see in the preceding figure. You can eliminate the letterboxes using the controls discussed in "Reframing a Clip with Motion Controls" in Lesson 6, which is a good solution when including one 4:3 clip in a 16:9 movie. If, however, all your clips are 4:3, you should restart the project using a 4:3 setting.

Choosing the Correct Setting

Premiere Elements offers dozens of different presets for ingesting source footage. By far, the easiest way to choose the right preset is to make sure that the first clip you import into your new project is from your primary camcorder. If so, and there's a mismatch between your preset and source footage, Premiere Elements will open the Mismatched Project Settings Preset dialog and ask if you want to change the preset to match your clips. Click Yes, and you should be set.

If you want to get it right the first time, here are the factors that you should consider when choosing a preset:

- **Source:** Consider the source. Premiere Elements has presets for AVCHD, DV, Flip, Hard disk and Flash memory camcorders, HDV camcorders, and video shot with HD video-capable DSLR camcorders, such as the Canon EOS family. So the first step is to find the presets that relate to your source.

- **Resolution:** Consider the resolution of the video next, which is typically either 1080i or 1080p (1920 horizontal, 1080 vertical); 720i or 720p (1280h, 720v); 720h, 480v resolution for DV; and sometimes 480p, which is 640h, 480v resolution. Find a preset that matches your source.

Complicating this resolution selection, however, is the pixel aspect ratio issue, which affects AVCHD and HDV camcorders, as well as DV. Specifically, all HDV camcorders that shoot in 1080i or 1080p actually capture video at 1440x1080 resolution and then stretch the video to 1920x1080 during display. That's why the HDV 1080i 30 HDV preset shows a frame size of 1440x1080 and a pixel aspect ratio of 1.333. This tells Premiere Elements to stretch the 1440 horizontal resolution by 1.333 to display it correctly on the Timeline. Although this might be confusing, this distinction never causes any problems, because all HDV 1080 video is stored in this manner.

On the other hand, when shooting 1080i or 1080p video, all AVCHD camcorders display the video at 1920x1080 resolution. However, like HDV, "HD" AVCHD video is stored by the camcorder at a resolution of 1440x1080, and each horizontal pixel must be stretched by a factor of 1.33 during display to achieve full resolution. In contrast, "Full HD" AVCHD video is captured at 1920x1080 resolution, so no stretching is required to produce the full 1920x1080 display. If you're shooting in AVCHD, check the specs of your camcorder to determine if you're shooting in Full HD or just HD.

Finally, all DV video is shot at 720x480 resolution, but 4:3 video has a pixel aspect ratio of .9091, which means that the pixels are shrunk about 10 percent during display, achieving the 4:3 aspect ratio. Widescreen DV video has a pixel aspect ratio of 1.2121, so the video is stretched during display, achieving the 16:9 aspect ratio. This is seldom confusing, however, because you'll probably know whether you shot in 4:3 or widescreen, and you can choose the preset accordingly.

- **Progressive or interlaced:** After you identify the right resolution and aspect ratio, you must choose whether the video is interlaced or progressive. Technically, interlaced video presents each frame in two fields— one consisting of the odd lines and the other of the even lines. Progressive video displays all lines simultaneously. TV is almost always interlaced, whereas film-based movies are always progressive. Most modern camcorders shoot in both modes (or at least simulate both modes effectively); just check the settings on your camcorder to see if you shot in progressive or interlaced, and then choose your preset accordingly.

- **Frames per second:** Most camcorders can shoot at multiple speeds, including 23.976 fps, 24 fps, 29.97 fps, 30 fps, 59.94 fps, and 60 fps. Again, check the settings on your camcorder to see which frame rate you used, and then choose your preset accordingly.

Once you understand and incorporate all these factors into your preset selection, you should be able to choose the right preset, if it's available. What do you do if you can't find a preset that matches the precise specs that you shot in? Let Premiere Elements decide. Choose the closest preset that you can find, drag in a clip, and click Yes if Premiere Elements opens the Mismatched Project Settings Preset dialog.

Working with Project Preferences

For the most part, once you have the right project setting selected, you can jump in and begin editing with Premiere Elements. However, at some point you may want to adjust several program preferences that impact your editing experience. Here are the preferences that will prove relevant to most video editors.

1 To open the General Preferences panel, choose Edit > Preferences > General (Windows) or Adobe Premiere Elements 10 > Preferences > General (Mac OS). Multiple preferences are in this panel; most important are the Video and Audio Transition Default Durations and the Still Image Default Duration. The latter controls the duration of all still images added to your project.

● **Note:** Adjusting these default durations will impact only edits made after the adjustment. For example, if you change the Still Image Default Duration to 120 frames, Premiere Elements will assign this duration to all still images added to the project thereafter but won't change the duration of still images already inserted into the project.

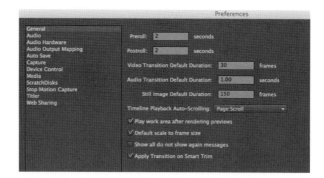

2 Click Auto Save to view the Auto Save preferences.

3 Click ScratchDisks to view the ScratchDisks preferences. These preferences identify the folders used to store audio and video clips that Premiere Elements creates while producing your project. This includes clips captured from your camcorder, video and audio previews, and media encoded for recording onto DVD or Blu-ray Disc. By default, Premiere Elements stores this content in the same folder as the project file. If you run short of disk space, you can change the location of the scratch disk by clicking the Browse button next to each category of content and choosing a different location on a separate disk. Close the Preferences dialog.

The preceding preferences are the most critical to consider before starting your first project. With these settings configured, let's explore other options for customizing your workspace.

Better Saved than Sorry

With Auto Save enabled, Premiere Elements automatically saves a copy of your project at the specified duration, which you can customize. You can also change the number of separate projects that Premiere Elements saves.

Premiere Elements saves all Auto Save files in a separate subfolder titled Premiere Elements Auto-Save, which is located in the folder containing your current project file.

It's good practice to manually save your project periodically during editing to preserve your work in the event of a power outage or other random crash. Should a crash occur, you may be able to recover some of the editing that you've done subsequent to your last manual save by loading the most recent project automatically saved by Premiere Elements.

You load these projects just like any other project: Click File > Open Project, navigate to the Premiere Elements Auto-Save folder, and choose the newest project file.

Customizing the Workspace

Premiere Elements uses a docking system to fit all the panels into the available space of the application window. However, panels can be moved and resized so that you can create a workspace that best fits your needs.

With Premiere Elements open, notice that the Monitor panel, the Tasks panel, and the My Project panel are separated by solid vertical and horizontal dividing lines. These dividers can be quickly repositioned to give you more space to work in one of the panels when you need it.

1   To increase the height of the My Project panel, hover your pointer over the dividing line between the My Project and Monitor panels until it converts to a two-headed cursor, and then drag it up toward the Monitor panel.

You can use a similar technique to expand the size of the Monitor panel by dragging it to the right or expand the Tasks panel by dragging it to the left.

2 To reset the panels to their default layout, choose Window > Restore Workspace. Notice how everything snaps back to its original position. Consider restoring your workspace if you find that your screen becomes cluttered.

To save space on your screen, the panel docking headers, which contain the title and sometimes panel menu and Close buttons, are hidden by default in Premiere Elements.

3 To show the docking headers, choose Window > Show Docking Headers. To hide them again, choose Window > Hide Docking Headers.

Although the default workspace layout docks every panel into a specific position, you may find it helpful from time to time to have a more flexible environment. To do this, you can undock, or float, your panels.

● **Note:** The Tasks panel is the only panel that cannot be undocked.

4 If the docking headers are not currently visible, choose Window > Show Docking Headers. Then click the docking header of the My Project panel and drag it a short distance in any direction. As you drag the header, the panel becomes translucent. When you release the pointer, the My Project panel becomes a floating window, allowing the Monitor panel and the Tasks panel to expand toward the bottom of the main window.

▶ **Tip:** When you work with multiple monitors, you can choose to display the application window on the main monitor and place floating windows on the second monitor.

5 Close the My Project panel by clicking its red Close button (🔴) in the upper-left corner.

6 Reopen the panel by choosing Window > My Project. Notice that the panel opens where you previously placed it. The reason is that Premiere Elements remembers the locations of the panels and retains them as part of the customized workspace.

7 Choose Window > Restore Workspace to return to the default workspace layout.

Review Questions

1 What's the most important factor to consider when choosing a project setting?

2 Why is it so important to choose the right setting at the start of the project?

3 In most instances, what's the right answer when Premiere Elements displays the Mismatched Project Settings Preset dialog?

4 What is letterboxing, and what's a common cause for having letterboxes appear in your project?

5 What is Auto Save, and where do you adjust the Auto Save defaults in Premiere Elements?

6 What command do you use to restore your workspace to the default panel configuration?

Review Answers

1 Choose a setting that matches the primary video that you will use in the project. For example, if you're shooting in widescreen DV, you should use a Widescreen DV project setting.

2 It's critical to choose the right setting when starting a project because, unlike most Premiere Elements configuration items, you can't change the Project Setting after you create the project. In some instances, you may have to start the project over using the correct setting to produce optimal results.

3 In most instances, the correct answer is Yes.

4 Letterboxing is a display technique characterized by black bars on the sides or on the top and bottom of video in the Monitor panel. One of the most common causes of letterboxing is a discrepancy between the display aspect ratio of the project setting and the display aspect ratio of a video file imported into the project. For example, if you import 4:3 video into a 16:9 project, Premiere Elements will display letterboxes on both sides of the video in the Monitor panel.

5 The Auto Save function in Premiere Elements automatically saves a copy of the project file at specified intervals, guarding against loss of work due to power outages or other random crashes. You can adjust the Auto Save defaults in the Preferences panel by choosing Edit > Preferences (Windows) or Adobe Premiere Elements 10 > Preferences (Mac OS).

6 Choose Window > Restore Workspace.

3

VIDEO CAPTURE AND IMPORT

Lesson overview

This lesson describes how to capture and import video from your camcorder and other devices for editing in Adobe Premiere Elements, and introduces the following key concepts:

* Connecting a camcorder to your PC

* Capturing video from a DV/HDV camcorder

* Using the Video Importer to import video from a Flip, AVCHD, or DVD camcorder; digital still camera; DVD; smart phone; or other similar device

* Importing audio, video, or still images from your hard drive into a Premiere Elements project

 This lesson will take approximately one hour.

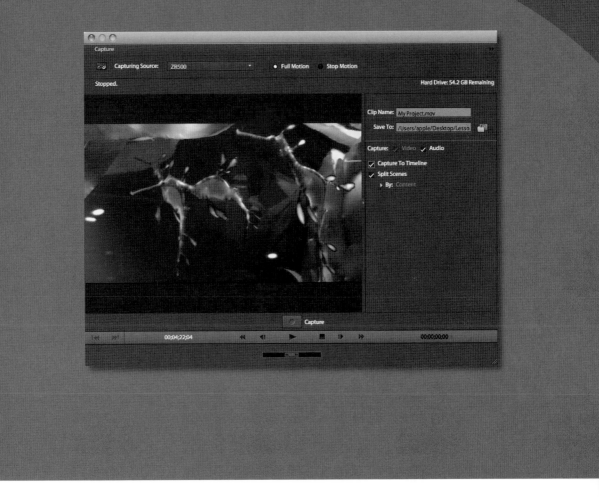

Capturing a weedy sea dragon video
from your DV camera.

Capturing Video with Premiere Elements

When videographers and video enthusiasts started editing video on computers, the typical source was an analog camcorder. Today, although some Premiere Elements users still shoot analog video, most will start with DV or HDV source footage, AVCHD, video shot with a digital still camera or digital Single Lens Reflex (DSLR) camera, or even video imported from a previously created DVD.

Whatever the source, Premiere Elements includes all the tools necessary to capture or import your footage so you can begin producing movies. Although the specific technique will vary depending on the source, Premiere Elements guides your efforts with device-specific interfaces. All you have to do is connect the device to your computer as described in this lesson and choose the appropriate icon from Get Media view in the Organize workspace.

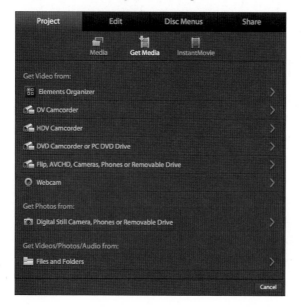

Premiere Elements has two basic interfaces for capturing or importing video. After a quick overview of these interfaces, this lesson will detail how to capture video from a tape-based camcorder and then explain how to import content from an AVCHD camcorder or any other device that stores video on a hard drive, on Compact Flash media (such as an SD card), or on optical media. All the concepts in this section and the specific Premiere Elements features that support them are described in more detail in the Premiere Elements User Guide.

● **Note:** Premiere Elements lets you add video, audio, graphics, and still images to your project from numerous sources. In addition to capturing footage, you can import image, video, and audio files stored on your computer's hard drive, card readers, mobile phones, DVDs, Blu-ray Discs, CDs, digital cameras, other devices, or the Internet.

Capture Interfaces

When you shoot video, it's stored locally on your camcorder, whether on tape, SD media, a hard drive, or even an optical disc like a DVD. Before you can edit your movie in Premiere Elements, you must transfer these clips to a local hard drive. In addition to capturing or importing video from a device, you may have existing content on your hard drive to import into a project.

Tape and Live Capture vs. Clip-based Import

Premiere Elements provides three interfaces for accomplishing captures and imports. If you're capturing video footage from a tape-based camcorder, such as a DV or HDV model, or live from a webcam, you'll use the Capture panel.

If you're importing file-based clips stored within the camera on a hard drive, flash media, or optical media, you'll use the Video Importer. You can also use this interface when importing clips from an SD card that you've removed from a camcorder and plugged into a USB adapter. Again, to open the appropriate interface, just connect your device and click the appropriate icon in Get Media view in the Organize workspace; Premiere Elements will do the rest.

If the audio, video, or still image files are already on your computer's hard drive, click the PC Files and Folders icon in Get Media view in the Organize workspace, navigate to the files, and select them as you normally would. Details concerning this procedure are at the end of this lesson.

Capturing Tape-based or Live Video

If you're capturing from a DV or HDV camcorder, or a webcam, you'll use the Capture panel, which you access by choosing Project > Get Media and then selecting the source that you'll be capturing from. This lesson will discuss some preliminary concepts relating to these devices and then detail the procedure. (For information on importing video from an AVCHD camcorder, see the "Using the Video Importer" section later in this chapter.)

Connecting Your Device

The simplest way to capture DV or HDV video is to connect the camcorder to a computer via an IEEE 1394 port. Premiere Elements supports a wide range of DV devices and capture cards, making it easy to capture DV source files.

Some DV and HDV camcorders also have USB 2.0 ports. USB 2.0 is a high-speed transfer protocol similar to IEEE 1394. When present on a DV/HDV camcorder, the USB 2.0 connector is typically used for transferring to the computer only digital still images rather than tape-based video shot by the camcorder. When both connectors are present, use the IEEE 1394 connector for video capture.

Note: Although it's extremely rare, sometimes when connecting your computer to your camcorder via an IEEE 1394 connector, an electrical charge from the computer can damage the camcorder. To minimize this risk, always turn off both devices before capture, connect the IEEE 1394 cable, turn on your computer, and then turn on the camcorder.

System Setup

Before you attempt to transfer video from a DV/HDV camcorder, make sure your system is set up properly for working with digital video. The following general guidelines will help to ensure that you have a DV-capable system:

- **IEEE 1394 port:** Make sure your computer has an IEEE 1394 port. Most currently manufactured computers include onboard IEEE 1394 cards.

- **High data transfer rate:** Make sure your hard drive is fast enough to capture and play back digital video. The speed at which digital video files transfer information—the data transfer rate (often shortened to data rate)—is 3.6 megabytes per second (MB/sec). The sustained (not peak) data transfer rate of your hard drive should meet or exceed this rate. To confirm the data transfer rate of your hard drive, see your computer or hard drive documentation.

- **Extra storage:** Consider using a secondary hard drive for extra capacity during capture and production, and to enhance capture performance. In general, most internal hard drives should be sufficiently fast for capture and editing. However, external drives that connect via USB 2.0 and IEEE 1394, although excellent for data backup chores, may be too slow for video capture. If you're looking for an external drive for video production, a newer technology called eSATA offers the best mix of performance and affordability, but you may have to purchase an internal eSATA adapter for your computer or notebook.

- **Sufficient hard drive space:** Make sure you have sufficient disk space for the captured footage. Five minutes of digital video consumes about 1 GB of hard drive space. The Capture panel in Premiere Elements indicates the remaining space on your hard drive. Be certain beforehand that you will have sufficient space for the intended length of video capture. Also, some capture cards have size limits on digital video files ranging from 2 GB and higher. See your capture card documentation for information on file size limitations.

- **Defragment:** Make sure you periodically defragment your hard drive. Writing to a fragmented disk can cause disruptions in your hard drive's transfer speed, causing you to lose or drop frames as you capture. You can use the defragmentation utility included with Windows or purchase a third-party utility.

- **Updates:** The state of high-end video hardware changes rapidly; consult the manufacturer of your video capture card for suggestions about appropriate video storage hardware.

Capture Video

How to connect your DV camcorder to your computer

* DV = i.LINK = FireWire = IEEE1394a = 1394

Most DV/HDV camcorders have a 4-pin IEEE 1394 connector, whereas most computers have a larger, 6-pin connector. Note, however, that some computers—particularly notebooks—may also have a 4-pin IEEE 1394 connector. When purchasing an IEEE 1394 cable, make sure it has the appropriate connectors.

Note that most recent Macintosh computers have 9-pin IEEE 1394b 800 connectors rather than 4- or 6-pin IEEE 1394a 400 connectors. To connect your camcorder to these Macs, you'll need an IEEE 1394b–to-IEEE 1394a adapter, which typically costs less than $15 or so.

If you're capturing from a webcam or WDM Device (Windows)/Webcam (Mac OS), Premiere Elements will capture the video from the USB 2.0 connector used to connect the device to your computer.

Capture Options

When you capture video from a tape or live source, you have multiple capture options, including whether to capture audio and video, capture to the Timeline, and split scenes. Let's briefly discuss each option before working through the capture process.

Capturing video or audio only

By default, Premiere Elements captures audio and video when capturing a clip. You can change this default in the Capture Settings dialog that appears in the Capture panel, which opens after you select your video source. In the top line of the dialog, Video and Audio are selected by default. To capture only audio, deselect the Video check box. To capture only video, deselect the Audio check box.

Note that you can easily remove either the audio or video portion of the captured clip during editing. Unless you're absolutely certain that you won't use either the audio or the video, capture both and remove the undesired media during editing.

Capturing to the Timeline

The Capture to Timeline option automatically inserts all captured clips into the My Project panel. By default, this option is selected. If you'd prefer to manually drag all clips to the My Project panel, deselect this option.

Capturing video clips with Scene Detect

During capture, Premiere Elements can split the captured video into scenes, which makes it much easier to find and edit the desired content. Premiere Elements can use one of two scene-detection techniques to detect scenes: Timecode-based and Content-based.

About Timecode

When capturing video, it's important to understand the basics about timecode. Timecode numbers represent the location of a frame in a video clip. Many camcorders record timecode as part of the video signal. The timecode format is based on the number of frames per second (fps) that the camcorder records and the number of frames per second that the video displays upon playback. Video has a standard frame rate that is either 29.97 fps for NTSC video (the North American and Japanese TV standard) or 25 fps for PAL video (the European TV standard). Timecode describes a frame's location in the format of hours;minutes;seconds;frames. For example, 01;20;15;10 specifies that the displayed frame is located 1 hour, 20 minutes, 15 seconds, and 10 frames into the scene.

—From Premiere Elements Help

Timecode-based scene detection is available only when capturing DV source video. As the name suggests, this technique uses timecodes in the video to break the capture clips into scenes. Specifically, when you record DV, your camcorder automatically records a time/date stamp when you press Stop or Record. During capture, Premiere Elements creates a new scene each time it detects a new time/date stamp and creates a separate video file on your hard drive for each scene.

Content-based scene detection, which is your only option for HDV or webcam videos, analyzes the content after capture to identify scene changes. For example, if you shot one scene indoors and the next outdoors, Premiere Elements would analyze the video frames and detect the new scene.

When detecting scenes using Content-based scene detection, Premiere Elements stores only one video file on your hard drive and designates the scenes in the Organize and Edit workspaces. After capture, while scanning the captured video for scene changes, Premiere Elements displays a status panel describing the operation and apprising you of its progress.

During capture, Premiere Elements defaults to Timecode-based scene detection for DV source video and defaults to Content-based scene detection for HDV and webcam-based videos. I suggest leaving Scene Detect enabled during video capture and using these defaults. To change these defaults in the Capture panel (which you'll learn how to open shortly), do the following:

1   To disable Scene Detect entirely, deselect the Split Scenes check box in the Capture settings on the right of the Capture panel.

2   If you're capturing DV, you can opt for either the Timecode-based or Content-based scene detection. In most instances, the former will be faster and more accurate. To change from Timecode-based to Content-based scene detection, select the Split Scenes check box, click the By: triangle if necessary to view both options, and click the Content radio button.

Capturing clips with device control

When capturing clips, device control refers to the ability to control the operation of a connected video deck or camcorder using controls within the Premiere Elements interface rather than using the controls on the connected device. This mode of operation is more convenient because Premiere Elements offers controls like Next Scene or Shuttle that may not be available on your camcorder's controls.

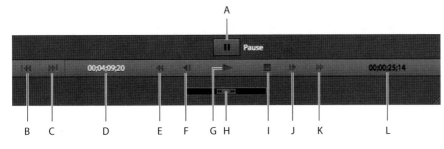

Capture panel controls:
A. Capture/Pause
toggle.
B. Previous Scene.
C. Next Scene.
D. Current Position—
Timecode Display.
E. Rewind.
F. Step Back (Left).
G. Play/Pause.
H. Shuttle.
I. Stop.
J. Step Forward (right).
K. Fast-Forward.
L. Capture Duration
(active only during
capture).

You probably know most of these controls because they're similar to your camcorder or VCR. You may not be familiar with the Shuttle control, which you can drag with your pointer to the left or right to rewind or fast-forward the video. This control is position-sensitive; the farther you drag the shuttle widget from the center, the faster the tape fast-forwards or rewinds. The Previous Scene and Next Scene controls use Timecode-based scene detection to advance backwards or forwards to the previous or next scenes.

Premiere Elements should be able to establish device control with all DV and HDV camcorders, but it's not available when capturing from webcams, WDM Device (Windows)/Webcam (MacOS), or analog camcorders. You can still capture video from these sources without device control, but the capture procedure is slightly different. Procedures for capturing with and without device control are detailed in the following section.

Capturing with the Capture Panel

With the preceding information in this lesson as a prologue, let's look at the process for capturing video via the Premiere Elements Capture panel.

1 Connect the DV camcorder to your computer via an IEEE 1394 cable.

2 Turn on the camera and set it to the playback mode, which may be labeled VTR, VCR, or Play.

3 Launch Premiere Elements. Click New Project in the Welcome screen, and choose a project name and the appropriate preset.

4 In the Organize workspace, click Get Media.

5 In Get Media view, select DV Camcorder (![icon]) to follow along with this procedure. Selecting HDV Camcorder (![icon]), or Webcam, or WDM Device (Windows)/Webcam (MacOS) (![icon]) will also open the Capture panel, although some settings will be different from this example.

The Capture panel appears. Note that if you're capturing from videotape, your preview screen will be black until you actually start to play the video.

● **Note:** This exercise assumes that a DV camera has been successfully connected to your computer and that you have footage available to capture. If this is not the case, you can still open the Capture panel to review the interface; however, you will not be able to access all the controls.

Note: If your DV camera is connected but not turned on, your Capture panel will display Capture Device Offline in the status area. Although it is preferable to turn on your camera before launching Premiere Elements, in most cases turning on your camera at any point will bring it online.

Note: When capturing DV and webcam footage, you will see video in the Preview area of the Capture panel. When capturing HDV, you won't see any video in the Preview area and will have to watch the LCD screen on your camcorder to determine when to stop capture.

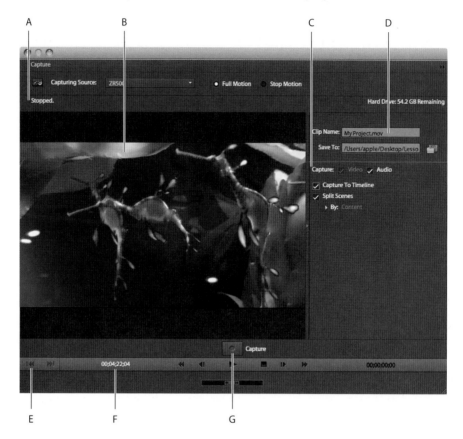

A. Status area—Displays status information about your camera. **B.** Preview area—Displays your current video as played through your camera. **C.** Capture settings—Enables you to change the capture settings. **D.** Clip Name—By default, Premiere Elements uses the project name to name the AVI or MOV movie clips. **E.** Device controls—Contains buttons used to directly control your camera. **F.** Current position—Timecode display. Shows you the current frame of your video, measured in the format of hours; minutes; seconds; frames. **G.** Capture/Pause button.

6   In the upper-right area of the Capture panel, type the desired Clip Name and Save To location for the captured files. Note that Premiere Elements defaults to the project name for Clip Name and uses the folder where you stored your project file for the default Save To location. If desired, change any of the default Capture settings.

7   At the bottom of the Capture panel, use the navigation controls to navigate to the first scene you'd like to capture.

8   Click the Capture button (▣). Premiere Elements automatically starts playing video on the DV camcorder, captures each scene as an individual movie clip, and adds it to your project.

9   After you click the Capture button, the button becomes the Pause button (▮▮). To stop capturing video, either click the Pause button or press the Esc key on your keyboard. If enabled, the Auto Analyze window will appear as Premiere Elements analyzes the clip and then close. Any clips you have already captured will remain in your project.

10 After you've completed capturing your video, close the Capture panel. Your captured clips appear in the Organize workspace in both the Media and Project views. If you enabled Capture to Timeline, Premiere Elements will also place each clip into your Sceneline in sequential order.

Using the Video Importer

As mentioned at the start of this lesson, you will use Premiere Elements' Video Importer to import video clips from Flip, AVCHD, and DVD-based camcorders, as well as smart phones with video cameras. You'll also use Video Importer to import videos from non-copy protected DVDs and to import photos from digital still cameras and phones. In essence, if the video is stored on a hard drive, SD card, optical disc, or other storage media other than tape, you'll import it with the Video Importer.

In this exercise you'll use the Video Importer to import video from an AVCHD camcorder. If you don't have an AVCHD camcorder, you can follow along using video captured on a digital still camera, DVD camcorder, or mobile phone, or even a nonencrypted DVD, such as one that you've previously produced with Premiere Elements. Note that Premiere Elements will not import video from DVDs that are encrypted, such as most Hollywood DVD titles.

● **Note:** When capturing without device control, use the camcorder's playback controls to navigate to a position about 20 seconds before the first scene you want to capture. Click Play, and about 10 seconds before the actual scene appears, click the Capture button (▣). Premiere Elements will start capturing the video. Capture the desired scenes, and about 10 seconds after the last target frame, click the Pause button (▮▮) to stop capture.

● **Note:** If you receive the error message "Recorder Error — frames are dropped during capture," or if you're having problems with the device control, it's likely that your hard drive is not keeping up with the transfer of video. Make sure you're capturing your video to the fastest hard drive available, for example, an external IEEE 1394 drive rather than a hard drive inside a laptop computer.

Debugging Device Control Issues

As mentioned, Premiere Elements should be able to establish device control with all DV and HDV camcorders. If you see the error message "No DV camera detected" or "No HDV camera detected," Premiere Elements can't detect your camcorder. In this case, you won't be able to establish device control and may not be able to capture video. Here are some steps you can take to attempt to remedy this situation.

1   Exit Premiere Elements and make sure your camcorder is turned on and running (and hasn't timed out due to inactivity) in VCR, Play, or other similar mode. Also, check to see that your IEEE 1394 cable is firmly connected to both the camcorder's and computer's IEEE 1394 ports. Then run Premiere Elements again and see if the program detects the camcorder.

2   If not, check your Project Settings and make sure they match your camcorder (DV project if DV camcorder; HDV project if HDV camcorder).

3   If you're still experiencing capture issues, you may have a configuration problem within Premiere Elements. In the upper-right corner of the Capture panel, click the two triangles to open the Capture panel menu and choose Capture Settings, which opens the Project Settings dialog to the Capture Format.

4   In this dialog, choose the correct capture device, either DV or HDV. Note that the Mac OS dialog will list HDV/DV/QuickTime (QTKit) in that order. Close the Project Settings dialog, and then close and reopen the Capture panel. If Premiere Elements still doesn't detect your camcorder, try step 5.

5   In the Capture panel menu, choose Device Control, which opens the Preferences dialog with the Device Control view visible.

6 In this dialog, make sure that DV/HDV is selected (note that the Mac OS dialog will have only two options: None and DV/HDV Device Control). Close the Preferences panel, and then close and reopen the Capture panel. If Premiere Elements still doesn't detect your camcorder, try step 7.

7 Most HDV camcorders can also record and play DV video. However, if you're capturing DV video and your camcorder is set to record HDV, Premiere Elements may detect an HDV camcorder rather than DV (or vice versa). For example, if you shot HDV in your last shoot but were capturing DV video from a previous shoot, Premiere Elements may detect an HDV camcorder rather than a DV camcorder. In this situation, set the camcorder to record DV video, and once you return to VCR or Play mode, play a few seconds of DV video, which may enable Premiere Elements to detect the DV camcorder.

● **Note:** Some AVCHD camcorders require that you set the camcorder to PC mode before connecting the USB 2.0 cable, others the reverse. Generally, when working with a camcorder that writes to removable SD cards or other Compact Flash media, it's easiest to remove the media and use an appropriate card reader to transfer the clips. Please check the documentation that came with your camcorder for additional details.

1 Connect your AVCHD camcorder (or SD card recorded therein) to your computer via the USB 2.0 port.

2 If you're capturing from a camcorder, turn on the camcorder and set it to PC mode, or whichever mode is used to transfer video from camcorder to computer.

3 Launch Premiere Elements. Click New Project in the Welcome screen, and choose a project name and the appropriate preset.

4 In the Organize workspace, click Get Media.

5 In Get Media view, select Flip, AVCHD, Cameras, Phones or Removable Drive (⊞) to follow along with this procedure. Selecting DVD Camcorder or PC DVD Drive (⊞), or Digital Still Camera, Phones or Removable Drive (⊡) will also open the Video Importer, although some settings will be different from this example.

The Video Importer opens (*see figure on next page*).

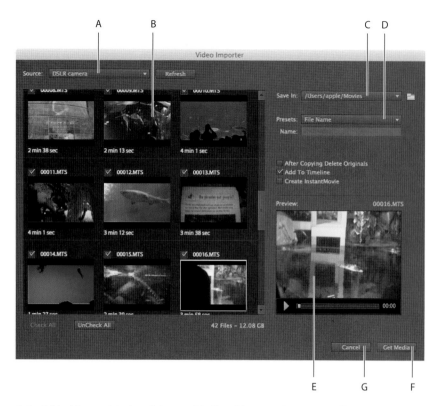

A. Available drives and devices. **B.** Importable files. **C.** Location for imported files. **D.** Naming convention. **E.** Preview window. **F.** Cancel button. **G.** Get Media button.

6   Under Source, choose the drive or device from the drop-down list.

Once you choose the drive or device, Premiere Elements will populate the Video Importer with thumbnails of all available video and still image files.

7   To preview a video file, double-click it, and Premiere Elements will load it in the preview window on the lower right. Click the Play/Pause button to play the file.

8   To specify a location for the saved files, do one of the following:

- To save files to the default location—which is the location where you previously stored files captured by the Video Importer—leave the location unchanged.

- To specify a new location for saving the files, click the folder icon to open the Browse for Folder window (Windows)/Open (MacOS) dialog and choose a folder, or click Make New Folder (Windows)/New Folder (MacOS) to create a new folder.

- Optionally, Premiere Elements saves imported files to one or more subfolders with multiple naming options.

- To create a single folder with a name of your choice, select Custom Name from the Create Subfolder(s) menu and enter the name of the folder in the text box that appears.

Capturing Stop-motion and Time-lapse Video

Using stop-motion and time-lapse video, you can make inanimate objects appear to move or show a flower grow and bloom in seconds. In these modes, you capture single video frames at widely spaced time intervals for later playback at normal frame rates.

You create stop-motion animations or time-lapse videos by using the Stop Motion button in the Capture panel. You can capture frames either from pre-recorded tape or from a live camera feed. Stop-motion capture lets you manually select the frames you want to capture; Time Lapse capture automatically captures frames at set intervals. Using Time Lapse mode you can reduce a lengthy event, such as a sunset or a flower blooming, to a very short span.

Note: You cannot capture stop-motion video from an HDV source.

—From Premiere Elements Help

To capture stop-motion from a tape-based device, do the following:

1 Connect your tape device to your computer and turn it on. Then do one of the following:

   • If you're capturing live from a camcorder, place the camcorder in Camera mode.

   • If you're capturing from videotape, place the device in Play, VTR, or VCR mode.

2 In the Capture panel, click the Stop Motion button.

3 Click the Create New Stop Motion button in the middle of the Capture panel preview pane.

4 If you're capturing from videotape, use the camcorder's controls to move to the desired frame. If you're capturing live, adjust your scene as desired. Click Grab Frame whenever the Capture panel displays a frame that you want to save to the hard drive. Each frame you grab will appear as a .bmp file in Project view with a sequential number in its filename.

5 Close the Capture panel and edit and save your project as you normally would.

> **Tip:** See "Capture stop-motion and time-lapse video" in Premiere Elements Help for more information.

9 To rename the files using a consistent name within the folder, select an option other than Do Not Rename Files from the Rename Files menu. When the files are added to the folder and to the Media panel, the file numbers are incremented by 001. For example, if you enter *Aquarium* as Custom Name under Rename Files, Premiere Elements will change the filenames to *Aquarium* 001.MTS, *Aquarium* 002.MTS, and so on.

10 In the thumbnail area, select individual files to add to the Media panel. A check mark by the filename indicates that the file is selected. By default, all files are selected. Only selected files are imported. Click a check box to deselect it, thus excluding the related file from being imported.

11 Click Get Media. This transfers the media to the destination location, which is typically your hard drive. You can click Cancel in the Copying Files dialog at any time to stop the process.

Files that you import using the Video Importer appear in the Media view in the Project workspace.

Converting Analog Video to Digital Video

Before DV camcorders were widely manufactured, most people used camcorders that recorded analog video onto VHS, 8mm, or other analog tape formats. To use video from analog sources in your Premiere Elements project, you must first convert (digitize) the footage to digital data, because Premiere Elements accepts only direct input from digital sources. To digitize your footage, you can use either your digital camcorder or a stand-alone device that performs analog-to-digital (AV DV) conversion.

You can perform a successful conversion using the following methods:

- **Output a digital signal.** Use your digital camcorder to output a digital signal from an analog input. Connect the analog source to input jacks on your digital camcorder and connect the digital camcorder to the computer. Not all digital camcorders support this method. See your camcorder documentation for more information.

- **Record analog footage.** Use your digital camcorder to record footage from your analog source. Connect your analog source's output to the analog inputs on your digital camcorder. Then record your analog footage to digital tape. When you are finished recording, Premiere Elements can then capture the footage from the digital camcorder. This is a very common procedure. See your camcorder documentation for more details on recording from analog sources.

- **Capture sound.** Use your computer's sound card, if it has a microphone (mic) input, to capture sound from a microphone.

- **Bridge the connection.** Use an AV DV converter to bridge the connection between your analog source and the computer. Connect the analog source to the converter and connect the converter to your computer. Premiere Elements then captures the digitized footage. AV DV converters are available in many large consumer electronics stores.

Note: If you capture using an AV DV converter, you might need to capture without using device control.

—From Premiere Elements Help

Importing Content from Your Hard Drive

Follow this procedure to import audio, video, or still-image content that's already on your hard drive.

1　In the Organize workspace, click Get Media.

2　Click Files and Folders (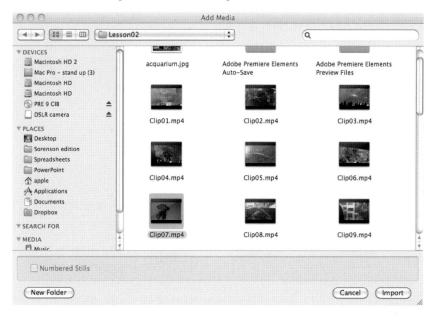).

Premiere Elements opens the Add Media panel.

3　To change to a new disk or folder, click the Look In list box (Windows)/Folder list box (Mac OS) and navigate to the Lesson02 folder you copied to your hard disk with all of the lesson files.

4　To display only certain file types in the dialog, click the Files of type list box (Windows-only), and choose the desired file type. The dialog displays only files of the selected type.

5　To import files, choose them in the dialog as you normally would, and click Open (Windows) or Import (Mac OS).

Files that you import using the Add Media dialog appear in the Organize workspace, as well as in Project view in the Edit workspace.

Review Questions

1 How do you access the Capture panel in Premiere Elements?

2 Why is having a separate hard drive dedicated to video a good idea?

3 What is Scene Detect, and how would you turn it on or off if you wanted to?

4 What is the Video Importer, and when would you use it?

5 What is device control?

Review Answers

1 Click Get Media from the Organize workspace, and then click the appropriate capture icon.

2 Video files take up large amounts of space compared to standard office and image files. A hard drive stores the video clips you capture and must be fast enough to store your video frames. Although office-type files tend to be fairly small, they can clutter a hard drive when scattered throughout the available space; the more free, defragmented space you have on a hard drive, the better the performance of real-time video capture will be.

3 Scene Detect is Premiere Elements' ability to detect scene changes in your video (based on timecode or by content) during video capture and save each scene as an individual clip in your project. You can select or deselect Scene Detect by Timecode and Scene Detect by Content in the Capture panel menu.

4 The Video Importer is a feature of Premiere Elements that enables you to import media from AVCHD camcorders, digital still cameras, smart phones and players, and DVDs, whether from a camcorder or PC DVD drive.

5 Device control is the ability of Premiere Elements to control the basic functions of your digital video camera (such as play, stop, and rewind) through the interface in the Capture panel. It's available on most DV and HDV camcorders.

4 ORGANIZING YOUR CONTENT

Lesson overview

Fast and efficient movie production is all about organization. In this lesson, you'll learn how to do the following:

- Manually tag your clips in the Organizer
- Apply Smart Tagging in the Organizer
- Create an album for backing up your projects to Photoshop.com
- Create an InstantMovie using manual and Smart Tagging
- Drag clips to the My Project panel from the Project view

This lesson will take approximately two hours.

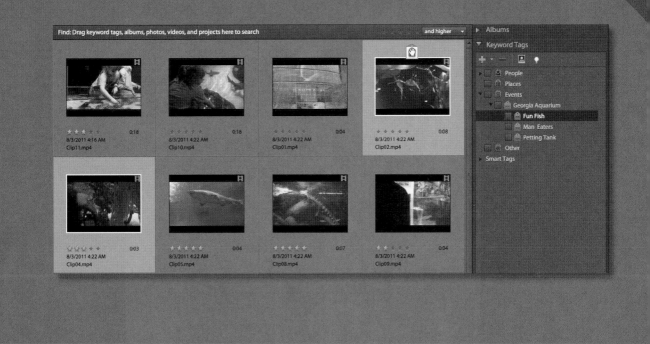

Tagging content in the Organizer.

Getting Started

Before you start working with the footage, let's review a final version of the movie you'll be creating.

1   Make sure that you have correctly copied the Lesson04 folder from the DVD in the back of this book onto your computer's hard drive. For more information, see "Copying the Classroom in a Book Files" in the "Getting Started" chapter at the beginning of this book.

2   Launch Adobe Premiere Elements.

3   In the Welcome screen, click the Open Project button. If necessary, click Open in the pop-up menu. The Open Project dialog opens.

4   In the Open Project dialog, navigate to the Lesson04 folder you copied to your hard drive. Within that folder, select the file Lesson04_Start_Win.prel (Windows) or Lesson04_Start_Mac.prel (Mac OS), and then click Open (Windows) Choose (Mac OS). If a dialog appears asking for the location of rendered files, click the Skip Previews button.

Your project file opens with the Monitor, Tasks, and My Project panels open.

5   Choose Window > Restore Workspace to ensure that you start the lesson with the default window layout.

Viewing the Completed Movie Before You Start

To see what you'll be creating in this lesson, you can take a look at the completed movie.

1   In the Project workspace in the Tasks panel, click the Media button ( ). In Media view, locate the file Lesson04_Movie.mov (which should be the only file available), and then double-click it to open the video into the Preview window.

2   In the Preview window, click the Play button ( ) to watch the video about a visit to the Georgia Aquarium, which you'll build in this lesson.

3 When you're finished, close the Preview window.

Working in the Project Workspace

When you first open Premiere Elements, you see the Project workspace. I described the separate views and functions within this workspace in Lesson 1, but because you're here now, let's review.

As you saw in the previous chapter, if you click Get Media (Get Media), you'll enter Get Media view where you'll capture or import video into your project.

Media view (Media) should be open when you first run Premiere Elements. This is a customized view of the Organizer, which you can open by clicking the Organizer icon (Organizer) in the top toolbar.

The InstantMovie icon (InstantMovie) starts a wizard that automatically and quickly steps you through the selection and editing portion of movie creation, allowing you to add theme-based effects, titles, transitions, and audio. You'll produce an InstantMovie of the aquarium shoot later in this chapter.

There's some overlap between Media view and the Organizer application, so let's look at their similarities and differences. The Organizer is a separate application that contains all audio, video, and still-image content that you've input into either Adobe Photoshop Elements or Premiere Elements since you first installed the programs. It's a great place to start many projects and provides access to a wide range of organization and collection functions.

Media view works neatly within Premiere Elements' Project workspace. It doesn't offer the breadth of capabilities enabled by the full Organizer, but it's convenient and provides a customized subset of functions that lets you efficiently find and deploy media within your movie projects. It also provides the ability to create certain types of media, such as titles, bars and tones, and color mattes, and the ability to organize your content into folders.

As mentioned, Media view is the default view in the Tasks panel and should be open when you run Premiere Elements for the first time. If it's not showing now, click Media in the Project workspace.

● **Note:** Previous versions of Adobe Premiere Elements had a Media view and a Project view. Both functions have been consolidated starting in Premiere Elements 10.

When you first run Premiere Elements, if you load an existing project, Media view will display all content that you've imported into the project. For new projects, there will be no content in Media view.

With this as background information, let's take a deeper look at how you can find clips in Media view.

Finding Clips in Media View

Let's load some clips into the project so you can work with them in Media view.

1   In the Organize workspace, click the Get Media button ( ).

2   Click Files and Folders ( ).

    Premiere Elements opens the Add Media dialog.

3   Navigate to the Lesson04 folder. Select the movie clips Clip01.mp4 through Clip13.mp4. Click Open (Windows)/Import (Mac OS).

Media view's role is to help you find files using different search methods. Some basic search methods are available without any action on your part, and you can access advanced methods after you've rated the clips or have applied keyword or Smart Tags to your clips. I'll discuss all of these options later in this lesson. In this short section, you'll learn how to use the basic tools in Media view to find and organize your content.

You can perform the following activities in Media view to view, create, and organize your files:

•   Browse through the entire catalog by using the scroll bar at the right side of Media view.

•   Change from List view to Icon view.

•   Create folders and subfolders to organize your content and navigate the various levels of folders and subfolders.

•   Sort by name or duration, either in ascending or descending order.

- Select which media type to show—or not to show—using icons on the right side of the Project view.

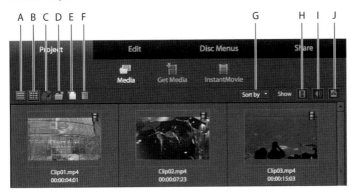

A. Switch to List view. **B.** Switch to Icon view. **C.** Go up one folder level.
D. Create folder. **E.** Create new item. **F.** Clear. **G.** Sort by Name and Duration
(ascending and descending). **H.** Show/Hide Video. **I.** Show/Hide Audio.
J. Show/Hide Still Image.

1 Click the List icon (▤) to switch to List view (if necessary). Once in List view, you can sort your content by clicking the column head of any column. The arrow in the column you choose shows whether the data is sorted in ascending view or descending view. For example, click the Name column head to see how it sorts the content in the Media view.

2 Click the Media view menu on the extreme upper right and choose Edit Columns to edit the columns presented and their order. Select the check box next to a column to include it in the Media view, and use the Move Up and Move Down buttons to change its order. Click OK to close the Edit Columns window.

3 Now you'll create a folder to organize your videos. Click the Folder icon (▣)
   to create a folder. Premiere Elements creates a folder named Folder 01 with the
   text highlighted so it's easy to change. Type in the word *Videos*, replacing the
   text "Folder 01."

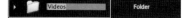

4 Drag the source videos from the aquarium shoot into the new folder. Select all the
   source videos in the Media view (all files with a .mp4 extension), and then drag
   them into the new folder. Twirl the triangle next to the Videos folder to close it;
   your Media view should become a whole lot tidier. When you're working with
   large projects with multiple video, still image, and audio files, creating folders is
   the best strategy for keeping your content organized and easy to find.

Clip09.mp4	Movie	30.00 fps	00:00:04:07
Clip10.mp4	Movie	29.97 fps	00:00:17:21
Clip11.mp4	Movie	30.00 fps	00:00:03:12
Clip1?.mp4	Movie	30.00 fps	00:00:07:06
?13.mp4	Movie	30.00 fps	00:00:04:19
Videos	Folder		

● **Note:** Sometimes
when you drop a clip
into the My Project
panel, you'll see a
message that says, "Clip
being dropped contains
solid background color.
Do you want to apply
Videomerge on this
clip?" Click No if you see
this message except as
directed in Lesson 6.

5 To add a still image, video, or audio file to your project from Media view,
   drag the file from Media view into the Timeline or Sceneline in the My Project
   panel. Click No if Premiere Elements asks if you want to fix any quality issues in
   the clip or poses any other questions.

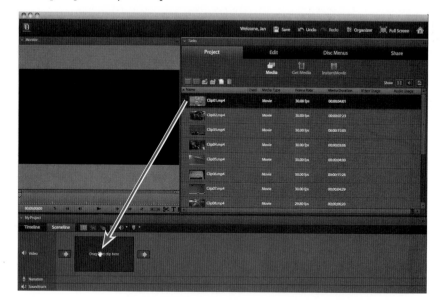

Tagging in the Organizer

Media view is great for quickly finding clips, but the Organizer is Premiere Elements' best tool for serious organization and search and retrieval work. You can open the Organizer by clicking the Organizer icon (▦ Organizer) in the top toolbar. This exercise will detail how to perform manual and Smart Tagging in the Organizer, and then how to search for clips using those tags in the Organizer.

Let's start with a brief description of tagging, which you perform in one or more of three ways: assigning star ratings (1–5), applying keyword tags, and using Smart Tags. At a high level, all tags allow you to more easily find the clips to include in a particular movie. For example, if you review and rate all your clips on a scale of 1–5, you can later search for only those clips that you rated 4 or higher—an easy way to find high-quality clips and eliminate poor-quality clips.

Keyword tags allow you to tag a clip by person, location, event, or other designation with customizable categories. For example, in this exercise, you'll apply several keyword tags to the clips from this project, and then search for clips containing these keyword tags.

When you run the Auto Analyzer on a clip, Premiere Elements analyzes the video to detect scenes based on content; you can hunt for scenes with faces and identify scenes that are out of focus, shaky, underexposed, or overexposed. Using this qualitative data, Premiere Elements then categorizes all clips as high, medium, or low quality. This serves as a valuable triage function that you can later use to search for the best clips for your movie. This analysis is also used for features like Smart Trimming, which you'll learn about in Chapter 5, and Automatic Quality Enhancement, which I'll discuss in Chapter 6.

For example, if you shot an hour of video on your last vacation, Smart Tagging allows you to identify medium-quality-and-higher clips containing faces (presumably family members), and produce a movie containing only these clips. What would literally take you hours to accomplish manually, Smart Tagging can produce in a few moments.

Using all these tags in any combination, you can hunt for clips to manually edit into a movie or create an InstantMovie, which is a professional-looking edited movie complete with titles, sound track, effects, and transitions that you'll produce using a fast and simple step-by-step process.

Tagging Clips in the Organizer

Let's open and explore operations in the Organizer. To open the Organizer, click the Organizer icon (![Organizer]) in the top toolbar. To make your Organizer look like the one in the figure, click the View menu and make sure that Details, Show File Names, and Show People Recognition are all selected.

● **Note:** Three keyboard shortcuts apply to all Premiere Elements' preview and playback controls: Press the spacebar to start and stop clip playback, and use the arrow keys to navigate frame by frame forward (right arrow) and backward (left arrow).

1 Double-click the video Clip11.mp4 to open the file in the Organizer's Preview view.

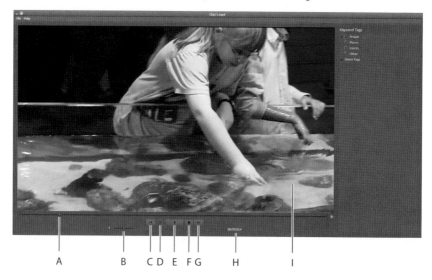

A. Current position. **B.** Volume. **C.** Start. **D.** Record. **E.** Play (spacebar). **F.** Stop. **G.** End. **H.** Current time. **I.** Preview window.

2 Click Play to play the video file, and use the playback controls to fast-forward, rewind, and otherwise experiment with these controls.

3 Close the Preview window to return to the Organizer.

Working with Star Ratings

Follow the procedures described in this section to apply and delete star ratings, and to search for clips based on the star ratings. Ratings range from 1 to 5.

● **Note:** You can position the Organizer anywhere onscreen by grabbing the docking header and moving the panel to the new location. You can also resize the panel by grabbing and dragging any edge to the desired size.

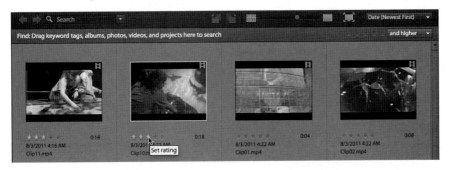

1 If you don't see the star ratings, choose View > Details in the Organizer menu.

2 Hover your pointer over the star ratings beneath any clip, and click the star that corresponds to the desired rating for that clip. Go ahead and rate a few clips so you can sort by rating in step 5.

3 To change a rating, use the same procedure and choose a different rating.

4 To delete the star rating, click the last selected star on the right (the fourth star in a clip rated four stars).

5 To find clips based on their assigned ratings in the Organizer (or in Media view), click the number of target stars and adjust the list box as desired. Premiere Elements displays only those files that meet the selected criteria.

B   A

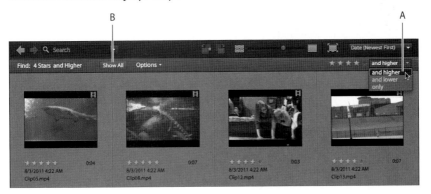

A. Target stars list box. **B.** Show All button.

6 Click the Show All button to view all clips in the Organizer (or in Media view).

Working with Keyword Tags

Premiere Elements includes general categories of keyword tags that you can apply as is or customize with your own categories or subcategories. In this lesson, you'll create and apply two custom categories in the Organizer, and then search for clips based on those keywords in Media view.

1 Under Keyword Tags in the Organizer, click and select Events. Do not select the checkbox, just click the text as shown in the figure.

2 Under Keyword Tags, click the Create New button (⊞) and choose New Sub-Category.

3 In the Create Sub-Category panel, type *Georgia Aquarium Visit* in the Sub-Category Name field. Then click OK.

Premiere Elements creates the new subcategory.

4 Repeat steps 2–3 to create three subcategories beneath Georgia Aquarium Visit called *Fun Fish, Man Eaters*, and *Petting Tank*.

5   In the Browser panel, click Clip02.mp4. Then press and hold the Ctrl key (Windows)/Command key (Mac OS), and click Clip04.mp4.

6   Drag the Fun Fish keyword tag to either of the selected clips. When you release the pointer, Premiere Elements applies the keyword tag to all selected clips.

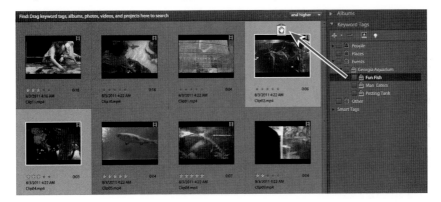

Note: If your Organizer shows multiple copies of any of the mentioned files, just choose any copy of that file.

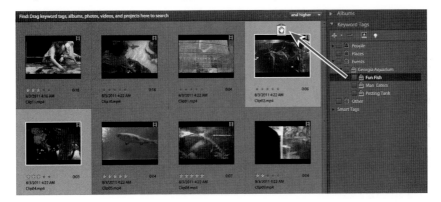

7   Use the same procedure to apply the Man Eaters tag to Clip05.mp4, Clip06. mp4, Clip08.mp4, and Clip09.mp4; the Petting Tank tag to Clip10.mp4, Clip11. mp4, and Clip12.mp4; and the Georgia Aquarium Visit tag to Clip01.mp4, Clip03.mp4, Clip07.mp4, and Clip13.mp4 (because they don't fall into any of the three more specific categories).

8   Click the box to the left of the Man Eaters subcategory, and a pair of binoculars will appear in the box. This tells the Organizer to display only those clips tagged with that keyword tag.

About the Auto Analyzer

As mentioned earlier, the Auto Analyzer analyzes your video clips for content and quality, and is integral to a number of functions, including Smart Tagging, Smart Trimming, and creating InstantMovies, which you'll learn to do later in this chapter. You can run the Auto Analyzer manually, as you'll learn in the next section, or run it as a background process. In fact, by default, the Auto Analyzer will run on clips that you've imported anytime your system is running and idle.

To access this preference option, in the Organizer, choose Edit > Preferences > Media-Analysis (Windows) Adobe Elements 10 Organizer > Preferences >

Media-Analysis (Mac OS). In the default setting, Premiere Elements will work in the background with imported media, so when you're ready to edit, you won't have to wait for the Auto Analyzer to run.

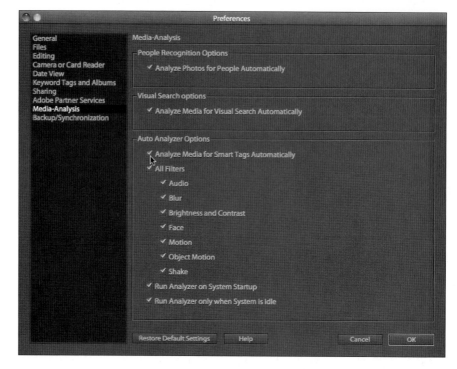

In most instances on most computers, background operation should work just fine. On older, less powerful computers and those configured with the minimum RAM, background operation may cause a noticeable drag on foreground operations, particularly when working with H.264-based, high-definition formats such as AVCHD and video shot by DSLRs. If you notice any sluggishness in your foreground operations after importing footage or experience any system instability, try disabling the Auto Analyzer as a background operation by deselecting the Analyze Media for Smart Tags Automatically check box.

Running the Auto Analyzer Manually

To manually run the Auto Analyzer and apply Smart Tags to the project clips, follow these steps.

1 If the Organizer isn't open, click the Organizer icon ( ) in the Project workspace to open the Organizer. Otherwise, press Alt+Tab (Windows) or Command+Tab (MacOS) to switch to Organizer view.

2 Click to select all clips, and then right-click and choose Run Auto-Analyzer. This can take a while, so you might want to try one or two clips first.

▶ **Tip:** As with keyword tagging, you can use the tags created via Smart Tagging by themselves or in conjunction with keyword tags or even star ratings. For example, in the Organizer, click three stars "and higher" in the top toolbar, click the Petting Tank tag in the Keyword Tags, and click In Focus in Smart Tags. Premiere Elements will display only those clips that meet these criteria.

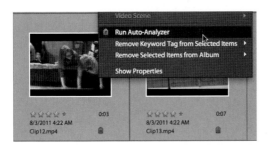

3   Premiere Elements starts analyzing the clips and reports its progress in the Elements Organizer. The duration of the process will vary by clip length, clip format, and the speed of your computer. After completion, Premiere Elements will open the Elements Organizer window to let you know the process has completed; click OK to close that window.

4   In the Organizer, if necessary, press Ctrl+D (Windows)/Command+D (MacOS) to ensure that Details are showing. A purple tag (■) beneath the clip's thumbnail indicates that Smart Tagging has been applied. Tags of different colors (■) indicate that keyword tags have been applied, whereas the Album tag (■) in the Organizer indicates only that the clip is in an album. To view which tags have been applied or which album(s) the clip was included in, hover your cursor over the respective tag in either the Organizer or Media view. Tagging details will appear beneath the Preview window.

5   To remove a tag, right-click the tag in the Organizer and delete the tag, or right-click the thumbnail in Media view and choose the tag to remove.

Working with Clips After Smart Tagging

Let's take a moment to understand what happens to clips after Smart Tagging. To review, during Smart Tagging, Premiere Elements breaks the clip into different scenes based on content changes (as opposed to timecode, like DV files); finds different types of content like faces; and rates the quality of each clip based on factors such as exposure, focus, and stability.

In the Organizer, you'll know that the clip has been split into multiple scenes if there is a Step Forward icon (▶) on the right of the clip. Click that icon, and Premiere Elements displays all scenes separately in the Organizer surrounded by a border that's a lighter gray than the rest of the Organizer. This lets you know that all the scenes are part of a single clip.

In the Organizer, you can treat each scene as a separate clip, for example, dragging it to the My Project panel to include it in a project or double-clicking it to play it in the Preview window. You can consolidate all scenes back into a single frame by clicking the Step Backward icon to the right of the final scene (). Note that you can expand and contract a clip into its separate scenes in Project view using these same controls.

Creating an InstantMovie

In this exercise, you'll create an InstantMovie from the aquarium clips that you tagged in a previous exercise. Again, an InstantMovie is a professional-looking edited movie, complete with titles, sound track, effects, and transitions that you'll create by following a simple wizard.

1   If necessary, switch to Media view. Then double-click the Videos folder to open it. Note how the Up One Folder icon becomes active once you're in this folder. After you create the InstantMovie, you can click this icon to navigate back to the root folder in Media view.

2   Press Ctrl+A (Windows)/Command+A (MacOS) to select all clips in the Media view, and then click the InstantMovie () button. Premiere Elements opens the InstantMovie Wizard. You can preview any Style by clicking it, and stop the preview by clicking it again.

3   Choose Fun Style and click Next. If this theme is not available, choose another.

● **Note:** The Apply to: radio buttons become active only when you apply a Theme to clips already inserted into the My Project panel, not when you create an InstantMovie from the Organizer.

4 Customize the Theme as desired. Accept the options as is, *or do any or all of the following*:

- Customize the Opening and Closing Titles.

- Select the Auto Edit check box to have Premiere Elements analyze your clips and edit them to fit the selected theme, which is recommended. If you don't select Auto Edit, Premiere Elements uses the clips as is and doesn't edit them. Also choose whether or not to apply the Auto Analyzer to clips that you haven't previously analyzed.

- In the Music box, choose the Theme Music radio button to use the background music from the selected Theme, or choose the No Music radio button. To use your own background music, click the My Music radio button, and then click the Browse button to choose the song you want. Then drag the Music/Sound FX slider to the desired setting, dragging to the right to prioritize audio captured with the video clips and to the left to prioritize the selected background music. If you have dialogue in your project (which these clips don't), select the SmartMix check box and Premiere Elements will reduce the volume of the music track when it detects dialogue.

- In the Speed and Intensity box, adjust the Effects and Cuts sliders as desired.

- In the Duration box, choose the desired option. Match Music produces a movie that matches the duration of the selected music and is recommended. Or, you can specify a duration or choose Use All Clips, which uses all clips at their original duration with no background music.

- In the Sequence box, choose Theme Order (recommended), which allows Premiere Elements to use clips as they best match the theme, or choose Time/Date, which uses the clips in the order that they were shot.

- In the Theme Content box, choose the content to incorporate into the InstantMovie and whether to replace any existing content with theme-based content.

- In the Render Preview box, choose Yes to render a preview of the InstantMovie after completion or No to preview in real time from the My Project panel (recommended).

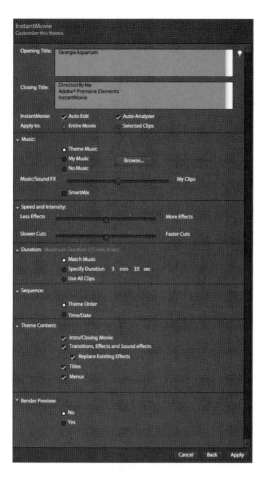

5   After selecting your options, click Apply to create the InstantMovie. Click
    No when the InstantMovie dialog opens and asks if you want to select more
    clips. Click No when Premiere Elements asks if you want to render the
    movie. Premiere Elements creates the InstantMovie and inserts it into the
    My Project panel.

6   Premiere Elements adds the InstantMovie to the My Project panel (either
    Timeline or Sceneline, whichever was selected) in consolidated form. To
    separate the InstantMovie into its components to edit them, click to select
    the new InstantMovie, right-click, and choose Break apart InstantMovie.

7 Use the playback controls in the Monitor panel to preview the InstantMovie.

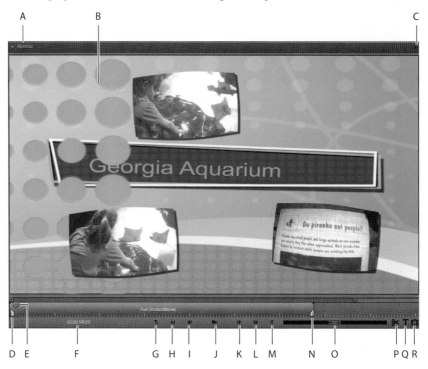

A. Docking header. **B.** Preview area. **C.** Monitor menu. **D.** In Point handle. **E.** Current position. **F.** Current time in movie. **G.** Go to previous edit point (page up). **H.** Rewind. **I.** Step back (left). **J.** Play/Pause toggle (spacebar). **K.** Step forward (right). **L.** Fast-forward. **M.** Go to next edit point (page down). **N.** Out Point handle. **O.** Shuttle. **P.** Split clip. **Q.** Add default text. **R.** Freeze frame.

Uploading Files to Photoshop.com

Depending on your membership level in Photoshop.com, you can back up at least 2 GB of video, audio, and still-image files to the site. To upload files, you must first create an album, and then add the video file to that album.

Follow this procedure to back up video files to Photoshop.com.

● **Note:** Photoshop.com services are currently available for Premiere Elements users only in the United States.

1 If necessary, click the Organizer icon (🔲 **Organizer**) in the Project workspace to open the Organizer.

2 Under Albums in the Project workspace, click the Create New Album or Album Group button and choose New Album. Premiere Elements opens the Create Album panel.

3   In the Album Name field, type *Georgia Aquarium*, and make sure that the Backup/Sync check box is selected. Then click Done to close the panel.

4   Because you also used Georgia Aquarium as the name of a subcategory in Events, Premiere Elements will open a dialog asking if you want to create an album with that name. Click OK to close that dialog. If you're not signed in, a dialog will appear asking you to enter your account information or to register.

5   In the Keyword Tags box, select the check box next to the Georgia Aquarium tag. The Organizer will display only those clips previously tagged with the Georgia Aquarium tag or a tag from any of the three subcategories.

6 Press Ctrl+A (Windows)/Command+A (MacOS) to select all clips.

7 Drag the Georgia Aquarium album tag to any of the selected clips. When you release the pointer, the album tag is applied to all selected clips.

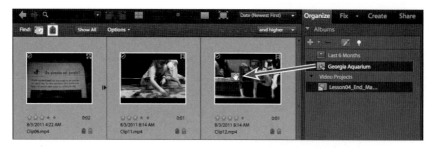

8 In the Organizer menu, choose Edit > Preferences > Backup/Synchronization (Windows) Adobe Elements 10 Organizer > Preferences > Backup/ Synchronization (Mac OS). In this panel, if not already selected, *do the following:*

- Select the Backup/Sync is On check box.

- Click the Advanced Backup/Sync Options disclosure triangle to reveal the advanced options. Here's where you can set options, such as which file types to archive and how to resolve conflicts between your online and desktop albums. Adjust these options as desired.

- Select the Sync check box for Georgia Aquarium.

9 Click OK to close the Preferences panel.

10 Unless you have a burning desire to store random videos from the Georgia Aquarium on your Photoshop.com site, under Albums in the Project workspace, click the Georgia Aquarium album, and then click the Delete Album button (■). Premiere Elements will delete the album and remove any files from that album previously uploaded to Photoshop.com.

● **Note:** You must be logged into Photoshop.com to view the Advanced Backup/Sync Options screen.

● **Note:** Synchronizing video files seems like a great idea, but remember that only ten minutes of DV or HDV video will consume the entire 2 GB of starter storage space on Photoshop.com. Keep that in mind when you select the file types to synchronize.

Working with Smart Albums

You know the drill. It's holiday time or perhaps birthday time, and you're thinking, man, I've gotta create a year-in-review video or perhaps a new photo collection. If you've been applying tags to your video all year long, you should be able to quickly search for what you want via some combination of tags, Smart Tags, star ratings, and date selection.

Alternatively, using a Smart Album in Premiere Elements, you can see all the relevant content with the click of a button. Simply stated, a Smart Album contains information based on search criteria that you insert when you create the Smart Album.

To create a Smart Album, click the Create New Album or Album Group button and choose New Smart Album. Premiere Elements opens the New Smart Album panel.

In the New Smart Album panel, you can add any number of search criteria, including keyword tags, date tags, and Smart Tags. In this example, the New Smart Album will identify all content tagged for any of my four daughters (Rose, Whatley, Franzi, and Vici) that was shot during 2011 and is judged High Quality and In Focus by Premiere Elements. When I'm ready to produce that year-end video, all I have to do is click the Kids—2011 Smart Album, and the content will be there waiting for me.

Review Questions

1 What's the difference between the Organizer that ships with Premiere Elements and the Organizer that ships with Photoshop Elements?

2 What is Smart Tagging? Are there any situations in which you wouldn't want to apply Smart Tagging?

3 After creating an InstantMovie, how do you break up the movie to edit it further?

4 How do you upload your clips to Photoshop.com?

Review Answers

1 This is a trick question—there is no difference. If you have Premiere Elements and Photoshop Elements installed, both programs can insert content into the same shared database and sort through and retrieve data from that database.

2 When you apply Smart Tagging to a clip, Premiere Elements analyzes the clip to detect scenes based on content, hunts for certain content types such as faces, and ranks the quality of your clips. Other than processing time, there's very little downside to applying Smart Tagging. Your video clips will be divided into useful scenes, and you can find high-quality clips much faster than you could manually.

3 Click the clip with your pointer to select it, and then right-click and choose Break apart InstantMovie.

4 To upload clips to Photoshop.com, create an album in the Organizer and drag the new album tag onto the target clips. Then access the Organizer Preferences panel and make sure that that album is synced with Photoshop.com.

5 EDITING VIDEO

Lesson overview

In Lesson 4, you learned to organize your video in Media view. In this lesson, you'll learn how to take that footage and shape it into a refined final version. You'll apply these basic editing techniques:

- Insert, delete, and rearrange clips in the Sceneline and Timeline
- Trim and split clips
- Quickly add a slide show to your video project
- Use Smart Trim mode to quickly remove lower-quality segments from your videos

Over the course of this lesson, you'll piece together a short video about a visit to the Georgia Aquarium. You'll be working with video and audio clips provided on the DVD that accompanies this book.

 This lesson will take approximately two hours.

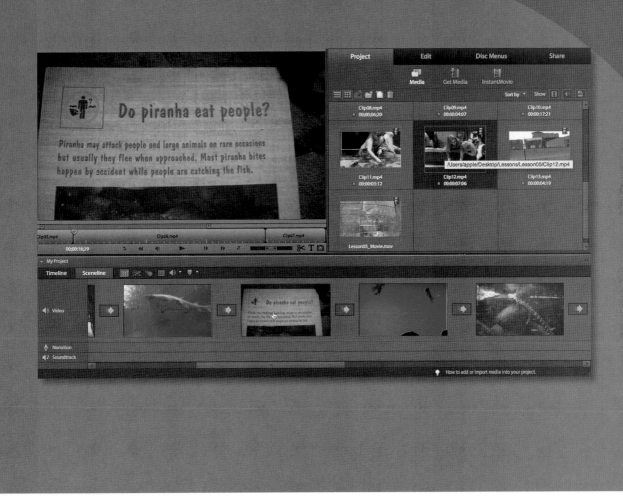

Working in the Sceneline.

Getting Started

To begin, you'll launch Adobe Premiere Elements, open the Lesson05 project, and review a final version of the movie you'll be creating.

1 Make sure that you have correctly copied the Lesson05 folder from the DVD in the back of this book onto your computer's hard drive. For more information, see "Copying the Classroom in a Book Files" in the "Getting Started" section at the start of this book.

2 Launch Premiere Elements.

3 In the Welcome screen, click the Open Project button, and then click the Open folder.

4 In the Open Project dialog, navigate to the Lesson05 folder you copied to your hard drive.

5 Within that folder, select the file Lesson05_Start_Win.prel (Windows) or Lesson05_Start_Mac.prel (Mac OS), and then click Open (Windows) Choose (Mac OS). If a dialog appears asking for the location of rendered files, click the Skip Previews button.

Your project file opens with the Monitor, Tasks, and My Project panels open.

6 Choose Window > Restore Workspace to ensure that you start the lesson with the default panel layout.

Viewing the Completed Movie Before You Start

To see what you'll be creating in this lesson, you can take a look at the completed movie.

1 In the Project tab in the Tasks panel, click Media ( ). In Media view, locate the file Lesson05_Movie.mov, and then double-click it to open the video in the Preview window.

2 In the Preview window, click the Play button ( ) to watch the video about a visit to the Georgia Aquarium, which you will build in this lesson.

3 When you're done, close the Preview window.

Working with the Monitor Panel

When you open the project for this lesson, you'll see multiple clips in the My Project panel in either Timeline or Sceneline view. Regardless of which view you choose, you'll preview your work in the Monitor panel. The Timeline and Sceneline are different panels for arranging clips and applying effects, and can show different views of the project.

In contrast, the Monitor panel shows one frame of the project, and one frame only. The displayed frame is at the location of the current-time indicator (   ). In the Sceneline, the current-time indicator is in the mini-timeline just below the preview area. In the Timeline, the current-time indicator is positioned directly on the Timeline.

Now let's explore the functions of the Monitor panel, particularly the multiple ways that you can move around the content presented in the My Project panel. This initial exercise will be in Sceneline view, so click the Sceneline button on the top left of the My Project panel to make sure that you're in that view.

1   In the mini-timeline beneath the Monitor panel, select the first clip in the Sceneline, and then click the Play button (   ) in the Monitor panel to begin playback. As the movie is playing, notice that the timecode in the lower-left corner of the Monitor panel is advancing. To pause playback, press the spacebar, or once again click the Play button, which becomes the Pause button (   ) during playback.

2   You can locate a specific frame in your movie by changing your position in time. Place your pointer over the timecode in the lower-left corner of the Monitor panel, and your Selection tool (   ) will change to a hand with two arrows (   ).

3 Drag the hand with two arrows icon to the right, advancing your video. The pointer will disappear while you're dragging and reappear when you stop. As long as you keep holding down the mouse button, you can move backward and forward through the video. This is known as *scrubbing* through your video.

A. Docking header. **B.** Preview area. **C.** Panel menu. **D.** Current-time indicator. **E.** Current time. **F.** Clip representation in mini-timeline. **G.** Playback controls.

● **Note:** To move to a specific frame in the movie—say, 9 seconds, 15 frames in—type the number *915*. This tells Premiere Elements to move to the ninth second and fifteenth frame of the movie.

4 The Shuttle control located in the lower-right corner of the Monitor panel lets you navigate through the movie in a similar fashion. To move forward through your video, drag the Shuttle control to the right. The farther to the right you move the Shuttle control, the faster you move through the video. This method is useful for quickly scanning a project for edit points.

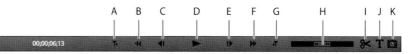

A. Go to Previous Edit Point (Page Up). **B.** Rewind. **C.** Step Back (left arrow key). **D.** Play/Pause toggle (spacebar). **E.** Step Forward (right arrow key). **F.** Fast-forward. **G.** Go to Next Edit Point (Page Down). **H.** Shuttle. **I.** Split Clip (Ctrl+K/Command+K). **J.** Add Default Text. **K.** Freeze Frame.

5 You can move to a specific point in your movie by entering the time in the Timecode control. Click the timecode in the lower-left corner of the Monitor panel, and it will change to an editable text field. Type the number *900*, and then press Enter/Return to move to the nine-second point of your project.

6 Click the Step Forward () button (right arrow key) repeatedly to advance your video one frame at a time. Video is simply a series of frames shown at a rate of approximately 30 frames per second. Using the Step Forward (■) or Step Back (◄) button (left arrow key) enables you to locate moments in time very precisely. You also can use the right and left arrow keys on the keyboard to accomplish the same functions.

7 Click the Go to Next Edit Point button (■) to jump to the first frame of the next clip. Notice in the mini-timeline that the current-time indicator (⬚) jumps to the beginning of the next clip representation. Click the Go to Previous Edit Point button (■) to jump to the previous edit. Or, you can use the Page Up and Page Down keys on your keyboard to accomplish the same functions.

8 Reposition the current-time indicator in the mini-timeline by clicking and dragging it to the left or to the right.

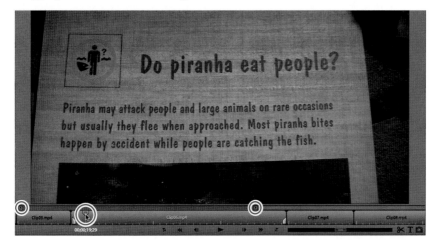

9 The Zoom controls, located just above the mini-timeline in the Monitor panel, enable you to zoom in to get a more detailed view of the clips, zoom out to see more of the entire movie in the mini-timeline, or scroll through the mini-timeline to find a clip. To work with the Zoom controls, *do any of the following:*

- To zoom in, drag the left Zoom Claw (■) to the right, or drag the right Zoom Claw to the left.

- To zoom out, drag the left Zoom Claw to the left, or drag the right Zoom Claw to the right.

10 Press the Home key on your keyboard to position the current-time indicator at the beginning of the movie. Press the End key on your keyboard to position the current-time indicator at the end of the movie. This is useful when you want to add content to the existing sections of your movie.

Previewing in Premiere Elements

Premiere Elements attempts to preview all movies at full frame rate and, typically, can do so when you're simply splitting, trimming, and moving clips around. Once you start to apply the effects discussed in Lesson 6, however, the display rate of the preview may slow down. If this occurs and you need to preview your project at full frame rate, you can render the entire project by pressing the Enter/Return key on your keyboard, or render a work area using a procedure defined in "Rendering a Work Area" in Lesson 6.

Working with the My Project Panel in the Sceneline

As mentioned, the My Project panel has two views: a Sceneline for basic movie editing and a Timeline for more advanced techniques. You can switch between the two views by clicking either the Sceneline or the Timeline button in the upper-left corner of the My Project panel.

Adding Clips in the Sceneline

In the Sceneline, each clip is represented by its first frame. This display makes it easy to arrange clips into coherent sequences without regard to clip length. As you learned in Chapter 1, this technique is referred to as *storyboard-style* editing.

1   If the My Project panel is not already in the Sceneline, click the Sceneline button.

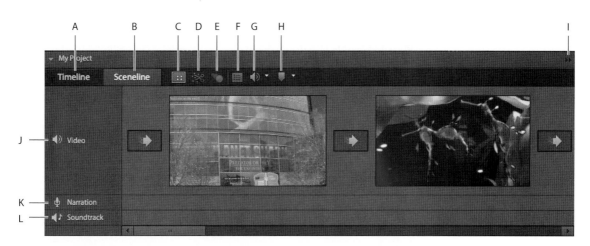

The Sceneline: **A.** Switch to Timeline. **B.** Switch to Sceneline. **C.** Pan and Zoom tool. **D.** Smart Trim mode. **E.** Motion Tracking mode. **F.** Properties. **G.** Audio tools. **H.** Markers. **I.** Panel menu. **J.** Change Track Volume (Scenes). **K.** Change Track Volume (Narration). **L.** Change Track Volume (Soundtrack).

2 To add clips in the Sceneline, do *any of the following*:

- **To add a clip at the end of the movie:** Use the scroll bar at the bottom of the My Project panel to scroll to the end of the movie (or press the End key). In Media view, click any clip, and then drag it onto the empty clip target at the end of the movie. If the SmartFix dialog opens and asks if you want to fix quality problems in the clip, click No.

- **To add a clip before another:** In Media view, click a clip, and then drag it onto an existing clip in the Sceneline. If the SmartFix dialog opens and asks if you want to fix quality problems in the clip, click No. Premiere Elements will insert the new clip before the clip it was dropped onto and will push the clip it was dragged onto and all subsequent clips to the right.

- **To add a clip after another in the Sceneline:** Select the clip after which you want to add the new clip. To do so in Media view, click the clip you want, and then drag it onto the Monitor panel. If the SmartFix dialog opens and asks if you want to fix quality problems in the clip, click No. Premiere Elements will insert the new clip after the clip currently selected in the Sceneline and will push all subsequent clips to the right.

3   Choose Edit > Undo three times to remove the clips that you added to the project during this exercise, or just reopen the project.

Moving Clips in the Sceneline

Working in the Sceneline makes it easy to move clips in your movie. Here's how it works.

1   To move a clip to a new position in the movie, click the clip in the Sceneline, and then drag it to a position before or after another clip. Release the pointer when a vertical blue line appears at the desired position.

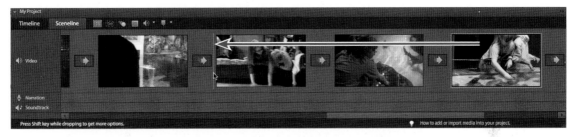

2   To move several adjacent clips to a new position in the movie, Ctrl-click (Windows)/Command-click (Mac OS) to select multiple clips in the Sceneline, and then drag them before or after another clip. Release the pointer when a vertical blue line appears at the desired position.

● **Note:** Although not shown in this exercise, a transition following a scene moves with the scene.

3   Choose Edit > Undo twice to undo the changes you made in this exercise.

Deleting Clips in the Sceneline

You may find, as your project develops, that you want to remove scenes you've imported into the Sceneline.

Note: When a clip is deleted from the Sceneline, the transition following the clip is also deleted. When a clip is deleted from the Timeline, the preceding and following transitions are deleted.

1   To delete a scene, right-click it in the Sceneline, and then *choose one of the following* from the context menu:

- **Delete Scene and its objects:** This option deletes the scene and any overlays it might have. Overlays are any items included above the scene, such as a title, graphic, or a picture-in-picture video. Note that the sample project that you're working with doesn't have any scenes with objects, so you'll choose the next option, Delete just Scene.

- **Delete just Scene:** This option deletes the clip but leaves the overlays in place.

The clips following the deleted clip move to the left to close the gap. This is the default behavior when deleting clips in Premiere Elements and is called a *ripple deletion.*

2   Choose Edit > Undo to restore the Scene that you just deleted.

Trimming Clips in the Sceneline

Although deleting unnecessary clips and thoughtfully rearranging the order of clips will make a better video, you'll inevitably want to shorten the length of some clips to create a more compelling movie. Here's how you'll accomplish this task.

Every clip has a beginning and an end. In editing terminology, these are referred to as the *In points* and *Out points.* Setting In and Out points does not actually delete frames from the hard drive; instead, it isolates a portion of the clip for use in your movie. When you trim a clip in Premiere Elements, you're simply changing the In and Out points.

1   In the Monitor panel, click Clip07.mp4 in the Project Task Area to open the Preview pane. Then press the spacebar to play the clip. You'll trim the first few frames from the start of this clip and the last few frames at the end.

2   Watching the timecode in the bottom left of the Monitor panel, drag the In point handle (▮) to the right until you see the 00;00;01;00 mark, which means

that you're trimming one second from the start of the clip. Notice that your Monitor panel has changed to a split screen: On the left, the Monitor displays the final frame of the scene *before* the one that you're trimming, and on the right, the Monitor displays the first frame of the scene that you're trimming.

3   Watching the timecode in the bottom left of the Monitor panel, click the Out point handle (▮) located on the right side of the current clip representation in the mini-timeline, and then drag it to the left until you see the 00;00;01;26 mark, which means that you're trimming one second and 26 frames from the end of the clip. The Monitor panel stays in split-screen view: On the left, it displays the final frame of the clip you're trimming, and on the right, it displays the initial frame of the *next* clip on the Sceneline.

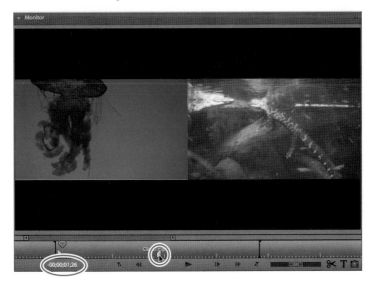

4   Click Clip07.mp4 again in the Sceneline. If necessary, click the Go to Previous Edit Point (⏮) button in the playback controls (or press the Page Up key on your keyboard) to move the current-time indicator to the start of the clip, and then press the spacebar to play the clip. Notice that you've trimmed away frames from the start and end of the clip, and have isolated the most usable segment.

Using the Split Clip Tool in the Sceneline

The Split Clip tool allows you to cut single clips into multiple clips. You can use this tool to split a clip into sections so you can delete one of them, which sometimes is more convenient than trimming. You can also use it to split a long clip into separate clips to edit them individually.

1   Click Clip06.mp4, and then press the spacebar to play the clip. The piranha sign certainly gets your attention, but the cutaway is pretty shaky. Let's cut this into two clips, one with the sign and one with a stable shot on the piranhas.

2   In the Monitor panel, position the current-time indicator around the 00;00;35;12 mark, which is about the last stable frame before cutting away from the sign.

3   To split the clip at the position of the current-time indicator, click the Split Clip button (✄) located near the right end of the Monitor panel just below the mini-timeline. You might have to resize the Monitor panel to its full width to see this icon. Or, choose Timeline > Split Clip. Premiere Elements will split the clip into two segments, both named Clip06.mp4.

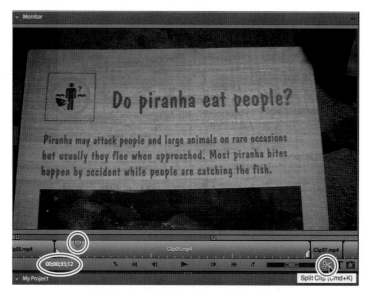

4 Now let's trim the unnecessary frames from the start of the second Clip06.
mp4 clip. Click the second Clip06.mp4 clip in the Sceneline or the Clip
Representation in Mini-Timeline. Watching the timecode in the bottom left of
the Monitor panel, drag the In point handle (▮) to the right until you see the
00;00;08;00 mark, which means that you're trimming eight seconds from the
start of the clip.

Note: After you split
a clip, Premiere Elements
treats each subclip as
a completely separate
clip, which you can trim
or reorder—just as with
any other clip.

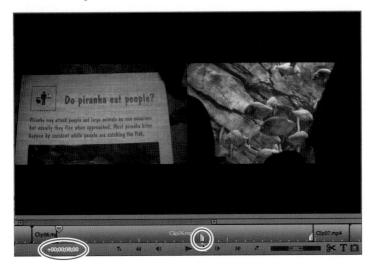

5 Click the first Clip06.mp4 clip, and then preview the video by pressing the
spacebar. You just cut eight seconds of unnecessary footage from the middle of
the clip by using the Split Clip tool and then by trimming in the Sceneline.

6 When you're finished reviewing the movie, choose File > Save As.

7 In the Save Project dialog, name the file *Lesson05_Win_work (Windows)*
or *Lesson05_Mac_work (Mac OS)* and save it in your Lesson05 folder.

Working with the My Project
Panel in the Timeline

Although you can perform most basic editing tasks in the Sceneline together with
the Monitor panel, you'll use the Timeline for many advanced editing tasks, especially those that involve *layering*, which means having multiple clips in the project
at the same location.

The Timeline graphically represents your movie as video and audio clips arranged
in vertically stacked tracks. Before beginning to work with the Timeline, follow the
instructions at the start of this lesson to load Lesson05_Start_Win.prel (Windows)
or Lesson05_Start_Mac (Mac OS).

1 In the My Project panel, click the Timeline button to switch to the Timeline. Depending on your monitor size, you might want to increase the height of the My Project panel to have more space to display additional video and audio tracks.

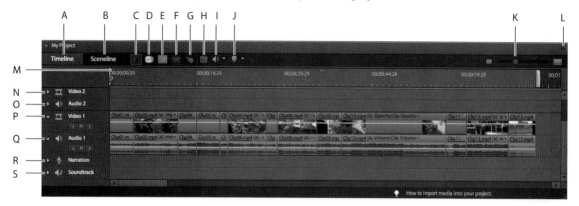

The Timeline: **A.** Switch to Timeline. **B.** Switch to Sceneline. **C.** Selection tool (V). **D.** Time Stretch tool. **E.** Pan and Zoom tool. **F.** Smart Trim mode. **G.** Motion Tracking mode. **H.** Properties. **I.** Audio tools. **J.** Markers. **K.** Zoom slider. **L.** Panel menu. **M.** Time ruler. **N.** Video track. **O.** Audio track. **P.** Set Video Track Display Style. **Q.** Set Audio Track Display Style. **R.** Narration track. **S.** Soundtrack.

The Timeline displays time horizontally. Clips that fall earlier in time appear to the left, and clips that come later in time appear to the right. Time is indicated by the time ruler near the top of the Timeline.

The Zoom controls in the Timeline let you change the timescale, allowing you to zoom out to see your entire video or zoom in to see time in more detail.

2 Click the Zoom In button (▦) once to zoom into the Timeline. Drag the Zoom slider to the right to zoom in farther.

Zooming in enables you to make precise edits in the Timeline. In doing so, however, you cannot see the entire Timeline at once.

3 To see other parts of your project, drag the scroll bar at the bottom of the Timeline to scroll through the Timeline.

4 Premiere Elements has keyboard shortcuts that enable you to quickly zoom in and out. Press the equals sign (=) to zoom in one step per keystroke; press the minus sign (-) to zoom out one step per keystroke. Press the Backslash (\) key to fit the entire video into the Timeline.

Adding and Deleting Tracks

As mentioned previously, the Timeline consists of vertically stacked tracks where you arrange media clips. Tracks let you layer video or audio and add compositing effects, picture-in-picture effects, overlay titles, sound tracks, and more.

You'll perform most of your editing in the Video 1 and the Audio 1 tracks. Directly above these are the Video 2 and Audio 2 tracks. Note that the stacking order of video tracks is important. The Monitor panel displays (and Premiere Elements produces) the tracks from the top down. Accordingly, any opaque areas of the clip in the Video 2 track will cover the view on the clip in the Video 1 track.

Conversely, the clip in the Video 1 track will show through any transparent areas of the clip in the Video 2 track. Below the Video 1 and Audio 1 tracks are two more audio tracks, Narration and Soundtrack. Audio tracks are combined in playback, and their stacking order is not relevant.

Premiere Elements starts with three open video tracks (Video 1, 2, and 3) and five open audio tracks (Soundtrack; Narration; and Audio 1, 2, and 3), which should be sufficient for most projects. Should you need additional video or audio tracks, you can add them by choosing Timeline > Add Tracks. You can delete any empty tracks by choosing Timeline > Delete Empty Tracks.

Changing the Height of Tracks

You can change the height of each track in the Timeline for better viewing and easier editing of your projects. As a track enlarges, it displays more information. Let's adjust the height of the Video 1 track.

1   If necessary, scroll down in the Timeline to see the Video 1 track.

2   At the left side of the Timeline, place your pointer between the Audio 2 and the Video 1 tracks. Your pointer should change to two parallel lines with two arrows (⬍). Drag up to expand the height of this track.

3   Right-click on any empty space in the My Project panel (not on an audio or video file), and choose Track Size > Small, Track Size > Medium, or Track Size > Large to change the track size for all tracks in the Timeline at the same time.

Customizing Track Views

You can display clips in the Timeline in different ways, depending on your preference or the task at hand. You can choose to display a thumbnail image at just the beginning of the clip; at the head and tail of the clip; or along the entire duration of the clip. For an audio track, you can choose to display or hide the audio waveform of the audio contents. Toggle through the various views of the video and audio tracks until you find the one that best suits your eye and working style.

1   By default, Premiere Elements displays all the frames in a video clip. However, at times you may find that you want to work with fewer visual distractions in your clip. Click the Set Display Style button (■) to the left of the Video 1 track to set the display style to Show Head and Tail. This will show you the first frame and last frame of all the clips in Video 1.

2   Click the Set Display Style button again to view only the head of the clip.

3   Click the Set Display Style button again to view the clip by its name only. No thumbnails will be displayed on the clip.

4   Click the Set Display Style button one more time to view the default style of all the frames.

Editing in the Timeline

Editing in the Timeline is very similar to editing in the Sceneline, although several controls are in different places. Most notably, when you switch to Timeline view, the mini-timeline beneath the Monitor panel moves to the Timeline, as does the current-time indicator. Other than that, all playback controls are identical.

Beyond the interface issues, most of the basic clip-related operations are also identical. For example, you add clips to the Timeline the same way you add them to the Sceneline. You move clips around the same way, and you delete clips the same way. If you repeat the exercises you've already completed in this chapter using the Timeline rather than the Sceneline, you'll quickly become adept at all of these operations.

Trimming and splitting clips is also very similar, but because these operations are so critical to everyday editing, let's run through them again in the Timeline.

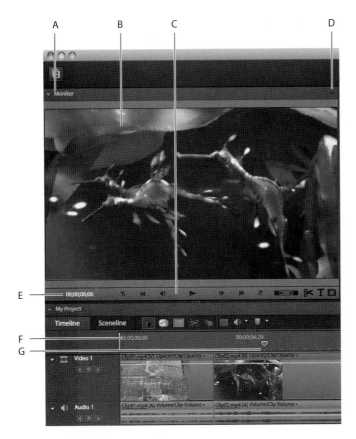

A. Docking header. B. Preview area. C. Panel menu. D. Playback controls.
E. Current time. F. Time ruler. G. Current-time indicator.

Trimming Clips in the Timeline

Every clip has a beginning and an end. In editing terminology these are referred to as the *In points* and the *Out points*, as described earlier in this lesson. Setting In and Out points does not actually delete frames from the hard drive; instead, it isolates a portion of the clip for use in your movie. When you trim a clip in Premiere Elements, you are simply changing the In and Out points.

1　Press the Home key to move the current-time indicator to the first frame of the project.

2　Press the Page Down key six times to move to the start of Clip07.mp4. Let's trim the same frames that you trimmed in the Sceneline a few lessons ago.

3　Click the Zoom In button (▦) at the top of the Timeline to magnify your view, and if necessary, drag the scroll bar on the bottom of the Timeline to center Clip07.mp4 in the Timeline. Zooming in and out to make these adjustments will feel awkward at first but will quickly become second nature.

4   Let's trim away unnecessary frames from the start of the clip. Hover the pointer over the left edge of Clip07.mp4 in the Timeline. The pointer changes to a two-headed drag pointer ((🔲) with the direction depending on the direction of your trim. Watching the current timecode in the bottom left of the Monitor panel, or in the text box that appears beneath the drag pointer, drag the edge of the clip to the right until you see the 00;00;01;00 mark, which means that you're trimming one second from the start of the clip. Notice that your Monitor panel has changed to a split screen: On the left, the Monitor displays the final frame of the scene *before* the one that you're trimming, and on the right, the Monitor displays the first frame of the scene that you're trimming. This gives you an ideal view of the transition from the first scene to the second.

5   Now let's trim the unnecessary frames from the end of the clip. Hover the pointer over the right edge of Clip07.mp4 in the Timeline. The pointer changes to a two-headed drag pointer (🔲). Watching the current timecode in the bottom left of the Monitor panel, or the text box that appears beneath the drag pointer, drag the edge of the clip to the left until you see the 00;00;01;26 mark, which means that you're trimming one second and 26 frames from the end of the clip. The Monitor panel stays in split-screen view: On the left, it displays the final frame of the clip you're trimming, and on the right, it displays the initial frame of the *next* clip on the Timeline.

6 Click the Clip07.mp4 clip again in the Timeline. If necessary, click the Go to Previous Edit Point (▶) button in the playback controls (or press the Page Up key on your keyboard) to move the current-time indicator to the start of the clip, and then press the spacebar to play the clip. Notice that you've trimmed away frames from the start and end of the clip, and have isolated the most usable segment.

Using the Split Clip Tool in the Timeline

The Split Clip tool allows you to cut single clips into multiple clips. You can use this tool to split a clip into sections so you can delete one of them, an alternative to trimming that you'll perform in this exercise. You can also use it to split a long clip into separate clips to edit them individually, although if you elect to Auto Analyze your clips, Premiere Elements will split most longer clips into separate scenes for you.

1 Press the Home key, and then press the Page Down key five times, which should take you to the start of Clip06.mp4. Then press the spacebar to play the clip. The piranha sign certainly gets your attention, but the cutaway is pretty shaky. Let's cut this into two clips, one with the sign and one with a stable shot on the piranhas.

2 Click the Zoom In button (▣) at the top of the Timeline to magnify your view, and (if necessary) drag the scroll bar on the bottom of the Timeline to center the Clip06.mp4 clip in the Timeline.

3 Position the current-time indicator at the 00;00;35;12 mark, which is about the last stable frame before cutting away from the sign.

4 To split the clip at the position of the current-time indicator, click the Split Clip button (✂) located near the right end of the Monitor panel just below the mini-timeline. You might have to resize the Monitor panel to its full width to see this icon. Or, choose Timeline > Split Clip. Premiere Elements will split the clip into two segments, both named Clip06.mp4.

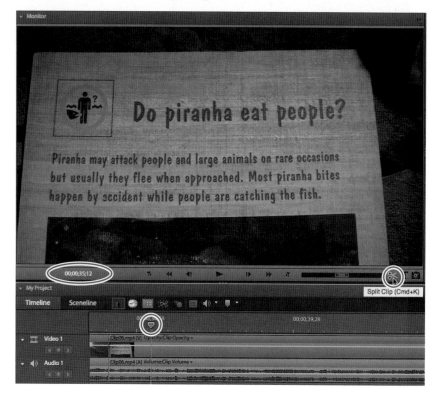

5 Now let's trim the unnecessary frames from the start of the second Clip06.mp4 clip. Hover the pointer over the left edge of the second Clip06.mp4 in the Timeline. The pointer changes to a two-headed drag pointer (⬌) with the direction depending on the direction of your trim. Watching the current timecode in the bottom left of the Monitor panel, or in the text box that appears beneath the drag pointer, drag the edge of the clip to the right until you see the 00;00;08;00 mark, which means that you're trimming eight seconds from the start of the clip. Then release the mouse to set the trim.

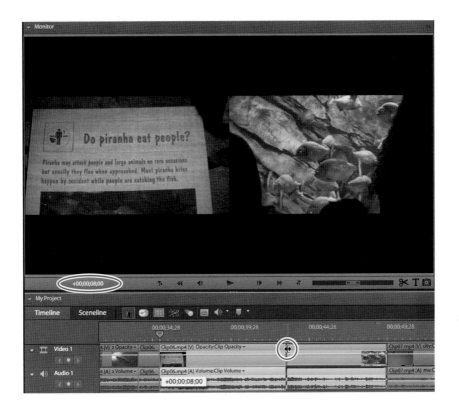

6   When you're finished reviewing the movie, choose File > Save As.

Creating a Slide Show

If you're like me, you like to shoot video and still-image shots of your events and travels, and it's fun to combine them into a single movie. Fortunately, Premiere Elements makes this very simple. Although you can add images in both the Sceneline and Timeline views, let's work in the former because it's more visual.

1   On the top left of the My Project panel, click Sceneline (Sceneline) (if necessary) to switch to the Sceneline view.

2   Press the End key on your keyboard to move to the end of the movie.

3   In the Project workspace, click the Get Media (Get Media) icon, and then click the Files and Folders button ( ). Premiere Elements opens the Add Media panel.

4   Navigate to the Lesson05 folder.

5   Select all JPEG files in the folder.

● **Note:** If you've previously saved the file, click Yes and replace the file. After you split a clip, Premiere Elements treats each subclip as a completely separate clip, which you can trim or reorder—just as with any other clip.

6 Click Open (Windows) Import (Mac OS) to import the files.

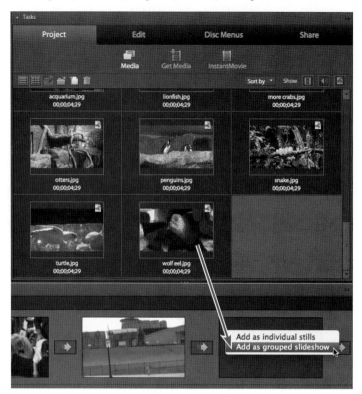

7 Ctrl-click (Windows)/Command-click (Mac OS) the photos in the order you want them to appear in the slide show. Drag the selected group to the first open scene in the Sceneline, release the mouse button, and choose "Add as grouped slideshow."

The Create SlideShow dialog opens.

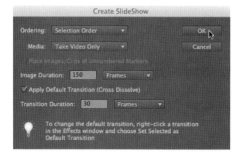

8 In the Create SlideShow dialog, choose Selection Order in the Ordering list box, leave all options at their default settings, and click OK. Premiere Elements adds each photo to the project in the order each was selected with a duration of 150 frames and a 30-frame transition between each photo.

9 In the Save Project dialog, name the file *Lesson05_Final* and save it in your Lesson05 folder.

Working in Smart Trim Mode

Smart Trim is an editing mode that can help you identify suboptimal regions within your videos so that you can either fix or delete them. Smart Trim relies on information gathered while Premiere Elements analyzes your clips, so you must Auto Analyze your clips before entering Smart Trim mode. You can operate Smart Trim either automatically or manually, although I recommend that you use Smart Trim manually until you understand how it works.

Let's reload the project to explore Smart Trim mode. Choose File > Open Project, navigate to the Lesson05 folder you copied to your hard drive, select the file Lesson05_Start_Win.prel (Windows) or Lesson05_Start_Mac.prel (Mac OS), and then click Open (Windows) Choose (Mac OS). If a dialog appears asking for the location of rendered files, click the Skip Previews button.

You can work with Smart Trim in either the Timeline or Sceneline; this exercise will demonstrate how it works in Timeline view. If necessary, to make your screen look like the figure in this exercise, click the Timeline button (Timeline) on the top left of the My Project panel to view the Timeline. Then click the Smart Trim icon ( ) atop the My Project panel to enter Smart Trim mode. If you haven't run the Auto Analyzer, Premiere Elements will run it now. Note that this could take a while, probably at least ten minutes on most computers.

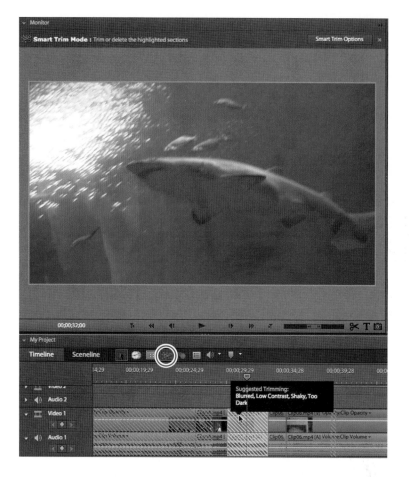

As you can see in the preceding figure, Smart Trim identifies problem areas via a zebra pattern. If you hover your mouse over the zebra pattern, a tool tip will detail the problems with the clip. You have multiple options regarding any clip, or portion of a clip, that Premiere Elements flags as a problem area.

Click any region with zebra striping to select it. You'll know you've selected the region when the zebra stripes turn bright white. Then you can right-click the region, and choose Trim, Keep, or Select All. Trim will delete the selected portion; Keep will retain it and turn off the zebra striping; and Select All will select multiple suboptimal regions within the same clip so you can trim or keep them all. In addition to these options, you can trim away any or all of the zebra striped regions of your clip by clicking and dragging an edge of the zebra striping to the new location, which is useful when you want to trim only a portion of the region originally identified by the zebra stripes.

How Smart Trim Works

Another approach to trimming a scene is to choose Smart Trim Options and adjust these options. Let's view the choices available by right-clicking any clip with zebra stripes and choosing Smart Trim Options.

As you can see, atop the Smart Trim Options window Premiere Elements uses two variables to identify suboptimal clips: Quality Level and Interest Level. Quality is simple to understand: If a clip is shaky or blurry, has poor contrast or lighting, or has other deficiencies that mar quality, Premiere Elements identifies the clip in Smart Trim mode as being below the Quality Level threshold, depending on how flawed the clip is and where you positioned the Quality Level slider.

By contrast, Interest Level analyzes qualities such as the amount of motion in a clip, the presence or absence of dialogue, and other criteria that tend to identify clips that are interesting to watch. If you shot a picture of a blank wall that was sharp, well lit, and completely stable, the Quality Level would be perfect, but Premiere Elements would flag it as lacking in the Interest Level department. That doesn't do much for those boring conversations with Uncle Harold, so you'll still have to delete those manually.

You can adjust the sliders to set the tolerance levels for either criterion: Moving the slider to the left increases the threshold for suboptimal clips, so that fewer and fewer clips will be flagged. Moving it to the right reduces the threshold so that more clips will be flagged.

For example, if you examine the clips in your project and find that most clips flagged by Premiere Elements look good to you, move the slider to the left and Premiere Elements will set the threshold higher and flag fewer clips. If clips left unflagged in Smart Trim mode look suboptimal to you for either Quality Level or Interest Level reasons, move the slider to the right.

Operating Modes

Note that there are two operating modes in the Smart Trim Options window: Manual and Automatic. In Manual mode, which is the default, Premiere Elements displays all suboptimal regions via the zebra stripes shown and discussed previously. If you opt for Automatic mode, Premiere Elements immediately deletes all suboptimal regions present on the Timeline. Thereafter, when you drag clips with suboptimal regions to the My Project panel, Premiere Elements presents a dialog asking if it's OK to remove Smart Trim sections.

There's an awful lot of bad video out there, and Smart Trim mode presents a very efficient way to identify it. In a real project, for example, when you've shot 30–60 minutes of footage and want to quickly isolate the best 3–5 minutes to include in your movie, Smart Trim mode can be a godsend. So check it out on your own projects and see how it works for you.

Two final points: First, when Smart Trim flags quality-related problems, you can either delete the offending sections or try to fix them, which you'll attempt to do in Lesson 6. So even if you decide to leave suboptimal clips in the project, Smart Trim helps by identifying sequences you can improve with corrective effects.

Second, to reiterate a comment I made earlier, I recommend that you *not* use Smart Trim in Automatic mode. Lots of "must have" sequences in your movies—such as your son blowing out the candles on his birthday cake or your daughter accepting her diploma—may not meet Premiere Elements' quality thresholds, but you still don't want to delete them. In Automatic mode, you don't get that choice.

Wonderful! You've finished another lesson and learned how to cut, trim, split, and arrange your raw video into a cohesive movie. Over the next few chapters, you'll polish it into a fine-tuned production.

Review Questions

1   What are the key differences between the Timeline and Sceneline?

2   What is an In point and what is an Out point, and what can you do with each?

3   What are two methods of shortening your video clips?

4   How does Premiere Elements combine video tracks at the same position on
    the Timeline?

5   What are the two criteria assessed by Premiere Elements in Smart Trim mode?

Review Answers

1   Premiere Elements offers two views in the My Project panel: Sceneline and Timeline.
    The Sceneline shows each clip as a separate thumbnail without regard to duration and
    doesn't show all available video tracks. The Timeline graphically represents your movie
    project as video and audio clips arranged in vertically stacked tracks with clip duration
    represented by the length. There are many common activities that you can perform in
    both views, including arranging clips, trimming frames from the beginning or end of
    a clip, splitting and deleting clips, and adding titles and effects. Many producers use
    both views in the course of a project—for example, adding and sequencing content in
    the Sceneline, and then switching over to the Timeline to add background music, titles,
    and other clips. Once you start working with multiple video clips at the same location,
    the Timeline becomes the superior view.

2   The In point is the first frame of your clip as seen in the Sceneline or Timeline, and
    the Out point is the last frame. You can move both the In and Out points to create a
    shorter or longer clip.

3   You can shorten your clips by trimming their In points and Out points, or by splitting
    the clip and deleting unwanted portions.

4   Premiere Elements renders the tracks from the top down. Any opaque areas of the clip
    in the Video 2 track will cover the view on the clip in the Video 1 track. Conversely,
    the clip in the Video 1 track will show through any transparent areas of the clip in the
    Video 2 track or if you reduce the Opacity of the clip in the Video 2 track.

5   Quality Level and Interest Level. The former concerns Premiere Elements' assessment
    of picture and audio quality on a technical level; the latter assesses multiple qualities,
    such as dialogue and motion, that tend to indicate whether or not a clip is interesting.

6 WORKING WITH EFFECTS

Lesson overview

In this lesson, you'll learn how to apply effects to the Georgia Aquarium clips that you used in previous lessons, and you'll also apply these effects to several new clips. Specifically, you'll learn how to do the following:

- Apply video effects to single and multiple clips

- Change effects and settings

- Improve the contrast and saturation of your videos

- Use Adobe Premiere Elements' Three-Way Color Corrector effect

- Copy effects and settings from one clip to another

- Animate a still image using Premiere Elements' Pan and Zoom effect

- Render your entire project and a work area within a project

- Control visual effects with keyframes

- Create a Picture-in-Picture effect

- Composite one video over another with Videomerge

- Apply Motion Tracking to a clip

- Apply Effect Masking to a clip

 This lesson will take approximately two hours.

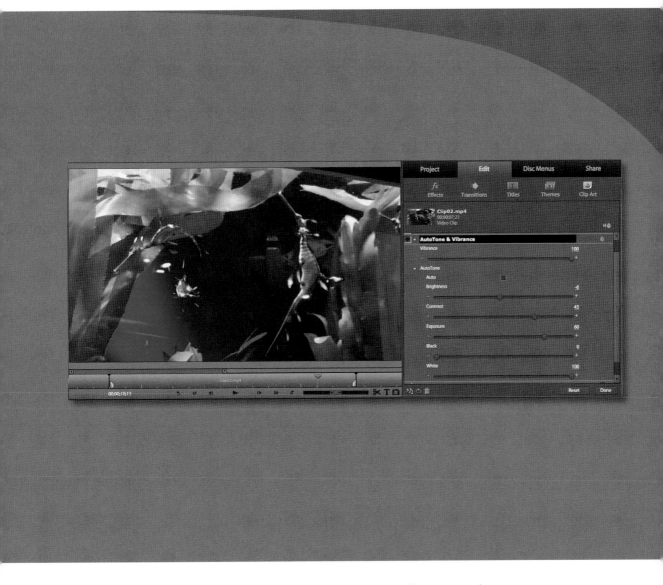

Using the AutoTone & Vibrance effect to improve the
contrast and saturation of these weedy sea dragons.

Getting Started

Before you begin the exercises in this lesson, make sure that you have correctly copied the Lesson06 folder from the DVD in the back of this book onto your computer's hard drive. For more information, see "Copying the Classroom in a Book Files" in the "Getting Started" section at the start of this book.

Now you're ready to begin working with the Lesson06 project file.

1 Launch Adobe Premiere Elements.

2 In the Welcome screen, click the Open Project button, and then click the Open folder.

3 In the Open Project dialog, navigate to the Lesson06 folder you copied to your hard drive. Within that folder, select the file Lesson06_Start_Win.prel (Windows) or Lesson06_Start_Mac.prel (Mac OS), and then click Open (Windows) Choose (Mac OS). If a dialog appears asking for the location of rendered files, click the Skip Previews button.

   Your project file opens with the Monitor, Tasks, and My Project panels open.

4 Choose Window > Restore Workspace to ensure that you start the lesson with the default panel layout.

Viewing the Completed Movie Before You Start

To see what you'll be creating in this lesson, you can play the completed movie.

● **Note:** Premiere Elements offers a large selection of diversified effects. It's a good idea to look up the gallery of video effects in your Premiere Elements Help file, which gives you a quick overview of all those effects actually applied to an image.

1 In the Project tab in the Tasks panel, click Media (![Media]).

2 In Media view, locate the file Lesson06_Movie.mov, and then double-click it to open the video into the Preview window.

3 In the Preview window, click the Play button (![Play ►]) to watch a video about a visit to the Georgia Aquarium, which you'll refine in this lesson.

4 When you're done, close the Preview window.

Using Effects

Effects (![Effects fx]) are located in two places in the Tasks panel's Edit tab. You'll find all "standard" effects in the Audio Effects folder or the Video Effects folder, organized by type. For example, all video effects that create a blur are grouped within the Blur & Sharpen folder within the Video Effects folder. As you'll see, you apply these effects by dragging them onto the target clip and configuring them in the Properties view.

Also, a small group of video and audio effects called "fixed" effects are applied automatically to each clip in your project. The two video effects are Motion and Opacity, and the audio effects are Volume and Balance. You access these fixed effects by clicking the clip in the My Project panel and then clicking the Properties button (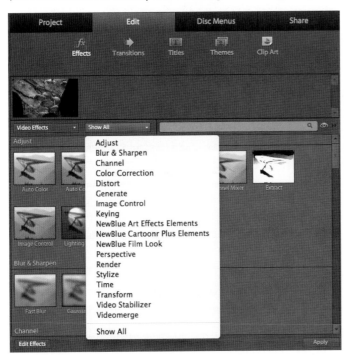).

Note: Premiere Elements for the Mac doesn't have as many effects as the Windows version, although all effects discussed in this chapter are available in both versions.

Fixed effects are provided for convenience; they're the effects that you'll use the most when editing your projects. You configure fixed and all other effects exactly the same way—you just have to apply standard effects before configuring them (the fixed effects are already there waiting to be configured).

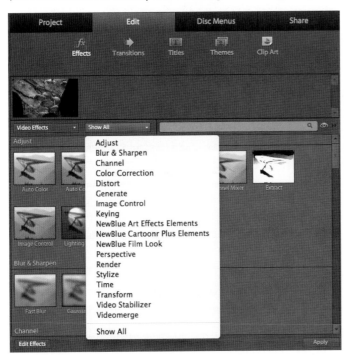

In addition to the fixed and standard effects designation, it's helpful to think about effects in the following categories:

- **Curative effects:** Curative effects correct problems in your video footage, including footage that's too bright or too dark, backlighted video, video that's too shaky because it was shot without a tripod, and even video that's a bit blurry. You can find curative effects in the Adjust folder (Auto Color, Auto Contrast, Auto Levels, Brightness & Contrast, Image Control, and Shadow/Highlight); Color Correction folder (AutoTone & Vibrance, Three-Way Color Corrector); Blur & Sharpen folder (Sharpen); Image Control folder (Black & White, Color Balance HLS, Color Balance RGB, Gamma Correction, Tint); and Video Stabilizer folder (Stabilizer).

- **Overlay effects:** Overlay effects allow you to composite one image over another. You can find overlay effects in the Keying and Videomerge folders.

- **Pan and Zoom effect:** This effect allows you to pan around and zoom into and away from still images and videos, allowing you to animate still images and add additional motion to videos. You can find this tool by clicking the Pan and Zoom icon (▦) in the My Project panel toolbar.

- **Artistic effects:** Most other effects are artistic effects that let you create a different look or feel from the original clip. These artistic effects can be quite powerful, like the Cartoonr Plus effect in the NewBlue Cartoonr Plus Elements folder that converts your videos to cartoons, and the Old Film effect in the NewBlue Film Look folder that can make your video look like old film by adding details like scratches and graininess. Other artistic effects let you add lightning to a clip (Lightning effect in the Render folder), add earthquake-like effects (Earthquake effect in the NewBlue Art Effects Elements folder), place a spotlight on a subject (Lighting effects in the Adjust folder), and apply many other looks and characteristics.

- **Speed controls:** You can speed up, slow down, or reverse your clips in the Timeline in the My Project panel by right-clicking the clip and choosing Time Stretch, or by choosing Clip > Time Stretch in the Premiere Elements menu.

● **Note:** Clicking the Properties (▤) button in the upper left of the My Project panel opens the Edit workspace in Properties view. There you'll find the functions of all fixed effects, which you open by clicking the disclosure triangle to the left of each effect.

- **Motion effects:** Motion effects also allow you to zoom into and around your original video clip or still image, and are used to adjust the framing of a video or create a pan and zoom effect. You adjust these parameters using the Motion controls found in the fixed effects that are automatically available for every clip in the My Project panel. Other fixed effects include the following:

  - **Image Control:** With Image Control you can control the brightness, contrast, hue, and saturation of clips.

  - **Opacity:** The Opacity effect lets you make a clip transparent, and by using keyframes, create fades and dissolves.

  - **Volume:** Volume lets you control the volume of audio clips.

  - **Balance:** Balance lets you adjust the balance of audio clips.

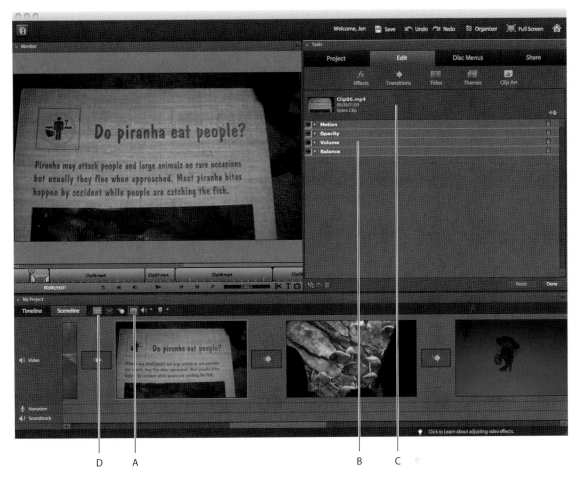

A. Properties button. **B.** Fixed effects. **C.** Properties view. **D.** Pan and Zoom tool.

After you apply an effect from the Effects panel to a clip, you can also adjust its parameters and set keyframes in the Effects Properties view. All effects that you add to a clip appear in the order in which you add them.

Although you can apply any and all of these effects at any time during the course of a project, the recommended workflow is to apply curative filters first, then adjust speed and motion, and then add other artistic effects. You can add an effect to any clip in the My Project panel and even apply the same effect numerous times to the same clip, but with different settings. By default, when you add an effect to a clip, it applies to the entire clip. If you want to apply an effect to only part of a clip, split it first using the Split Clip icon beneath the Monitor panel, and then apply the effect to the desired clip segment.

Working with SmartFix

Unless you disable the application of the Auto Analyzer in the Organizer, at some point Premiere Elements will analyze your clips, either in the background while you're performing other edits or after capture or import. While analyzing the clips, Premiere Elements looks for problems in the video.

As you saw with Smart Trim in the previous chapter, Premiere Elements uses some of this information to recommend which clips to trim away. In addition, you can instruct the application to use some of this information to fix common problems like shakiness and poor exposure. More specifically, if your video or still image is too bright or too dark, Premiere Elements will apply the Shadow/Highlight effect as you'll see in this exercise. If an SD video is too shaky, Premiere Elements will apply the Stabilizer effect. If you're working with shaky HD video, Premiere Elements won't apply the Stabilizer effect automatically because it's too processor-intensive, though you can apply the effect manually as you'll learn in a subsequent exercise.

This is how SmartFix works.

1   If necessary, click the Timeline icon (Timeline) on the top left of the My Project panel. Then press the End key on your keyboard to move to the end of the project.

2   In the Organizer workspace, click the Media icon (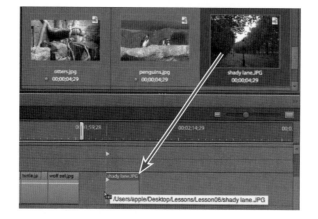) to enter Media view.

3   Scroll down until you find shady lane.jpg, a still image. If you haven't previously run the Auto Analyzer, click the image to select it, right-click, and choose Run Auto-Analyzer. Click and drag that clip into the Video 1 track on the Timeline. Premiere Elements opens the SmartFix window.

4   In the SmartFix window, click Yes to fix the quality problem in the clip.

5 In the Timeline, click the shady lane.jpg image to select it, and then click the Properties button (▣) at the top left of the Timeline. This opens the Tasks panel into Properties view. You'll see that Premiere Elements has applied the Shadow/Highlight effect to the clip.

If you click the eye icon next to the effect (officially called the "toggle the effect on or off" button), you'll see that the Shadow/Highlight effect does a marvelous job of brightening the shadows without "blowing out" the lighter regions. It's a wonderful effect for backlighted videos that you'll work with later in this chapter.

6 To return to the correct starting point for the rest of the chapter, either delete the image you just added to the project or reopen Lesson06_Start_Win.prel (Windows) or Lesson06_Start_Mac.prel (Mac OS) as described in the "Getting Started" section earlier in this chapter.

7 When Premiere Elements asks if you want to save your changes, click No.

▶ **Tip:** You can adjust the setting of any effect applied by Premiere Elements or disable or delete it. Unless you have a strong reason not to do so, it's generally a good idea to allow Premiere Elements to apply SmartFix whenever you add your clips to the My Project panel. It's not a panacea, but it's a great start towards improving clip quality.

Perfecting Your Clips

All projects are unique, and all source clips present unique issues. Outdoor projects shot during a nice, bright day are generally fairly simple to perfect. However, indoor shoots like the project you're working on here typically present a completely different range of problems, because lighting is often inadequate and camcorders sometimes have problems producing accurate colors when shooting under fluorescent or incandescent lighting. When your personal projects involve indoor shoots, you should experiment with the Brightness, Contrast, Hue, and Saturation adjustments in the Image Control effect, and the Auto Color, Auto Contrast, Auto Levels, and Shadow/Highlight effects in the Adjust folder. Often, applying the latter three—either individually or in concert—can produce quite remarkable improvements in minimal time and with little effort.

Whether you shot the source videos outside, inside, or both, typically you'll apply the curative effects first, fixing brightness, contrast, and color; then remove the shakes; and then reframe the video to get the best presentation possible. Thereafter, you can start to apply artistic effects.

Choosing and Applying Effects

Let's jump in and apply the AutoTone & Vibrance effect, which is a standard effect you'll apply from the Effects view. You can apply standard effects in either the Sceneline or Timeline; use the view that you feel most comfortable using, but I'll be in Sceneline.. Let's adjust Clip02.mp4, which shows several Weedy Sea Dragons, one of the coolest species in the aquarium.

Here's the problem. The clip was shot through the glass wall of a tank under less-than-stellar lighting conditions, and contrast is a bit low. Let's make those critters really pop.

1 If Clip02.mp4 isn't still selected, click to select it. Then select Effects (![fx Effects]) in the Edit tab in the Tasks panel.

2 In the list box next to Video Effects, click and select Color Correction.

3 To apply the effect, drag the AutoTone & Vibrance effect from Effects view and drop it onto Clip02.mp4. Premiere Elements applies the effect immediately, and you'll actually see the clip darken a bit.

4 Click the Properties button at the upper left of the My Project panel.

5 In Properties view, click the disclosure triangle to the left of the AutoTone & Vibrance effect to open the parameter settings.

6 Find the eye icon (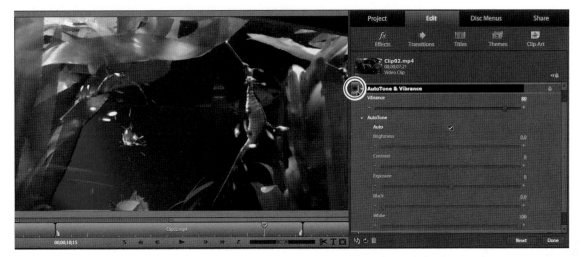) on the left side of the AutoTone & Vibrance effect. As mentioned previously, the eye icon toggles the effect on or off so you can compare the clip with and without the adjustments. Toggle the eye icon on and off a few times. In this application, the effect works almost perfectly, boosting contrast and saturation with no negative side effects.

The AutoTone effect uses automatic Premiere Elements settings for exposure, blacks, brightness, and contrast, and you can either use the default settings or adjust them manually by deselecting the Auto button. In contrast, the Vibrance slider, which adjusts clip saturation, must be adjusted manually.

7 Experiment with the Vibrance slider by dragging it to the left and right. Dragging to the left desaturates the clip, removing colors. At 100, the clip is at maximum saturation, though the difference between 80 and 100 is very slight. Let's leave it at 100.

8 Click the triangle next to AutoTone to see those options. Deselect the Auto check box, and then adjust the Brightness, Contrast, Exposure, Black, and White controls to your liking, using the values shown in the figure as a preliminary guide. Then select and deselect the Auto check box to compare your settings to the Auto settings to see if you're improving the automatic result. Toggle the eye icon (◉) on and off a few times to gauge the overall improvement in clip appearance.

● **Note:** You don't have to click Done to "set" the effect; you can simply click another clip and continue to edit. After you apply and configure an effect, it remains applied until you reset or delete the effect.

9 If you're satisfied with the results, click Done in the lower right of Properties view to return to the Project workspace.

10 To reset the Image Control parameters to their default values, click the AutoTone & Vibrance effect to select it, and then click Reset in the lower right of Properties view. This technique works for both fixed and standard effects. Choose Edit > Undo to undo the reset and keep the adjusted values.

11 Choose File > Save As and save your project as *Lesson06_Work.prel*.

Previewing and Rendering Effects

When you apply an effect to a clip or adjust a standard effect, Premiere Elements will show a very close approximation of the effect when you preview in the Monitor panel. In most instances, this is good enough to allow you to perfect your configuration options and move on to the next edit.

If the quality isn't sufficient, right-click the frame in the Monitor panel and choose Playback quality > Highest. This tells Premiere Elements to prioritize frame quality over playback speed. As a result, on slower computers, playback may be jerky, but frame quality should be very good. On the other hand, if playback speed isn't sufficient, right-click in the Monitor panel and make sure that Automatic is selected. This tells Premiere Elements to prioritize smoothness over frame quality. With Automatic selected, you might see some blurriness or pixelation in the frame, but playback should be smooth.

If neither setting gives you the preview quality that you need to finalize the edit, you'll have to render the clip. Start by clicking the Timeline icon (Timeline) at the top left of the My Project panel to enter Timeline view. If you applied the AutoTone & Vibrance effect detailed in the previous lesson, you should see a red line above Clip02.mp4 in the Timeline. In this instance, the red line tells you that an effect has been applied to the clip that hasn't been rendered.

In general, the red line tells you that some adjustment has been made to the clip that must be rendered before final production. For example, if you apply a title above a clip, you'll see the red line. If you insert a clip into a project that doesn't match the project preset—like the JPEG images inserted into the slide show at the end of the project—you'll see the red line as well. You don't have to render to preview your work; however, rendering will show you exactly how the final video will look.

To render the entire project, click Enter/Return. Premiere Elements opens the Rendering dialog, which tells you how many clips need to be rendered and how long it will take. After rendering, Premiere Elements turns the red bar to green, and you can start previewing your clips from the beginning.

Rendering a Work Area

In most instances, it's not necessary to render every edit, and sooner or later you'll have lots of red lines over your Timeline. At some point, you'll apply an effect that you do want to render. If you press Enter/Return to render, you render the *entire* clip, which can be time-consuming. As an alternative, you can simply render the work area that you're interested in.

● **Note:** Sometimes it may not be convenient to zoom out to see the entire clip and the edges of the Work Area bar. As an alternative to dragging the edges, you can also place the current-time indicator at the start of the work area and press Alt+[(Windows) or Option+[(Mac OS) to set the start of the work area. Then drag the current-time indicator to the end of the work area and press Alt+] (Windows) or Option+] (Mac OS) to set the end of the work area. Again, you don't need to render each effect to see it in its final form; in most instances, the real-time approximation produced by Premiere Elements should suffice. When you need to render, however, often it's more efficient to render a work area.

You don't have to render a work area with your Image Control adjustment to Clip02.mp4, because that should be the only clip with a red line, but next you'll learn how to render a work area using Clip02.mp4. To change the green line above the clip back to red, adjust any parameter in the AutoTone & Vibrance effect—for example, change the Brightness value to *14*.

1 Press the Backslash (\) key to show the entire project in the Timeline.

2 Drag the left edge of the Work Area bar to the start of Clip02.mp4.

3 Drag the right edge of the Work Area bar to the end of Clip02.mp4.

4 Press Enter/Return to render the work area. Premiere Elements will render the work area and start previewing at the start of Clip02.mp4.

Three-Way Color Corrector

The Three-Way Color Corrector effect lets you make subtle corrections by adjusting a clip's color and brightness in three separate ranges: shadows, midtones, and highlights. It's a professional quality tool that can really help you fine-tune your productions. Let's take a quick look at what it is and how it works. I'll conclude with a brief discussion on when to use it.

1 Click to select Clip12.mp4. Then select Effects (🔲 Effects) in the Edit tab in the Tasks panel.

2 In the list box next to Video Effects, click and select Color Correction.

3 To apply the effect, drag the Three-Way Color Corrector effect from Effects view and drop it onto Clip12.mp4.

4 Click the Properties button at the upper left of the My Project panel.

5 In Properties view, click the disclosure triangle to the left of the Three-Way Color Corrector effect to open the parameter settings. Select the Preview Tonal Ranges check box. Note that my current-time indicator is on 00;01;19;22; place yours there or thereabouts.

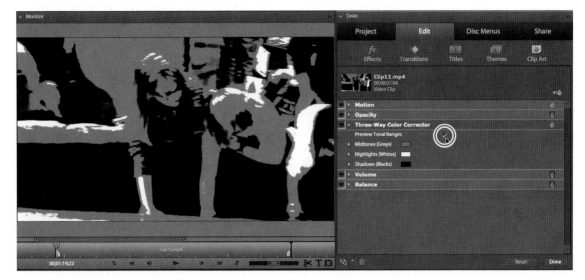

As shown in the figure, the Three-Way Color Corrector effect divides your image into three ranges based on the brightness of the pixels. The brightest pixels are called the highlights (whites), the darkest pixels are called the shadows (blacks), and the middle pixels are called the midtones (greys).

When you select the Preview Tonal Ranges check box, Premiere Elements shows you the three ranges in your video with midtones shown as gray, highlights shown as white, and shadows shown as black. Then, as you'll see in a moment, the Three-Way Color Corrector provides separate controls that let you adjust each tonal range separately. In contrast, most other effects, such as AutoTone & Vibrance, work on all pixels as a whole, so you can't fine-tune any specific tonal range.

Entire books have been written on how to use Three-Way Color Corrector effects, but you can get 95 percent of the benefit by taking the following steps.

6 In Properties view, deselect the Preview Tonal Ranges check box.

7   Click the disclosure triangle to the left of Highlights (Whites) to reveal those controls. Click the Set White Balance eyedropper next to the white color chip to select it, and then move into the frame and select an object that you know to be white. In this case, I used the white shirt on the girl to the right of my daughters. This tells Adobe Premiere Elements that these pixels should be white, and the program color corrects those pixels and all others in that tonal range accordingly.

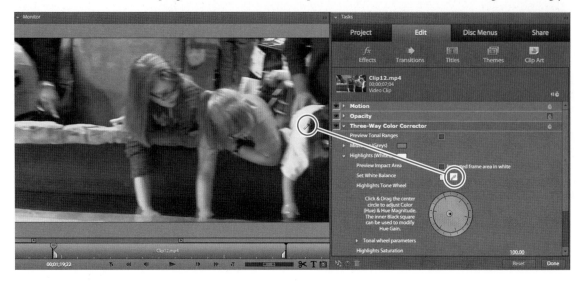

8   Click the disclosure triangle to the left of Shadows (Blacks) to reveal those controls. Click the Set Black Balance eyedropper next to the black color chip to select it, and then move into the frame and select an object that you know to be black. In this case, I used the petting tank wall on the extreme lower right of the frame. This tells Premiere Elements that these pixels should be black, and the program color corrects those pixels and all others in the tonal range accordingly.

9   Click the disclosure triangle to the left of Midtones (Greys) to reveal those controls. Select the "Impacted frame area in white" check box to reveal the tonal range impacted by the adjustment that you're about to make. You'll see a vast swath of white, including the skin of my daughters and others at the tank. Accordingly, you'll use this control to adjust skin tones, which are typically the most important pixels in the shot, because viewers tend to watch faces more than any other objects.

10 Deselect the "Impacted frame area in white" check box to reveal the normal frame. Note that you can't adjust colors when this or the Preview Tonal Ranges check box is selected.

11 Unfortunately, there is no equivalent of the absolute white or black pixels that you selected in the previous two steps, so you have to make a subjective call. Under the fluorescent lighting, the skin tones look a bit muted and grayish. Add some red in the skin tones by dragging the center of the color wheel towards red.

12 Toggle the eye icon on and off a few times to gauge the overall improvement in clip appearance.

13 If you're satisfied with the results, click Done in the lower right of Properties view to return to the Project workspace.

14 Save your project as *Lesson06_Work.prel*.

Now you've learned how to use two effects that can really improve the color and contrast of your clips: the AutoTone & Vibrance and Three-Way Color Corrector effects. When should you use one and not the other? Well, one obvious answer is to try both and see which works best. You'll do that in a moment.

As a general rule, however, I think you'll find that for relatively low-quality clips, like those in this project, which were shot under fluorescent lighting using auto-exposure without a tripod, the AutoTone & Vibrance effect can give you a quick boost in quality with minimal fussing. As your source videos improve with better lighting, manual exposure, and more stable footage, the Three-Way Color Corrector will let you fine-tune your videos with much more control. Obviously, it's great to have both options at your disposal.

● **Note:** If you click the disclosure triangle next to "Tonal wheel parameters" in each tonal range in the Three-Way Color Corrector, you can find precise numerical values for the adjustments in the color wheel, and the Adobe Premiere Elements Help file contains precise definitions of all configuration options. In this application, however, my preferred plan of action is the subjective "wiggle it until it looks right" approach rather than trying to fine-tune the settings with numerical values.

Copying Effects from One Clip to Another

Because effects are customized a single clip at a time, it would be quite time-consuming to place the same effect across numerous clips, especially if you had to drop the effect on each clip. This is especially true for color-related effects, which typically you have to apply to all shots from a specific scene. Fortunately, Premiere Elements provides several simple ways to copy effects and their settings from one clip to another.

Let's copy the AutoTone & Vibrance effect that you customized on those Weedy Sea Dragons in Clip02.mp4 onto my daughters in Clip12.mp4 to see how it compares with the Three-Way Color Corrector effect. Then, you'll delete the undesired effect.

● **Note:** You can also right-click in Properties view and choose Copy or press Ctrl+C (Windows)/ Command+C (Mac OS) to copy the selected effects.

1 Click Clip02.mp4 in either the Sceneline or Timeline to select it.

2 Click the Properties button in the upper left of the My Project panel to open the Effects Properties view.

3 Click the AutoTone & Vibrance effect in Properties view.

4 Choose Edit > Copy.

5 In either the Sceneline or Timeline, click to select Clip12.mp4. Click the Properties button on the upper left of the My Project panel to open Properties view.

6 Right-click in the blank gray area beneath the fixed and standard effects in Properties view, and then choose Paste. Premiere Elements applies the AutoTone & Vibrance effect to this clip with the same properties.

7 Toggle the eye icon () off and on for both effects to compare the two. Note that when both eye icons are visible, both effects are applied, which you don't want in this case. In this particular application, the AutoTone & Vibrance effect seems to do a better job, so you'll delete the Three-Way Color Corrector in a moment. But first, you'll save the AutoTone & Vibrance preset so it's easier to apply to other clips.

Saving a Preset

After you've created the ideal AutoTone & Vibrance or Three-Way Color Corrector settings for a particular scene, you'll probably want to apply it to all clips in that scene. The easiest way to do this is to save it as a preset.

1 Click Clip02.mp4 in either the Sceneline or Timeline to select it.

2 Click the Properties button in the upper left of the My Project panel to open the Effects Properties view.

3 Right-click the AutoTone & Vibrance effect in Properties view and choose Save Preset. Adobe Premiere Elements opens the Save Preset dialog.

4 Choose Scale for Type, and complete the name and any description. Then click OK to save the preset.

5 To view a custom preset, choose the My Presets folder from the drop-down list in the Effects view. From there, you apply it by dragging the effect onto a clip or clips, just like any other effect.

Note: Anchor to In Point and Anchor to Out Point control how clips with keyframes are applied to new clips. Because there are no keyframes in the AutoTone & Vibrance preset, choose Scale to apply the effect to the entire clip.

Deleting Standard Effects

You can't delete fixed effects, but to delete any standard effect, right-click to select it in Properties view, and then choose either Delete Selected Effect or Delete All Effects from Clip. Or, select the clip and click the trash can icon (■) on the lower left. Use either procedure to delete the Three-Way Color Corrector effect on Clip12.mp4.

Fixing Backlighted Video

● **Note:** Like the Three-Way Color Corrector, the Shadow/Highlight effect divides each video frame into three regions based on the original brightness of the pixels in the frame: Shadows (Blacks), Highlights (Whites), and Midtones (Greys). The Shadow and Highlight sliders let you customize the adjustments to these respective regions, but the effect doesn't modify the Midtone values.

The AutoTone & Vibrance effect works well with clips that need to be adjusted globally—for example, when the entire clip is too dark or lacks contrast. The Three-Way Color Corrector can adjust color values in different tonal ranges but is overkill for clips with simple backlighting problems, like Clip10.mp4. In that clip, the water in the middle of the frame is so bright that the camera darkened my daughter and the sharks and rays in the Georgia Aquarium's awesome petting tank. To improve this video, I want to brighten my daughter and the sharks and rays, but not the water.

So let's use the Shadow/Highlight effect, which lets you brighten just the shadows in the clip without adjusting other regions. This effect is perfect for fixing *backlighting*, which often occurs when shooting against a bright background and is characterized by dark faces, such as those in Clip10.mp4.

1. Click the Properties button in the upper left of the My Project panel, and then click the Edit tab to enter Effects view (if necessary).

2. In the list box next to Video Effects, click and select Adjust.

3. Drag the Shadow/Highlight effect from the Effects view onto Clip10.mp4. If necessary, drag the current-time indicator to 00;01;01;27 to view that frame.

Working with Multiple Clips Simultaneously

The Shadow/Highlight effect is as close to a panacea as I've seen in any video editor. Although none of the photos in the slide show at the end of the movie were dark enough to trigger SmartFix's application of the Shadow/Highlight effect, some could use brightening.

One great feature in Premiere Elements is the ability to apply any effect—including Shadow/Highlight—to multiple clips. To try this, in Timeline mode, select all clips on the Timeline, and then drag the Shadow/Highlight effect onto any one of them. Premiere Elements applies the effect to all selected clips.

If you change your mind, you can delete the effect from all clips simultaneously as well. Again, just click and select all clips, right-click, and choose Remove Effects > Video Effects. Premiere Elements will remove all effects from all video clips. Give both operations a try—you'll find they're real time-savers.

4   Click the Properties button at the top left of the My Project panel or the Edit Effects button at the lower left of the Effects view to open the Effects Properties view.

5   In the Properties view, click the eye icon next to the Shadow/Highlight effect to toggle it on and off. Note how the effect brightens the darker regions without adjusting the brighter regions like the water in the upper middle of the frame.

6   Click the disclosure triangle to the left of the Shadow/Highlight effect to open the parameter settings.

7   The default parameters may be too conservative for this clip. Let's try to improve the results. To adjust the effect manually, deselect the Auto Amounts check box.

8   To adjust the darker regions, drag the Shadow Amount slider to the right to increase the brightness of pixels in the shadows (including the faces in this clip) and to the left to decrease the brightness. Try to increase brightness as much as you can without fading the video. I suggest a setting of about 40.

9   To adjust the brightest regions, drag the Highlight Amount slider to the right to reduce the brightness of highlight pixels. Try a setting of about 20. Click the eye icon to the left of the Shadow/Highlight effect to toggle the effect on and off.

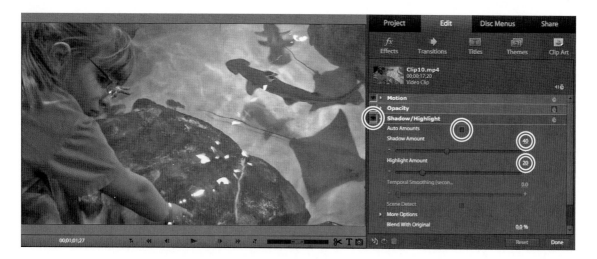

These are the most important manual controls in the Shadow/Highlight effect; to learn about the others, check the Premiere Elements Help file.

10 Save your project as *Lesson06_Work.prel*.

Reframing a Clip Using Motion Controls

Let's take a look at the fixed effects that you'll probably use the most: the Motion controls. In this exercise, you'll learn how to use these effects to reframe a shot; later in the lesson, you'll learn how to use these controls to create a pan and zoom effect within an image.

The clip you'll edit is the sixth clip of the project, the first portion of Clip06.mp4. It's the shot of the piranha sign, but it's not quite centered in the frame. In this lesson, you'll use Motion controls to reframe the shot.

1 In either the Sceneline or Timeline, click the first Clip06.mp4.

2 If you're not already in Properties view, click the Properties button in the upper left of the My Project panel.

3 In Properties view, click the disclosure triangle to the left of the Motion effect to open the parameter settings.

4 Zoom into the video and make it larger. Drag the Scale slider to the right until it reaches the value of 115 (or click the numeric entry to make it active, type *115*, and then press Enter/Return).

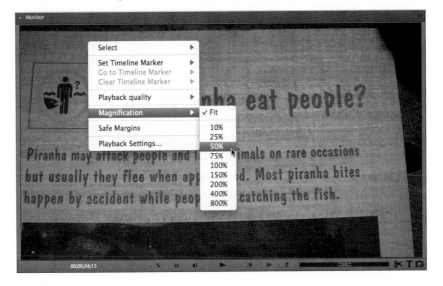

5   Now let's reframe the image. In the Monitor panel, right-click the frame and choose Magnification > 50%. If you're working on a notebook or very small monitor, choose Magnification > 25%.

6   Click the frame to make the center crosshair active. You should see a white box outside the visible frame in the Monitor panel. As you've probably guessed, this is an outline of the entire video, which you can drag around to optimize positioning within the visible area in the Monitor panel. As you drag the frame

▶ **Tip:** Whenever you're repositioning a clip like this, scroll through the entire video to make sure that you don't obscure some critical action in the shot.

around, note that the numeric Position parameters on the right are updated as you move it. You can position the frame either by dragging it directly as you just did or by typing in new numeric parameters. I used 716 and 360, which shifted the video to the right while maintaining the same vertical position.

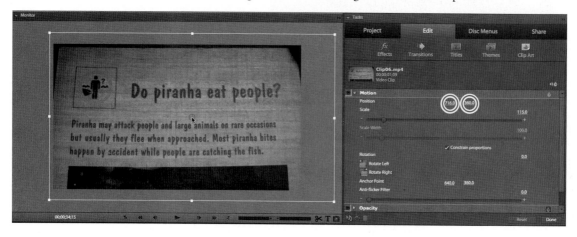

● **Note:** If you zoom too far into a clip, you can cause some blurriness or softness in the clip. If blurriness results from your reframing efforts, you can minimize it to some degree by applying the Sharpen effect.

7   In the Monitor panel, right-click the frame and choose Magnification > 100%. This sets your preview at a pixel-for-pixel preview, which is helpful when previewing Motion control adjustments.

8   Click the Play button in the Monitor panel to preview the effect.

Stabilizing Shaky Footage

One common problem with home video footage is excessive shakiness, which can occur anytime you don't use a tripod. Via the SmartFix function, Premiere Elements will stabilize the worst of the SD clips, but for HD clips like those we're using in this project, you'll have to do it manually. I didn't bring a tripod into the Georgia Aquarium, so all clips are a bit shaky, but one of the worst is Clip11.mp4. In this exercise, you'll apply the Stabilize filter to correct this problem.

1   In the list box next to Video Effects, click and select Video Stabilizer.

2   Drag the Stabilizer effect from Effects view and drop it onto Clip11.mp4.

3   Click the Properties button in the upper left of the My Project panel or the Edit Effects button in Effects view to open Effects Properties view.

4   In Properties view, click the disclosure triangle to the left of the Stabilizer effect to open the parameter settings.

5   Render and preview the clip. There's no problem with this application of the Stabilizer effect, but sometimes you'll notice a black bar on the top, bottom, or sides of the clip where the adjustment was too strong and extended beyond the frame's edge. To correct this, in Properties view, select the Limit To Zoom check box, which limits the stabilization to the edges of the frame.

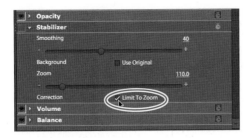

6 Drag through the rest of the clip to see if any other bars appear. If not, click Done on the lower right in Properties view to move on to your next edit.

Play the clip, using the eye icon to the left of the Stabilizer effect to toggle it on and off. The clip is definitely easier to watch with the Stabilizer effect applied.

Changing Playback Speed

Changing playback speed is a commonly used effect, and Premiere Elements offers two techniques for speeding up or slowing down your video. In this exercise, you'll learn how to adjust the speed of clips bounded by others in the Timeline. In a subsequent exercise, you'll learn how to adjust the speed of a clip that doesn't have a clip immediately after it on the Timeline.

Specifically, in this exercise, you'll adjust the speed of the first Clip06.mp4—which is a bit too short to let the viewer read the entire sign—slowing it down to 25 percent of its original speed. Note that you can implement this effect only in the Timeline, so step 1 will switch over to the Timeline view of the My Project panel.

1 If you're currently working in the Sceneline, in the My Project panel, click the Timeline button to switch to Timeline. If necessary, zoom into the Timeline so you can easily see the individual clips.

2 Right-click the first Clip06.mp4 and choose Time Stretch. Premiere Elements opens the Time Stretch panel.

3 Type 25 in the Speed box (where it will appear as 25%), and select the Maintain Audio Pitch check box.

4 Click OK to close the panel. Premiere Elements extends the clip to its new duration and pushes back all subsequent files. Drag the current-time indicator to the start of the clip, and press the spacebar to play the clip and observe the slow motion. Press the spacebar again to stop playback. Though the pitch is correct, the audio sounds like the track from a bad horror movie. Don't worry; you'll cover it up with narration and some music in Chapter 9.

● **Note:** As you probably can guess, the Reverse Speed check box, when enabled, will reverse the clip, making the video play backward.

5 Save your project as *Lesson06_Work.prel*.

Creating a Pan and Zoom Effect

I'm the designated shooter in all family events, so I'm hardly ever in the actual video, which gets old after a while. Fortunately, the Georgia Aquarium offers a photo service that can shoot the whole group, which I gladly purchased. Now let's integrate that shot into the video using Premiere Elements' new Pan and Zoom tool.

1   Click the Project tab to enter Media view. Click to select aquarium.jpg; then right-click the image, and choose Run Auto-Analyzer. This allows Premiere Elements to detect the smiling faces in the image.

2   In the My Project panel, click Sceneline (Sceneline) to enter Sceneline view. Drag and release aquarium.jpg atop Clip02.mp4 (the Weedy Sea Dragons) to insert the still image before that video clip. Note that you can perform these edits in Timeline view, but I thought Sceneline was better to illustrate where I inserted the image.

3   In the My Project panel, click the Pan and Zoom icon (▦) to open the Pan and Zoom tool.

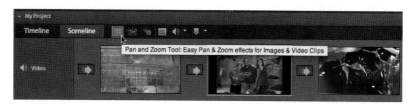

4   In the upper-left toolbar in the Pan and Zoom tool, click Face Frames (Face Frames). This tells Premiere Elements to create a project that pans to all faces in the project.

5   On the bottom of the Pan and Zoom tool, click Play Output (Play Output ▶) to watch the effect. It's a good start, but I'm not sure we want to zoom in that close. Let's explore how the tool works and then make some adjustments.

The basic unit of operation of the Pan and Zoom tool is the focus frame, and the tool creates motion by moving from focus frame to focus frame. If your image has faces, like aquarium.jpg, Premiere Elements will insert a focus frame around each face after analyzing the image. If there are no faces, you insert the focus frames manually by clicking the area in the frame that you want to focus on.

The focus frames in the image are presented in the thumbnail view at the bottom of the dialog. You can change the order by dragging the thumbnails into the desired order. Click Play Output to preview the Pan and Zoom effect at any time.

Once created, you can control the size of the focus frames. You can also control the pan duration, or how long it takes to move from one focus frame to another, as well as hold time, which is the duration that the effect stays on that focus frame.

A. Zoom controls for the image. **B.** Clear frames. **C.** New frame. **D.** Face frame. **E.** Hold time. **F.** Delete frame. **G.** Zoom controls for focus frame. **H.** Resize handlers for focus frame. **I.** Focus frame number. **J.** Pan duration. **K.** Focus frame markers. **L.** Focus frame thumbnails.

Customizing the Pan and Zoom Effect

Now that you have a bit of background, let's customize the pan and zoom effect. In general, I want to start out with a very wide shot, and then zoom closer and closer into the faces.

1   If you're still in Preview mode, click the Exit Preview button on top of the preview window (or click escape on your keyboard) to exit preview mode. In the Pan and Zoom thumbnail view, click the first thumbnail to select it. Then use the resize handlers at the corners of the image to make it span across the entire image, as shown in the figure. Be careful not to click outside the frame, or you'll create another focus frame.

2   In the Pan and Zoom thumbnail view, click the second thumbnail to select it. Then use the resize handlers at the corners of the focus frame to frame it so it's closer than the first focus frame, as shown in the figure. Again, be careful not to click outside the frame, or you'll create another focus frame.

3 Let's shorten the pan time between the first focus frame and the second. Click the "5s" text on the Pan line on the right to open the Pan Time dialog. Drag the time to the left so that it equals 00;00;03;00. Click OK to close the Pan Time dialog.

4 In the Pan and Zoom thumbnail view, click the third thumbnail to select it. Then use the resize handlers at the corners of the focus frame to create the medium close-up shown in the figure.

5 Ah, one big happy family—mommy logging some retail therapy at Phipps Plaza and daddy getting some quality time with the girls, and now in the video! Let's savor the moment even further by expanding the duration of the hold time at the end of the third focus frame. Click Hold:1s (Windows) or 0s (Mac OS) on the upper left of the focus frame to open the Hold Time dialog, and drag the duration to 00;00;02;00 as shown. Then Click OK to close the Hold Time dialog.

6 On the bottom of the Pan and Zoom tool, click Play Output (Play Output ▶) to watch the effect. It's bringing tears to my eyes; how about you? Well, let's just agree that it's close enough to perfect to click Done on the bottom right of the Pan and Zoom Tool dialog, and move on to the next edit.

Note: You can use the Pan and Zoom tool with video, but you can't use the Face Frames option.

Working with Keyframes

Every clip in the Timeline, and most effects that you apply to them, can be modified over time. This involves a concept called *keyframing*. Essentially, a keyframe is a location in the Timeline where you specify a value for a specific property. When you set two keyframes, Premiere Elements interpolates the value of that property over all frames between the two keyframes, effecting a change gradually over time, basically creating an animated effect. For example, in the next exercise, you'll use keyframes to animate the appearance of an effect.

Keyframes give you significant flexibility and creativity in your projects. Although they sound challenging at first, if you work through the next few exercises, you'll quickly grasp their operation and utility.

Using Keyframes to Animate Effects

Animating an effect using keyframes is a very powerful capability: Essentially, it lets you create custom transitions using any Premiere Elements' effect.

One word of caution: This section is more advanced than some users of Premiere Elements may need, so feel free to skip to the next lesson. But before you do, you should know that keyframing is the basis of animation in programs such as Adobe Premiere Pro and Adobe After Effects, which means this could be a useful introduction to using those tools, and the exercise is not difficult to complete. If you do choose to skip it, you can always revisit it later.

In this exercise, you'll be animating the NewBlue Metallic effect to create a unique transition that you'll apply to the start of several clips.

1 Select Effects ( ) in the Edit tab in the Tasks panel, and in the list box next to Video Effects, click and select NewBlue Art Effects Elements.

2 Press the Home key to move your current-time indicator to the start of the project. Increase the magnification of the Timeline if needed.

3 Drag the Metallic effect from Effects view and drop it onto Clip05.mp4 to apply it. You'll see the effect applied in the Monitor panel.

4 Click the Edit Effects button in Effects view, and then click the disclosure triangle next to Metallic to reveal the controls.

5 In the top right of Properties view, click the Show Keyframes ( ) button. You may need to expand the size of Properties view to better view the keyframes.

6 Note the mini-timeline at the top of Properties view, which has the same values as the Timeline in the My Project panel for the selected clip and has a matching current-time indicator. With the current-time indicator at the start of the

clip, click the small stopwatch to the right of the Metallic controls to enable animation for this property. After you click the stopwatch, a small diamond appears in the mini-timeline within Properties view to the right of the three configurable properties in the Metallic control. These are the initial keyframes.

7 When producing your own movies, you might want to adjust the effect settings to customize them for your video. Let's keep things simple here and accept the default values.

8 Now you'll set the second set of keyframes. In the mini-timeline in Properties view, drag the current-time indicator to the right about two seconds into the clip.

9 Drag the Metal slider all the way to the left (to a 0.00 value) and the Picture slider all the way to the right (to the 100.00 value), which essentially turns off the effect.

Changing the value automatically adds a second keyframe, which is represented as a second diamond in the Timeline in Properties view. Once animation has been turned on, Premiere Elements automatically animates the effect between the two values. Note that Premiere Elements didn't create a new keyframe for the color value because you did not adjust that option.

● **Note:** The time codes that you see in the figure below will probably be different from what you're seeing in your program right now. That's because Adobe Premiere Elements uses different default times for the Pan and Zoom effect in Windows and on the Mac, and those times were being finalized while I was writing the book. Sorry for any convenience or confusion.

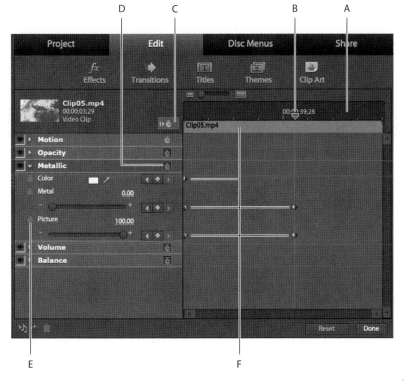

A. Mini-timeline. **B.** Current-time indicator. **C.** Hide Keyframes. **D.** Toggle Animation button (enables keyframes). **E.** Keyframable configuration options in the Metallic effect. **F.** Keyframes.

Note: If you hadn't set the second set of keyframes, the Metallic effect would have continued without change through the end of the clip but wouldn't continue on to subsequent clips.

10 Drag the current-time indicator to the start of Clip05.mp4, and then press the spacebar to play the clip and the effect. The clip starts out with the Metallic in full effect and returns to a normal appearance at the 00;00;40;05 mark. Press the spacebar again to stop playback.

11 Save your project as *Lesson06_Work.prel*.

Creating a Fade Out Using Keyframes

You can control keyframes in two locations in Premiere Elements: Properties view and the Timeline. In this exercise, you'll adjust the opacity keyframes of a video clip in the Timeline.

1 Click to select the Wolf eel.jpg image, which is the last image in the Timeline. You may need to scroll to the right in the Timeline to fully see the image.

2 Let's make the video tracks as large as possible to provide some working space. To the right of the Wolf eel.jpg clip, right-click a blank area on the Timeline and choose Track Size > Large. You may have to adjust the scroll bars on the right of the Timeline to see the clip after adjusting the track size.

3 Drag the current-time indicator to about two seconds from the end of the project.

4 Click the Zoom In tool (▦) in the Timeline to increase your view of the clip.

When you're working with clip keyframes, it's often helpful to increase the magnification. The orange line spanning horizontally across the clip is the connector line (or graph) between keyframes. By default, all clips have the Opacity property enabled.

5 Working with the Wolf eel.jpg, place your pointer over the orange connector line at the location of the current-time indicator. The pointer changes to a double-arrow icon (▦).

6 Drag the connector line down towards the bottom of the clip. As you drag, you'll see a small window with changing numbers. The numbers represent the opacity values. Drag the connector line down to approximately the 50% level. Don't worry if you can't get an exact number. When you release the pointer, you'll see that the clip now has an opacity value of only 50% and is much darker than before.

7 Drag the connector line back up towards the top of the clip to restore the clip's opacity to 100%.

Now you'll add keyframes to help Premiere Elements create a fade to black at the end of the movie.

8 The current-time indicator should be positioned about two seconds from the end of the clip. Then position your pointer on the orange connector line where it intersects with the current-time indicator line; the pointer should change to a small cross icon (⊞).

9 With the double-arrow icon as your pointer, hold down the Ctrl/Command key and click the connector line once. You should see a small yellow diamond added to the orange connector line at the beginning of the clip, representing your first keyframe.

10 Press the Page Down key to move the current-time indicator to the end of the movie. Using the same procedure, create a keyframe at that location.

11 Click the keyframe at the end of the movie clip and drag it down to the bottom of the track. The number on the right of the yellow box next to the pointer is the Opacity value; drag it until that value equals 0.00.

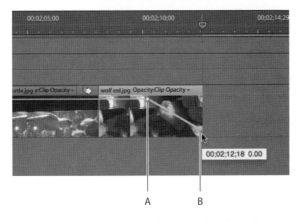

A. First keyframe (opacity at 100%). **B.** Second keyframe (opacity at 0%).

12 To view the Opacity fade out, move your current-time indicator to the beginning of the Wolf eel.jpg clip, and then press the spacebar.

13 Save your project as *Lesson06_End.prel*.

In Lesson 7, you'll learn how to create a similar effect using the Dip to Black transition. Although the visual effect is similar, working with keyframes lets you customize the effect to a much greater degree.

Working with Keyframes

After you've set a keyframe, you can modify it by dragging it to a new location or value. To delete a keyframe, right-click it and choose Delete.

The other keyframe-related controls shown in the context menu are advanced options that control the rate and smoothness of change applied by Premiere Elements. For more on those options, search the Help file for "Controlling change between keyframes."

Finally, you can access all keyframes inserted on the Timeline in Properties view. Select Wolf eel.jpg, and then click the Properties (▣) button in the upper left of the My Project panel. This opens Properties view.

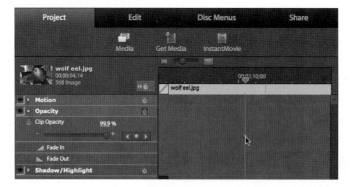

If necessary, click the Show Keyframes (▯⌚) button at the top right in Properties view to view the keyframes. Then click the disclosure triangle to the left of the Opacity effect to open the parameter settings and view the keyframes that you created in the Timeline.

You can set and modify opacity-related keyframes in either or both locations. In general, the Timeline is best for fast and simple adjustments, like the fade out that you just applied, whereas Properties view is a better choice for complicated, more precise adjustments.

This concludes the main lesson. Next, you'll learn how to implement several additional effects using other source clips in a separate project file.

Creating a Picture-in-Picture Overlay

Premiere Elements can superimpose multiple tracks of video. In this exercise, you'll superimpose one video clip in a small frame over your preexisting background clip that covers the entire screen. This effect is called a Picture-in-Picture (PiP) overlay.

1 To load the project file containing the new content, click File > Open Project, and then navigate to the Lesson06 folder you copied to your hard drive.

2 Within that folder, select the file Greenscreen_Win.prel (Windows) or Greenscreen_Mac.prel (Mac OS), and then click Open (Windows) or Choose (Mac OS). If a dialog appears asking for the location of rendered files, click the Skip Previews button.

3 Choose Window > Restore Workspace to ensure that you start the lesson with the default panel layout.

4 In the Timeline, click Rockshow.mov, the only clip. The selected clip appears in the Monitor panel.

5 In Media view, locate the Gina_guitar.mov clip. Click once to select the clip, hold down the Shift key, and drag the clip towards the upper-left corner of the Rockshow.mov clip in the Monitor panel.

6 Release the pointer and choose Picture-in-Picture from the menu that appears.

7 Click No in the Videomerge panel (if it appears).

Note: If the superimposed clip is longer than the background clip, it appears over successive clips in the Sceneline for its entire duration and appears superimposed over those clips during playback.

8 Click to select the superimposed clip, and notice that the clip changes appearance. There are now handles on the edges, indicating that the clip is active.

9 Choose Window > Properties to open Properties view.

10 In Properties view, click the arrow to the left of Motion to reveal its properties. Make sure the Constrain proportions check box is selected.

11 Place your pointer over the value for Scale, and then drag the value to 45. As you change the scale, the Gina_guitar.mov clip expands to 45 percent of its original size.

12 If necessary, you can reposition the clip using the Position controls, or simply drag the clip to the desired position in the Monitor panel.

13 Press the Home key to go to the start of your project, and then click the Play button to review your work.

14 Save your project as *Lesson06_pip.prel*.

Compositing Two Clips Using Videomerge

Compositing is the process of merging two clips together, one atop the other, while removing the background color of the top clip to reveal the second. This allows you to place your subject in a variety of environments, both real and simulated.

Premiere Elements' Videomerge effect makes compositing as easy as drag and drop. Videomerge automatically determines the background of the top clip and makes it transparent. Video or image clips on the tracks below it become visible through the transparent areas. You'll get the best results with Videomerge if you shoot the clip to be composited using the following rules:

- Create a strong (preferably dark or saturated), solid, uniform-color background to shoot against.

- Make sure the background is brightly and uniformly lit to avoid shadows.

- When choosing a background color, avoid skin tones and colors that are similar to the subject's clothing or hair color. (Otherwise, the skin, clothes, or hair will become transparent, too). Bright green and blue are the best choices.

With this information as background, reload the Greenscreen.prel project file (you should have already saved the first project as Lesson06_pip.prel) and follow this procedure.

1 In the Timeline, click Rockshow.mov, the only clip. The selected clip appears in your Monitor panel.

2 In Media view, locate the Gina_guitar.mov clip. Click to select the clip, hold down the Shift key, and drag the clip onto the Rockshow.mov clip in the Monitor panel.

3 Release the pointer and choose Place on Top and Apply Videomerge.

Premiere Elements inserts Gina_guitar.mov in the Video 2 track over Rockshow. mov, automatically detects the blue background, and makes it transparent. The result needs a bit of work. Let's try a manual adjustment.

4 In the Timeline, click Gina_guitar.mov to select it, and then click the Properties (▤) button on the upper left of the My Project panel.

5 In Properties view, click the disclosure triangle to the left of the Videomerge effect to open the parameter settings.

6 Select the Select Color check box, and then click the eyedropper (▨) to select it. The background behind Gina will reappear. Press Ctrl/Command, and then click the blue background close to Gina's head. This tells Videomerge which color to eliminate, and pressing Ctrl/Command averages a 5x5-pixel block surrounding the pixel that you clicked to achieve a smoother result. Much better.

7 You can try adjusting the Tolerance slider, but it makes no noticeable difference. I think we're done here.

8 Press the Home key to go to the start of your project, and then click the Play button to review your work. The clip looks good, so let's move on to the next edit.

Changing Speed Using the Time Stretch Tool

Previously, you learned how to change the speed of clips bounded in the Timeline by other clips on both sides. Now you'll learn how to use the Time Stretch tool to accomplish the same task but in a more visual way.

Here's the problem you'll solve. The Rockshow.mov clip used as a background in the previous two exercises is 31 seconds long, and the Gina_guitar.mov clip is about 27 seconds long. You could just trim the Rockshow clip to the same duration, but that would delete content at the end of that clip.

A more elegant solution is to use the Time Stretch feature to speed up the Rockshow.mov clip so that it's the same duration as Gina_guitar.mov.

1 In the Timeline, click the Time Stretch icon (▣) at the upper left of the My Project panel.

2 Hover your pointer over the right edge of the Rockshow.mov clip until the Time Stretch icon (▣) appears.

3 Drag the right edge of the Rockshow.mov clip to the left until it aligns with the end of the Gina_guitar.mov clip.

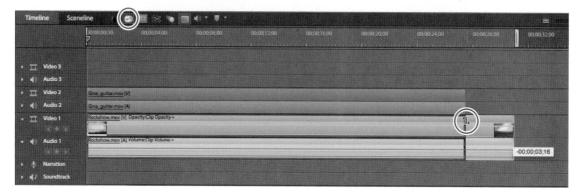

4   Click the Selection tool () at the upper left of the My Project panel to restore the normal pointer.

5   Right-click Rockshow.mov and choose Time Stretch.

Premiere Elements opens the Time Stretch panel. Note that the speed should have increased to 112.86, which is precisely the correction needed to make Rockshow.mov the same duration as Gina_guitar.mov. In most instances, you would click Maintain Audio Pitch to maintain the pitch of the clip, but because Rockshow.mov has no audio, that isn't necessary in this case.

6   Save your project as *Lesson06_videomerge.prel*.

Working with Motion Tracking

Motion Tracking gives you the ability to automatically track moving objects in a project so you can add labels, thought bubbles, or other effects to the moving object. This exercise teaches you how to use this function.

1   To load the project file containing the new content, click File > Open Project, and then navigate to the Lesson06 folder you copied to your hard drive.

2   Within the Lesson06 folder, select the file Motion_Tracking_Win.prel (Windows) or Motion_Tracking Mac.prel (Mac OS), and then click Open (Windows) or Choose (Mac OS). If a dialog appears asking for the location of rendered files, click the Skip Previews button.

3   Click to select the clip in the My Project panel, Alfie.mov.

4   Select the Motion Tracking icon () at the upper left of the Timeline to turn on Motion Tracking mode. If the dialog opens, click Yes in the Motion Tracking window to enable Premiere Elements to track moving objects in the clip. The Auto Analyzer starts to run.

5   Drag the current-time indicator to 00;00;02 where a big yellow box enters the frame. Motion Tracking starts by tracking the largest object in the frame. You could jump to step 8 here and add the thought bubble, but I want to track Alfie's head, which is more precise than tracking the entire body. So click the yellow box (which then turns blue), and then right-click and choose Delete Selected Object.

6 On the upper right of the Monitor panel, click the Add Object button (Add Object). Premiere Elements adds a scalable box to the Monitor panel. Drag the box over the object that you'd like to track (in this case Alfie's head), and then drag the edges to fit the object.

● **Note:** In addition to thought bubbles, you can use Motion Tracking with other clip art, titles, graphics, and Picture-in-Picture effects.

7 In the upper-right corner of the Monitor panel, click Track Object (Track Object). Premiere Elements analyzes the clip to track the moving object.

8 Click the Edit tab to enter the Edit workspace, and then click Clip Art (Clip Art) to view that content. In the Filter By: list box, click and choose Thought and Speech Bubbles. Click SpeechBubble05-LEFT and drag it over the box that you just created.

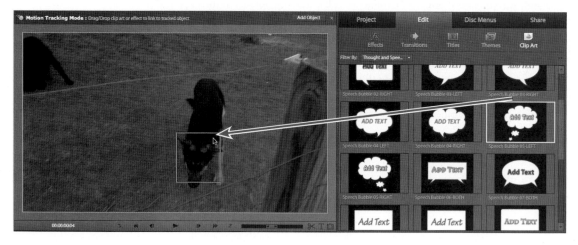

9 In the Change Text dialog, type *Feed me!* Then click OK to close the dialog.

10 Drag the Position controls to finalize placement of the thought bubble over Alfie's head.

● **Note:** You can use the Add Object/Track Object procedure to add and track multiple objects in a single video.

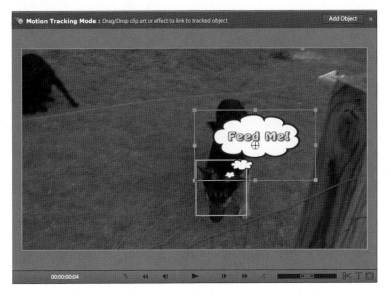

11 Press the Home key to move to the start of your project, and then click the Play button to review your work. Watch how the thought bubble moves with Alfie.

12 Save your project as *Lesson06_Alfie.prel*.

Working with Effect Masking

Effect Masking gives you the ability to constrain an effect to a certain section of an image, and if that section is moving, to track it around the frame. For example, reload the project file from the previous exercise—Motion_Tracking_Win.prel (Windows) or Motion_Tracking Mac.prel (Mac OS)— and work through steps 1–7 again. But this time don't save the project you created in the previous section. Then follow these steps.

1 Select Effects (fx Effects) in the Edit tab in the Tasks panel, and in the list box next to Video Effects, click and select NewBlue Cartoonr Plus Elements.

2 Drag the Cartoonr Plus effect from Effects view and drop it onto the little box you created in the Alfie.mov clip. You should see the Monitor panel flash briefly. If the box shifts a bit, re-drag the edges to the desired coverage.

3 Click Alfie.mov to select it, click the Edit Effects button in Effects view, and then click the disclosure triangle next to Cartoonr Plus to reveal the controls. You can experiment with the different presets, but Pencil Test worked best for me.

● **Note:** In my version of Premiere Elements, this exercise ran correctly only one time, which was the first time the application analyzed Alfie.mov. After that, the rectangle didn't reappear. If you want to run the exercise again, go to the Elements Organizer and delete Alfie.mov. The next time you run the project, Premiere Elements will have to reanalyze the clip, and the exercise should work as detailed here.

● **Note:** You can apply a static mask to any clip by right-clicking the clip and choosing Effects Mask > Apply.

Premiere Elements applies the effect only within the box (called a mask), and the box follows Alfie's motion in the video.

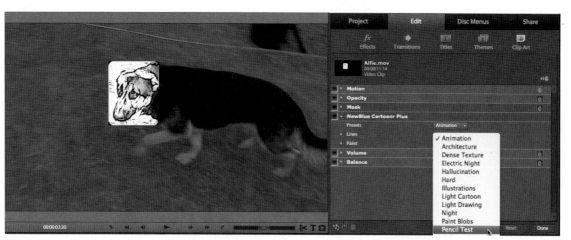

● **Note:** I used the Cartoonr Plus effect because it's cool, and because I wanted to show it to you. If you're looking for the witness-protection look, which may make more sense in this application, try either the Gaussian Blur effect (in the Blur & Sharpen group) or the Mosaic effect (in the Stylize group).

Exploring on Your Own

Congratulations! Now you understand how to apply video settings, change effects and settings, copy effects from one clip to another, create an image pan, animate an effect with keyframes, create a Picture-in-Picture effect, and composite one video over another with Videomerge. You also know how to use Motion Tracking and how to "mask" an effect. Here are some effects that you can experiment with on your own.

1 Create a PiP effect using two or more clips on the same screen.

2 Experiment with alternative effects such as Adjust > Brightness & Contrast, or Distort > Bend. To get a sense of the different effects available in Premiere Elements, choose Help > Premiere Elements Help, or press F1 to access the Help guide. The Applying Effects section includes a gallery of video effects.

3 Experiment with the various effects presets located in the Effects panel— specifically, the Horizontal and Vertical image pans.

Review Questions

1 What are curative effects, and when should you apply them?

2 What's the quickest way to apply identical effects and settings to multiple clips?

3 What are fixed effects, and what is their purpose?

4 What is a keyframe, and what does it contain?

5 How do you modify keyframes once they've been added to a clip?

6 How do you apply the same effect to multiple clips on the Timeline?

Review Answers

1 Curative effects improve one or more aspects of a clip, such as exposure, backlighting, or excessive shakiness. You should apply curative effects to a clip before applying artistic and other effects.

2 After selecting the clip that contains the effect or effects that you want to copy, click an effect to select it in the Properties panel or Shift-click to select multiple effects. Copy your selection by choosing Edit > Copy. Then select the clip to which you want to transfer the effects, and choose Edit > Paste.

3 Fixed effects are the Property parameters that every clip in Premiere Elements has enabled by default. These effects are Motion, Opacity, and Volume. Within the Motion effect, Scale, Position, Rotation, and Anchor Point are all properties that can be adjusted to create, for example, a PiP effect.

4 A keyframe contains the values for all the controls in an effect and applies those values to the clip at the specific time.

5 Once keyframes have been added to a clip, they can be adjusted by clicking and dragging them along the connector line. If there are two keyframes, moving one keyframe farther away from the other extends the duration of the effect; moving a keyframe closer to another keyframe shortens the effect.

6 Select all target clips in the My Project panel and apply the effect to any single clip.

7 CREATING TRANSITIONS

Lesson overview

If you've followed the lessons in this book in order, you should now feel comfortable adding and deleting footage in your project, and trimming clips to improve the pacing of the movie you're producing. In this lesson, you'll take a project in which your clips have already been sequenced and trimmed, and add nuance and dimension using transitions between the clips. You'll learn how to do the following:

- Apply a transition using Transitions view

- Preview transitions

- Modify transition settings

- Apply the default transition to multiple clips

- Copy and paste transitions

- Create fade-ins and fade-outs

- Render transitions

 This lesson will take approximately one hour.

Inserting a Dip to Black transition
at the start of the movie.

Getting Started

You'll modify scenes in this lesson's project by adding transitions in stages. But first you'll open the Lesson07 project and prepare your Adobe Premiere Elements workspace.

1 Make sure that you have correctly copied the Lesson07 folder from the DVD in the back of this book onto your computer's hard drive. See "Copying the Classroom in a Book Files" in the "Getting Started" section at the start of this book.

2 Launch Premiere Elements.

3 In the Welcome screen, click the Open Project button, and then click the Open folder.

4 In the Open Project dialog, navigate to the Lesson07 folder.

5 Within that folder, select the file Lesson07_Start_Win.prel (Windows) or Lesson07_ Start_Mac.prel (Mac OS), and then click Open (Windows) Choose (Mac OS).

   Your project file opens with the Monitor, Tasks, and My Project panels open.

6 Choose Window > Restore Workspace to ensure that you start the lesson in the default panel layout.

Viewing the Completed Movie Before You Start

To see what you'll be creating in this lesson, you can play the completed movie.

1 In the Project tab in the Tasks panel, click Media ( ). In the Media view, locate the file Lesson07_Movie.mov, and then double-click it to open the video in the Preview window.

2 In the Preview window, click the Play button ( ) to watch the video showing a visit to the Georgia Aquarium, which you will build in this lesson.

3 When you're done, close the Preview window.

Working with Transitions

Transitions phase out one clip while phasing in the next. The simplest form of a transition is the cut. A cut occurs when the last frame of one clip is followed by the first frame of the next. The cut is the most frequently used transition in video and film, and the one you will use most of the time. However, you can also use other types of transitions to achieve effects between scenes.

Transitions

Using transitions, you can phase out one clip while phasing in the next, or you can stylize the beginning or end of a single clip. A transition can be as subtle as a cross dissolve, or as emphatic as a page turn or spinning pinwheel. You generally place transitions on a cut between two clips, creating a double-sided transition. However, you can also apply a transition to just the beginning or end of a clip, creating a single-sided transition, such as a fade to black.

When a transition shifts from one clip to the next, it overlaps frames from both clips. The overlapped frames can either be frames previously trimmed from the clips (frames just past the In or Out point at the cut), or existing frames repeated on either side of the cut. It's important to remember that when you trim a clip, you don't delete frames; instead, the resulting In and Out points frame a window over the original clip. A transition uses the trimmed frames to create the transition effect, or, if the clips don't have trimmed frames, the transition repeats frames.

—From Adobe Premiere Elements Help

Using Transitions View in the Tasks Panel

Premiere Elements includes a wide range of transitions, including 3D motion, dissolves, wipes, and zooms. The animated thumbnail view that appears when you click on a specific transition gives you a good idea of how it might be applied to your project. Transitions are grouped into two main folders in Transitions view: Audio Transitions and Video Transitions.

1   To access Premiere Elements transitions, click the Transitions button (![Transitions]) in the Edit tab in the Tasks panel. Click a transition to see an animated preview, and then click again to stop the preview.

2   Select Video Transitions (if it's not already selected) from the category menu in the upper-left corner of Transitions view. Then select NewBlue Motion Blends Elements from the adjacent menu to see only the different types of transitions in Transitions view. You'll use the Shake transition from that category in a moment.

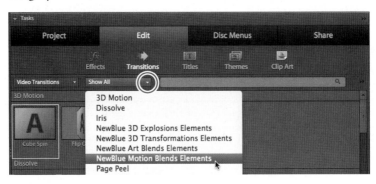

Applying a Transition

Understanding how transitions work is essential to using them successfully. For a transition to shift from one clip to another, the transition must overlap frames from both clips for a certain amount of time.

<aside>
● **Note:** You don't need to reposition the current-time indicator to place transitions between clips. However, it's often helpful in locating the correct point in your project.
</aside>

1   In the Monitor panel, position your current-time indicator at around the 00;00;12;01 mark, which should be the edit point between aquarium.jpg and Clip02.mp4. You'll be placing a transition between these two clips.

2   If Sceneline is not already selected in the My Project panel, switch to it now.

3   From Transitions view, which should still be showing the content of the NewBlue Motion Blends Elements, drag the Shake transition to the rectangle between aquarium.jpg and Clip02.mp4 in the Sceneline. You'll know the transition has been added because its icon is visible in the rectangle between the two clips in the Sceneline.

4   In the Monitor, drag the current- time indicator to around the 00;00;09;00 mark, and then press the spacebar to preview the transition. After the transition ends, press the spacebar to stop playback.

● **Note:** To delete a transition, right-click it and choose Clear (in the Timeline) or click to select it and press the Delete key (in the Sceneline).

Viewing Transition Properties

When you add a transition to a clip, the default length of the transition is determined by your preferences. You can change the length of transitions after applying them. Additionally, there are several other attributes of transitions that you can adjust. These include alignment, start and end values, border, and softness.

In this exercise, you'll add a Push transition that pushes one image offscreen to replace it with the next clip. You will then modify the various attributes of the transition in Properties view.

1 In Transitions view in the Edit tab, choose Video Transitions from the category menu. Make sure Show All is selected in the menu next to it. Then click in the text search box to the left of the magnifying glass icon () and type the word *push*. Premiere Elements automatically searches the list of video transitions and locates the Push transition.

2 If necessary, scroll to the right in the My Project panel until you can see the two Clip06 clips: The first is the sign about piranhas; the second is a shot of the fish themselves. Drag the Push transition from Transitions view to the rectangle between these two clips in the Sceneline.

3 In the Monitor panel, position the current-time indicator a few frames before the transition. Press the spacebar to view the transition. The Push transition will push the first clip off to the side. After the transition ends, press the spacebar to stop playback.

4 Select the Push transition in the Sceneline, and then click the Edit Transition button (Edit Transition) in the lower-left corner of Transitions view. This will load the transition's parameters into Properties view where you can edit them.

5   Click the Show Keyframes button () at the top of Properties view to view
    a magnified version of your Timeline. This enables you to view the transition
    as it is applied between your two clips. If necessary, resize the Properties panel
    or just its Timeline to better see this Timeline.

6   In the Timeline in Properties view, drag the current-time indicator back
    and forth over the transition to preview your transition effect.

Stay in this window. You will now modify your transition's settings.

Modifying Transition Settings

All transitions have default settings. To achieve specific results, you can customize the settings in Properties view. Modifying the length of a transition is easy, as you will see in this exercise. You'll adjust the transition using the actual clip, so click the Show Actual Sources (📷) icon just below Start/End Points before getting started.

● Note: On my Mac, I had to choose 00;00;00;16 in the Duration field for Premiere Elements to input 00;00;00;15. No biggie, but I didn't want you to drive yourself nuts trying to dial in the right number.

1   To change the length of a transition in Properties view, place your pointer over the Duration value, and then drag to the left to change the Duration to 00;00;00;15 (15 frames). Remember that there are 30 frames in one second of NTSC video; therefore, 15 frames represent a half second of time. For a small preview of the adjusted transition, click the Play button immediately above the Duration field. This converts to a Stop button once pressed, and you can click Stop to end the preview.

● Note: If you don't see all the controls in the Transition Properties panel, expand the panel to make it wider.

2   For a big-screen preview, drag the current-time indicator—in either the Monitor panel or Properties view—to a position before the Push transition, and press the spacebar to preview the transition. After the transition ends, press the spacebar to stop playback. If you should accidentally click the track area of your Sceneline, you will deselect the transition and its parameters will vanish from Properties view. Don't worry; just click the transition in your Sceneline to select it again and display its parameters in Properties view.

3   In Properties view, click the Alignment drop-down list to view the options. Note that you can set the transition to start at the cut between the two clips (Start at Cut), or end at the cut between the two clips (End at Cut), or position it at the center of the cut (Center at Cut). Experiment with these settings to get a feel for the different looks they create, but choose Center at Cut before moving on to step 4.

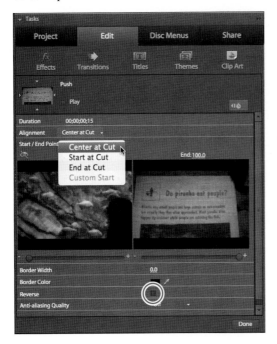

4   In Properties view, select the Reverse check box (see the circled item in the preceding figure). This reverses the transition so that the second clip now pushes the first clip to the left. Depending on the size of your monitor, you may need to scroll down and resize Properties view or its Timeline to see this check box.

5   Click the Timeline button in the upper-left corner of the My Project panel to shift into Timeline mode. Zoom into the Timeline, if necessary, to see the transition.

6   Drag your current-time indicator to approximately halfway through the transition, at roughly the 00;00;47;09 mark.

Because you're in the middle of the transition, your screen will be split in half. This makes it easier to preview the modifications you'll apply in the next steps.

7   If necessary, scroll down Properties view to view the additional controls. Click the value for Border Width, type the number *10*, and then press Enter/Return.

This creates a 10-pixel border on the edge of your transition. The default color of the border is black, but you can modify this as well.

8   Click the black color swatch next to the Border Color. This opens the Color Picker dialog.

9   In the color slider, which displays the spectrum of colors in a vertical strip, click in the blue hues.

10 In the larger color spectrum, click the lower-right corner to select a medium blue.

11 Click OK to close the Color Picker dialog. The border of your transition is now 10 pixels wide and blue.

12 Drag your current-time indicator to a position before the transition, and then press the spacebar to play your modified transition. After the transition ends, press the spacebar to stop playback.

13 Choose File > Save As, name the file *Lesson07_Work.prel* in the Save Project dialog, and then click Save to save it in your Lesson07 folder.

Replacing a Transition

Replacing an existing transition between two clips is done in essentially the same way as adding a new transition: Simply drag the transition from the Media panel onto the existing transition in the Sceneline. You can do this repeatedly to compare the effects of different transitions.

To practice adding and replacing transitions—this time using the Timeline—you will now apply a Checker Board transition between the two Clip06 sections, and then replace it with an Iris Diamond transition.

1 In the My Project panel, click the Timeline button. If necessary, use the Zoom controls and scroll your view so that the aforementioned clips are visible.

2 Press the Page Up and Page Down keys to position the current-time indicator at the edit line between the two clips. You might want to click the Zoom In tool (■) to magnify the view at this edit line.

3 If necessary, click the Transitions button to open Transitions view in the Edit tab, and then click the Categories tag and choose NewBlue 3D Transformations Elements.

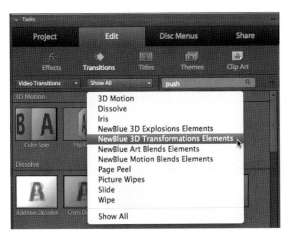

Tip: For more information about transition alignment, search for "transition alignment options" in Premiere Elements Help.

4   In this step and the following step, do not release the pointer until instructed. Drag the Checker Board transition over the edit line between the two Clip06. mp4 clips; do not release the pointer. Pay careful attention to the appearance of your pointer.

5   Move your pointer on top of the edit line between the two clips. Notice how your pointer changes to the Center at Cut icon ( ). Release the pointer to center the transition over the cut.

Note: When working with transitions in the Timeline, you may need to zoom into the Timeline using the zoom slider on the upper right of the Timeline to see the transitions up close.

6   Preview the Checker Board transition by dragging your current-time indicator before the transition and then pressing the spacebar. When the transition is over, press the spacebar to stop playback.

Notice how the transition is represented by a swooshing arrow above the cut between the clips in the Timeline.

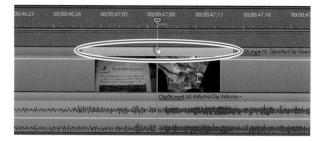

7   In Transitions view, select the Iris Diamond transition in the Iris category and drag it on top of the Checker Board transition in the Timeline to replace it. You can have only one transition between two clips.

8   Preview the new transition by dragging the current-time indicator before the transition and pressing the spacebar to start playback. After the transition ends, press the spacebar to stop playback.

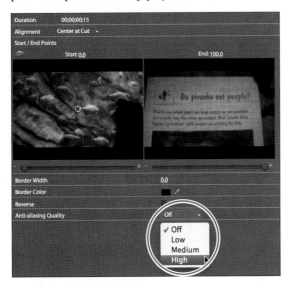

9   Select the Iris Diamond transition in the Sceneline, and then click the Edit Transition button (Edit Transition) in the lower-left corner of Transitions view.

This transition's parameters are loaded into Properties view where you can edit them.

10 Find the Anti-aliasing Quality control on the bottom of the Transition Properties view. Click the list box and choose High, which will smooth rough edges in some regions of the wipe.

● **Note:** Anytime you insert a transition with diagonal lines, ovals, or other edges that aren't exactly vertical or horizontal, jagged edges can appear, particularly in standard definition (SD) clips. Smooth them out with the Anti-aliasing Quality control used in this exercise.

Adding a Single-sided Transition to Create a Fade-in

Transitions do not necessarily need to be located between two clips. For example, you can quickly add a fade-in and fade-out to the beginning and end of your movie.

1   If you're not already in Timeline view, in the My Project panel, click the Timeline button. Press the Home key to position the current-time indicator at the beginning of the first clip.

2   In the Transitions view in the Edit tab, select the Dissolve transition category.

3 Drag the Dip to Black transition from the Transitions view to the beginning of Clip01.mp4 on the Video 1 track.

4 Press the spacebar to play the transition. The beginning of the transition starts at black and then fades into the video. After the transition ends, press the spacebar to stop playback.

5 To extend the duration of these transitions by a half second, grab the right edge of each transition box one at a time, and drag it to the right until the text box next to the drag pointer indicates that you've added 00;00;00;15. Release the pointer.

6 Save your project as *Lesson07_End.prel*.

GPU (Graphics Processing Unit) Transition Effects

Premiere Elements comes with many GPU-accelerated transitions, including Card Flip, Center Peel, Page Curl, Page Roll, and Sphere. You can find all of them in the GPU Transitions menu in the Transitions view. These transitions take advantage of the added video processing capabilities offered by video display cards that have Graphics Processing Unit (GPU) chips. These display cards help with graphics acceleration, so transitions can be previewed and rendered more quickly than by the CPU alone. If you have a display card that supports DirectX 9.x, Pixel Shader (PS) 1.3 or later, and Vertex Shader 1.1 or later, you can use the GPU-accelerated transitions. They are visible only if you have a card with a GPU, and they reside in the Video Transitions folder in the Transitions view.

—From Adobe Premiere Elements Help

Applying the Default Transition to Multiple Clips

There's no rule that says you need to use transitions between all clips in your movies. However, rather than using cuts between clips, many producers insert very short cross-dissolve transitions between clips to smooth out any visual jarring between the clips. A feature in Premiere Elements makes this very simple to do. In this exercise, you'll start by changing the duration of the default transition and then applying it to multiple clips simultaneously.

1   Choose Edit > Preferences > General (Windows) or Adobe Premiere Elements 10 > Preferences > General (Mac OS) to open the Preferences panel.

2   Highlight the number in the Video Transition Default Duration box to make it active, type in 5, and press Enter/Return.

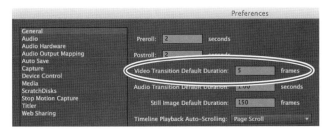

3   Click OK to close the Preferences panel.

4   If you're not already in Timeline view, in the My Project panel, click the Timeline button. Press the Backslash (\) key to display the entire contents of the project in the Timeline.

5 Drag to select Clip07.mp4 through Clip13.mp4 on the Timeline.

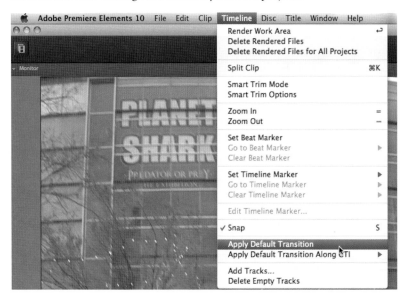

6 In the Premiere Elements menu, choose Timeline > Apply Default Transition.

7 Click OK if the "Insufficient media" error message appears. This appears because you're using short, mostly untrimmed clips in this exercise; you shouldn't see this message too often in your own projects.

● **Note:** You can also copy and paste a transition to multiple clips by copying the transition, selecting the target clips, and pasting the transition on the selected clips.

8 Premiere Elements applies the default transition between all selected clips. In practice, if you applied the default transition to clips with existing transitions, Premiere Elements would replace the transitions but wouldn't change the duration of the previously inserted transitions, which you'd have to adjust manually if you wanted them to match that of the newly inserted clips.

9 Drag the current-time indicator around the project and preview the transitions. You'll notice that the effect is subtle but smoothes the flow from clip to clip.

Making Transitions Work in Your Movie

Now that you know the how of transitions, let's spend a bit of time discussing the when and why. Although there are few absolutes about the art of transitions, your productions will benefit by incorporating these two concepts into your creative decisions.

First, recognize that you don't need to include a transition between every clip in your movies. If you watch a Hollywood movie, for example, you'll see that noticeable transitions (that is, those longer than four or five frames) are seldom used between clips *within a scene* but are often used *between scenes*.

Why? Because the transition lets the viewer know that there's been a change in time or location. That is, if a scene jumped from a kitchen at night to the backyard the next day, simply jumping from scene to scene would confuse the viewer. You can imagine the viewer saying, "Hey, what happened here? One second they were in the kitchen drinking milkshakes at night, and the next second they were playing dodgeball in the yard in sunlight." However, if the editor inserts a fade to black between the two scenes, the viewer understands that there is a change of time or location.

Within the context of the aquarium project, there are two distinct scenes—the videos and the slide show. These would be the natural locations for noticeable transitions within this project. You inserted the Dip to Black at the start of the clip in this chapter, and in the project going forward, you'll notice the same transition between the video and the slide. These transitions are all one-second long, so they're meant to be noticed. The dissolves between movie clips are all five frames, which is one-sixth of a second. You may recall that the transitions you inserted in the slide show back in Lesson 5 were all one-second long as well, which worked because each slide was like a separate scene.

Of course, with family videos, your goal is to produce smiles, not to win an Academy Award. If you'd like to use transitions as content rather than in their traditional role, feel free to add as many as you'd like, anywhere you'd like. Just be sure to consider the following rule.

When using transitions, you should match the tone of the transition to the tone of the movie. In a fun, family video like a trip to the aquarium or other vacation, you could use any transition that Premiere Elements offers—in some cases, the zanier the better. This is why highly noticeable transitions are used frequently in children's shows like *Barney & Friends* or *The Wiggles*.

On the other hand, when shooting a solemn event—say, a wedding or graduation—the tone is usually much more serious. In these instances, you'd probably want to use only cross-dissolves or the occasional Dip to Black transition to maintain that tone.

Exploring on Your Own

My compliments; that's another lesson well done! You've discovered how transitions can make your projects more professional-looking by adding continuity between clips. You've learned about placing, previewing, modifying, and rendering different transitions, as well as applying them en masse.

As you continue to edit with transitions, you'll get a better idea of how to use them to enhance the tone or style of your project. The best way to develop that style is by trying different transitions and discovering how they affect your movie. So here's your task list for further experimentation:

1   Make the changes discussed in "Making Transitions Work in Your Movie" to your project.

2   Experiment with different transitions; preview their animated icons in Transitions view. Remember that dragging a transition onto an existing transition will replace it.

3   Be sure that you're comfortable modifying the default parameters of your transitions. One by one, select the transitions you've added and explore their settings in Properties view.

Review Questions

1 Where are Video Transitions located, and what are two ways to locate specific transitions?

2 How do you modify transitions?

3 How can you extend the duration of a transition?

4 How can you apply a transition to multiple clips simultaneously?

Review Answers

1 Video Transitions are located in Transitions view, which you can access at anytime from your Edit workspace. You can browse for individual transitions, which are organized in categories and by transition type. Additionally, you can find a specific transition by typing its name or part of its name into the search field in Transitions view.

2 Click the transition you want to modify to select it, and then choose Edit Transition in Properties view.

3 One method of extending the duration of a transition is to change its length in Properties view. Select the transition in the Sceneline to access its properties. You can also change the duration of a transition by dragging its edges in the Timeline of the My Project panel.

4 You can use two techniques to apply transitions to multiple clips: One is to select multiple clips on the Timeline and choose Timeline > Apply Default Transition. Premiere Elements will insert the default transition between all selected clips. You can also copy a previously applied transition, select multiple clips on the Timeline, and then paste the transition onto any selected clip.

8   TITLES AND CREDITS

Lesson overview

In this lesson, you'll learn how to create original titles and rolling credits for a movie about our visit to the Georgia Aquarium. You'll be adding still titles and rolling titles, placing images, and using the drawing tools in the Monitor panel. Specifically, you'll learn how to do the following:

- Add and stylize text

- Superimpose titles and graphics over video

- Create and customize rolling titles

- Use title templates

 This lesson will take approximately two hours.

Creating a full-screen title in Adobe Premiere Elements.

Working with Titles and Title-editing Mode

Within Adobe Premiere Elements, you can create custom graphics and titles. When you add a title over one of your video clips, it's also added to your Media view as a new clip. As such, it's treated much like any other clip in your project. It can be edited, moved, deleted, and have transitions and effects applied to it.

Premiere Elements allows you to create original titles using text, drawing tools, and imported graphics. However, to help you quickly and easily add high-quality titles to your project, Premiere Elements also provides a number of templates based on common themes, such as Sports, Travel, and Weddings.

Getting Started

To begin, you'll launch Premiere Elements and open the Lesson08 project file. Then you'll review a final version of the project you'll be creating.

1 Before you begin, make sure that you have correctly copied the Lesson08 folder from the DVD in the back of this book onto your computer's hard drive. See "Copying the Classroom in a Book Files" in the "Getting Started" section at the beginning of this book.

2 Launch Premiere Elements and click the Open Project button in the Welcome screen. If necessary, click Open in the menu that appears. If Premiere Elements is already open, choose File > Open Project.

3 Navigate to your Lesson08 folder and select the project file Lesson08_Start_Win.prel (Windows) or Lesson08_Start_Mac.prel (Mac OS). Click the Open button (Windows) or Choose (Mac OS) to open your project. If a dialog appears asking for the location of rendered files, click the Skip Previews button. The Premiere Elements work area appears with the Edit workspace selected in the Tasks panel.

4 The project file opens in Properties view and the Media, Monitor, and My Project panels in view. Choose Window > Restore Workspace to ensure that you start the lesson with the default panel layout.

Viewing the Completed Movie Before You Start

To see what you'll be creating as your first project in this lesson, you can play the completed movie.

1 In the Project tab in the Tasks panel, click the Media button (). In Media view, locate the file Lesson08_Movie.mov, and then double-click it to open the video into the Preview window.

2 In the Preview window, click the Play button () to watch the video about a visit to the Georgia Aquarium, which you'll continue to build in this lesson.

3 After watching the complete movie, close the Preview window.

Creating a Simple Title

You can add titles to your movie—whether simple still titles, advanced titles with added graphics, or styled text scrolling across the screen horizontally or vertically—directly in the Monitor panel in Premiere Elements. To begin, you'll create a basic still title. Working with the Georgia Aquarium project, you'll add a title clip at the beginning of the movie. But first, you'll add a few seconds of black video over which you can then type the title text.

1 In the Sceneline in the My Project panel, click the first clip to select it. In the upper-right corner of Media view, click the New Item button ( ), and then choose Black Video from the menu that appears.

2 Premiere Elements inserts a five-second black video clip after the first clip in the Sceneline. To move the black video clip to the beginning of the movie, drag it to the left of the first clip in the Sceneline.

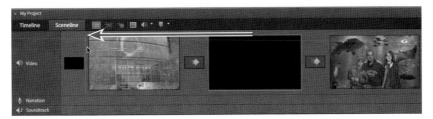

3 With the black video still selected in the Sceneline, choose Title > New Title > Default Still. Premiere Elements places the default title text over the black video in the Monitor panel and switches to title-editing mode. In the mini-timeline in the Monitor panel, notice the bluish-gray-colored clip representation for the new title clip that's placed on top of the lavender-colored clip representation for the black video clip. Also, notice the text and drawing tools now visible on the right side of the Monitor panel, and the text options, text styles, and text animation choices accessible from Properties view.

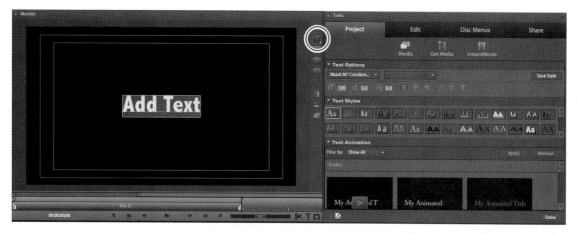

● **Note:** In the Type Tool button, the Horizontal Type tool is grouped with the Vertical Type tool. To switch between the two, click and hold the Tool button, and then choose from the menu that appears.

4 The Horizontal Type tool should be selected by default. If it's not, click the Type Tool button (T) to the right of the Monitor panel to select it now.

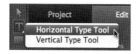

5 Click in the text box and drag your pointer over the default text to select it. Type the words *Our Visit to,* and then press the Enter/Return key to create a new line. Next, type the words *The Georgia Aquarium.*

6 To reposition your text, click the Selection tool () in the upper-right corner of the Monitor panel, and then click anywhere inside the text to select the text block. Drag to reposition the text so it appears centered in the upper third of your title window. Two white margins display in the title window. These are referred to as the title-safe and action-safe margins. Stay within the inner margin (title-safe) while repositioning your text. Don't worry about the exact position for now; you'll reposition the text later in this lesson.

▶ **Tip:** You can add multiple text entries to a single title, or you can create multiple titles, each containing unique text strings.

7 Choose File > Save As. In the Save As dialog, name the file *Lesson08_Work.prel*, and then click Save to save it in your Lesson08 folder.

Premiere Elements treats basic titles, such as the one you just created, like still image files. After you've created a title, an image file is automatically added to your Media view. In this case, the new title was superimposed over the black video clip at the beginning of the movie, but as you'll see, you can also place it over any other clip in your movie.

Modifying Text

After creating and adding a title to the project, you can change text or its appearance at any time, much as you would in a word processor or page layout program. In this exercise, you'll learn how to adjust the alignment of your type as well as its style, size, and color.

Changing the Text Alignment, Style, and Size

To begin, let's switch over to the Timeline, so you can see how Premiere Elements displays titles in that view.

Title-safe and Action-safe Margins

The title-safe and action-safe margins visible in the Monitor panel when you're in title-editing mode designate the title's visible safe zones. These margins are visible by default.

Safe zones are useful when producing DVDs or other video that will be viewed on a traditional TV set rather than on your computer. The reason is that when displaying video, most consumer TV sets cut off a portion of the outer edges of the picture, which is called *overscan*. The amount of overscan is not consistent across TVs, so to ensure that everything fits within the area that most TVs display, keep text within the title-safe margins and keep all other important elements within the action-safe margins.

If you're creating content for computer-screen viewing only, the title-safe and action-safe margins are irrelevant because computer screens display the entire image.

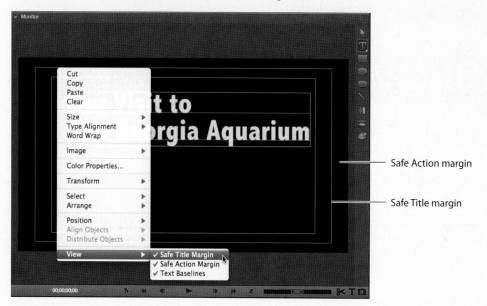

To turn title-safe and action-safe margins on or off, right-click inside the Monitor panel and choose View > Safe Title Margin or View > Safe Action Margin from the Monitor panel menu. The margin is visible if a check mark appears beside its name.

1   Click Timeline in the upper-left portion of the My Project panel to open Timeline view. In the Timeline, double-click the new title (Title 01), which should be on the Video 2 track.

2   To center the text in its text box, use the Selection tool () to select the title text box, and then click the Center Text button (▤) located under Text Options in Properties view.

3   In the Monitor panel, choose the Type tool and drag it in the text box to select the first line of text. Under Text Options in Properties view, choose Comic Sans MS from the font menu and Bold from the style menu next to it. Choose another font and style if you don't have this font on your system.

4   With the first line of text still selected, to change the font size, *do the following*:

    • Under Text Options in Properties view, place the pointer over the number to the right of the Change Text Size icon (▦). The pointer will change to a hand with two black arrows (▥).

- Drag to change the Size value to 75. If you have difficulties getting a precise value by dragging, click the size value once, and then type *75* into the text field.

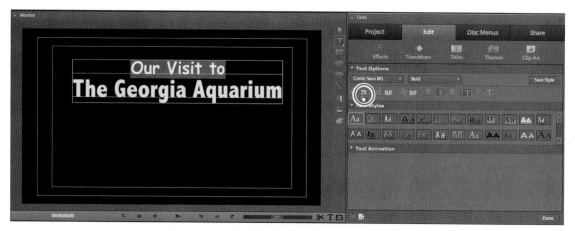

5   In the Text Styles box, scroll down until you can see the LithosPro Pink 28 style. Then select the second line of text—the words "The Georgia Aquarium"—with the Type tool, and choose LithosPro Pink 28. This changes the text font.

▶ **Tip:** You can also change the size of text by selecting its text box and then dragging one of the anchor points. Hold down the Shift key as you are dragging to maintain a proportional height and width of the text box and the type therein.

6   With the words "The Georgia Aquarium" still selected, change the font size to 90, either by dragging the Size value to the right or by clicking the size value once and typing *90* into the text field.

7   Next, you'll condense the letters in the bottom line of text. Select the words "The Georgia Aquarium" with the Text tool (if not already selected), and *do the following*:

- Under Text Options in Properties view, locate the Kerning value next to the Kerning icon (▩). Position the pointer over the numerical value, and it will change to a hand with two black arrows (▥).

- Drag the size value to -10. If you have difficulties getting a precise value by dragging, click the size value once, and then type *-10* into the text field.

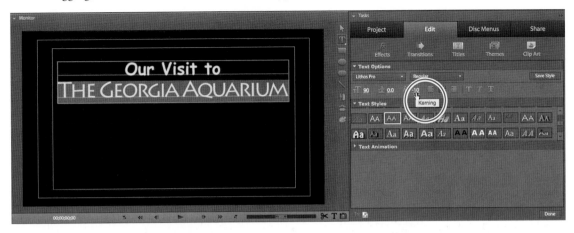

8 Now you'll increase the spacing between the two lines of text. Select both lines of text with the Text tool, and *do the following*:

- Under Text Options in Properties view, place the pointer over the Leading value (■). The pointer changes to a hand with two black arrows (■).

- Drag the size value to 15. If you have difficulties getting a precise value by dragging, click the size value once, and then type *15* into the text field.

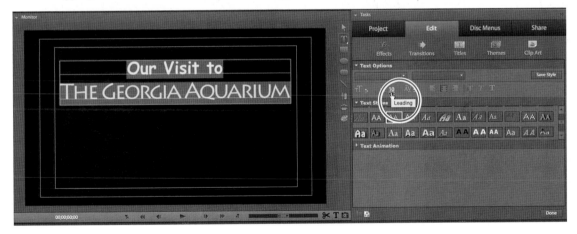

9 Choose File > Save to save your work.

Centering Elements in the Monitor Panel

At this point, your title probably isn't precisely centered horizontally within the frame. You can fix this manually, or you can let Premiere Elements do the work for you.

1   Using the Selection tool, click the text box to select the title.

2   Choose Title > Position > Horizontal Center. Or, right-click the text box, and then choose Position > Horizontal Center. Premiere Elements centers the text box horizontally within the frame. Depending on how you positioned the box earlier in this lesson, you might see little or no change.

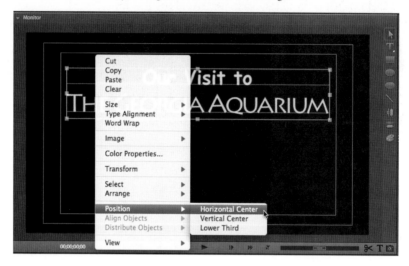

3   Choose File > Save to save your work.

Changing the Color of Your Type

As you've seen, changing the style and size of your type is easy. You can change all text within a text box equally by first selecting the text box using the Selection tool and then applying the change. Or, you can restrict the change to portions of the text by selecting them using the Type tool. You will now change the color of the words "The Georgia Aquarium."

1   Select the Horizontal Type tool (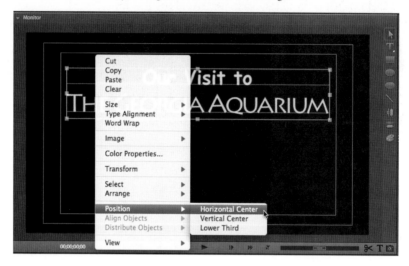), and then drag over the words "The Georgia Aquarium" to highlight the text.

Next, you'll change the gradient of the type. Note that any changes you make will apply to only the selected type.

2   Click the Color Properties button () at the bottom of the tool buttons in the Monitor panel to open the Color Properties dialog. In the middle of the dialog, note the Gradient list box. If it's not already selected, choose the 4 Color Gradient option. This means that the gradient is composed of the four colors

in the boxes at the corners of the yellow rectangle beneath the gradient list box. Experiment with the different options in the list box, and notice how they change the appearance of the text. Return to the 4 Color Gradient. Next, you'll change the upper-left and lower-right corners of the gradient to sea green.

3 Click the box on the top left of the gradient rectangle to select it. Set the RGB values to R: *84*, G: *84*, and B: *255*. Then click the box on the lower right of the gradient rectangle to select it, and set the RGB values to R: *84*, G: *84*, and B: *255*.

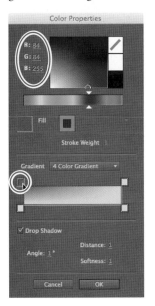

4 Click OK to close the Color Properties dialog. Use the Selection tool and click outside the text box in the Monitor panel to deselect the text and review your work.

5 Choose File > Save to save your work.

Adding an Image to Your Title Files

To add an extra element of depth and fun to your titles, you can import and insert images from any number of sources. For instance, you can use photos from your digital still camera as elements in your title file. In this exercise, you'll use a still image taken from a video clip and place it in the lower half of the title image.

1   With the Monitor panel still in title-editing mode, choose Title > Image > Add Image, or right-click the Monitor panel, and then choose Image > Add Image.

▶ Tip: If you have overlapping frames, you can change the stacking order by right-clicking on a selected frame and then using one of the Arrange commands from the context menu. To align multiple frames, select the frames you want to align, right-click, and then choose any of the Align Objects commands.

The file Open dialog appears. By default, the dialog may point you to the list of files in Premiere Elements' Logos folder. These are the default images that were installed with the application. Feel free to use these in your other projects, whether from this book or otherwise.

2   In the Open dialog, navigate to the Lesson08 folder. Within that folder, select the file marquee.psd, and then click Open (Windows) or Choose (Mac OS) to import the image into your title.

3   The image appears stacked in front of the text box in your title. Use the Selection tool to drag the placed image downward, making sure that the bottom of the image stays above the action-safe area (if this were text, you'd have to make sure it was within the title-safe zone).

4   If you're unhappy with the size of the image you've inserted, drag any anchor
    point to resize the placed image. Hold down the Shift key while dragging to
    maintain the height and width proportions of the image.

5   Right-click the image, and choose Position > Horizontal Center.

6   Choose File > Save to save your work.

Creating Fade-in and Fade-out Effects

Any transition that you use on video clips can also be added to title clips. In this
exercise, you'll add a fade-in and fade-out effect to the title clip.

1   In the Timeline view in the My Project panel, click Title 01, which should be on
    the Video 2 track. Click the Zoom In button to zoom into approximately the
    amount of detail shown in the following figure. If necessary, click the disclosure
    triangle next to Video 2 to see the detail shown in the figure.

2   At the upper left of the My Project panel, click the Properties button (▣).

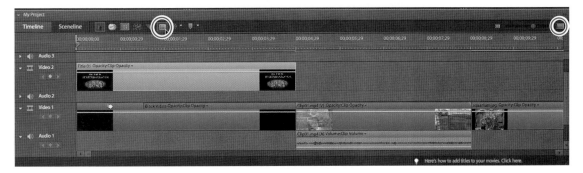

3 In Properties view, click the disclosure triangle next to Opacity to see the Opacity controls.

4 Under Opacity in Properties view, click the Fade In button once. The title image seems to disappear from the Monitor panel. Drag the current-time indicator in the Timeline to the right to see the image fade in.

If you adjusted the default transition duration to five frames as detailed in Chapter 7, after five frames the clip's opacity is at 100 percent and fully visible again. Although five frames is an appropriate length for interscene dissolves, fade-ins should be one full second. You'll fix that next.

5 In the Timeline, drag the second keyframe in the Video 2 track to the 01;00 second mark. That extends the fade-in from five frames to one full second.

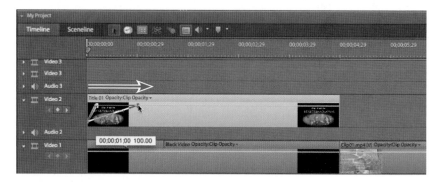

▶ **Tip:** Because the video on Video 1 is pure black, there's no reason to fade in that video. If the video on Video 1 was any other color, you would have to fade in both tracks that made up the title to achieve the desired effect.

Animate a Still Title

You can easily apply a preset animation to any still title. Text animation presets quickly and easily animate the characters in your title so that they fade or pop characters into view, or fly in from the top or bottom of the screen. For example, using the Fade In By Characters preset instantly makes each character in your title fade into view until the title is complete.

To preview an animation, position the pointer on the animation thumbnail in the Text Animation section in the Tasks panel. (To see the Text Animation section, you must select a title so that the Tasks panel is in Title Editing view.)

1 *Do one of the following*:

   - In the Sceneline, select the superimposed clip. In the Monitor panel, click the clip, and then double-click the title text.

   - In the Timeline, double-click the title clip.

   The Tasks panel changes to Title Editor view, displaying the text options.

2 In the Tasks panel, select an animation preset under Text Animation.

3 *Do one of the following* to apply the preset to the title:

   - Click Apply.

   - Drag the preset to the Monitor panel and drop it on top of the title text.

4 Click Preview to view the changes you have made to the title.

5 Click Done at the bottom of the Tasks panel to exit Title Editing view.

⬤ **Note:** To remove an animation from a title, select the title text and click the Remove button in the top-right corner of the Text Animation section in the Tasks panel.

—From Adobe Premiere Elements Help

Superimposing a Title over Video Clips

Inserting titles over a black background video works well for opening titles, but Premiere Elements also lets you superimpose titles directly over video clips. Although you can add titles in both the Timeline and Sceneline, in this exercise, you'll work in the former, adding a title to the shark clip (Clip05.mp4). Then you'll copy the title to the start of the slide show and customize the text for that location.

1 With the Timeline selected in the My Project panel, press the Home key to move to the start of the movie. Then click the Page Down key six times to move to the start of Clip05.mp4.

2 Choose Title > New Title > Default Still. With the Text tool, select the default text and type *Scary Critters*.

3 Drag the text to select it and click to apply the LithosPro White 94 text style.

4 Right-click the title text, choose Position > Lower Third, and then choose Position > Horizontal Center. The title should be horizontally centered right above the title-safe line at the bottom of the frame.

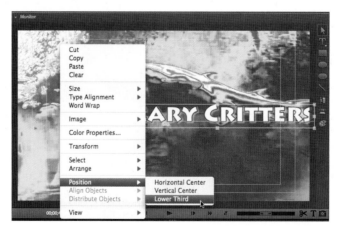

Because you chose a style with an outline and a shadow, it's actually pretty legible against the moving background. To make it even more legible, you can add a colored rectangle behind the text, as explained in the following steps.

5   Select the Rectangle tool (■) from the tools on the right side of the Monitor panel. The cursor changes to a crosshair. Drag to create a rectangle over the text you just created. Don't worry about obscuring the text; in a moment, you'll position the rectangle behind the text.

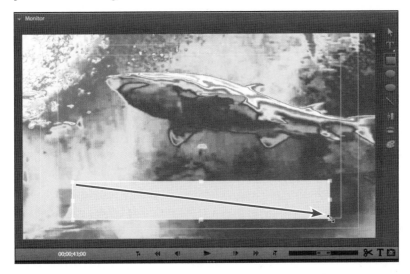

6   Click the Color Properties button (■) at the bottom of the tool buttons in the Monitor panel to open the Color Properties dialog. Set the color to black by clicking the large black color chip on the upper right of the Color Properties dialog. Click OK to apply the color to the rectangle you created, and close the Color Properties dialog.

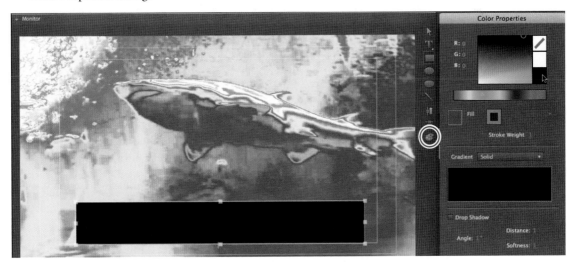

7 Let's soften the black color by making the background slightly transparent. Right-click the rectangle, and choose Transform > Opacity. The Opacity panel opens. Type *60.00* into the Opacity % field, and click OK to close the panel.

8 Now you'll shift the new rectangle behind the text. Right-click the rectangle and choose Arrange > Send to Back to place your rectangle behind your white type. The white text is now clearly visible over the rectangle. If necessary, you can edit the size of the rectangle by clicking it to make it active and then dragging any edge to a new location. You can also trim the right edge of the title so that it doesn't extend over the first Clip06.mp4 clip, where it would obscure the piranha text.

When you add multiple elements, such as text, squares, or circles, to a title, you create a stacking order. The most recent items added (in this case, the rectangle) are placed at the top of the stacking order. You can control the stacking order—as you did here—using the Arrange commands from the context menu or the Title menu. To quickly add matching titles at the same position in other clips, you can use the Copy and Paste commands.

9 Using the Selection tool, click to select the rectangle, and then Shift-click to select the text frame as well. Choose Edit > Copy.

10 Drag the current-time indicator to around 00;01;44;14, which should be close to the start of the slide show.

11 Choose Title > New Title > Default Still to switch to title-editing mode. Use the Selection tool to select the default text that was added, and then choose Edit > Clear.

12 Choose Edit > Paste to add the black rectangle with the words "Scary Critters" at the same position as in the original clip. Using the Type tool, select the words "Scary Critters" and replace them by typing *Slideshow*.

13 Use the Selection tool to select the black rectangle, and then adjust its width to the new text length by dragging the right-center anchor point to the left.

14 Center the Slideshow text by clicking to select it, right-clicking, and choosing Position > Horizontal Center. Then do the same with the background rectangle.

15 Review your movie, and then save your project.

Creating a Rolling Credit

The titles you have created to this point have been static, but Premiere Elements can create animated titles as well. There are two types of animated titles: rolls and crawls. A rolling credit is defined as text that moves vertically up the screen, like the end credits of a movie. A crawl is defined as text that moves horizontally across the screen, like a news ticker. In this exercise, you will create a rolling credit at the end of the project.

1 Press the End key to move to the end of the project.

2 Choose Title > New Title > Default Roll. Premiere Elements switches to title-editing mode and inserts a new rolling title.

3 Using the Type tool, select the text Main Title at the top of the Monitor panel. In the Text Options area, click the Center Text (▤) icon to center the text. That way, whatever you type will continue to be centered. Making sure that the Main Title text is still selected, type *The End*.

4 Click the other text box, press Ctrl+A/Command+A to select all text, and then click the Center Text icon again to center the text. Type *Starring:* and press Enter/Return twice. Then, type *Whatley*, press Enter/Return; type *Eleanor*, press Enter/Return; type *Daddy*, press Enter/Return twice; type *and the*, press Enter/Return; and type *Georgia Aquarium.*

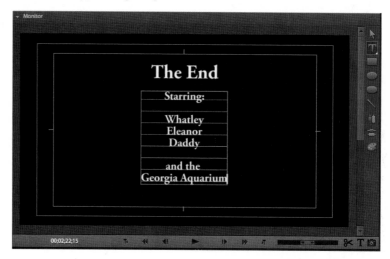

5 Choose Title > Roll/Crawl Options.

6 In the Roll/Crawl Options dialog, make sure Roll is selected for Title type and that both Start Off Screen and End Off Screen options are also selected. Finally, make sure that Preroll, Ease-In, Ease-Out, and Postroll values are all set to 0. Click OK to close the dialog.

When you play the clip, the text box with the credits will move—in the five-second default length of the title—from bottom to top across the monitor.

7 Place your current-time indicator just before the beginning of the rolling credits. Press the spacebar to play the rolling credits clip, and then save your project.

Changing the Speed of a Rolling Title

When Premiere Elements creates a rolling title, it spreads the text evenly over the duration of the title. The only way to change the speed of a rolling title is to increase or decrease the length of the title clip. The default duration for titles is five seconds. If you want the text to move more slowly across the screen, you need to increase the clip length.

● **Note:** If your titles do not display smoothly, they may need to be rendered. Pressing the Enter/ Return key will render all effects, transitions, and titles in a project.

1 In the Timeline, place your pointer over the end of the Title 06 rolling title clip. When the pointer changes to a red bracket pointing to the left (▨), drag the clip to the right. Note that as you drag, a small context menu shows you how much time you are adding to the clip. Add about five seconds to the length of the clip, and then release the pointer.

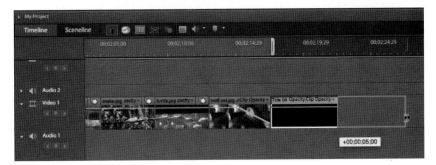

2 Place your current-time indicator just before the beginning of the rolling credits. Press the spacebar to play the rolling credits clip. Notice how your titles are now moving more slowly on the monitor.

3 Save your project as *Lesson08_End.prel*.

Using Title Templates

Creating your own titles, as you have done in the exercises in this lesson, will give you the most flexibility and options when it comes to customized titles. However, this involves performing a considerable number of steps from start to finish. To help you get started designing your titles, Premiere Elements ships with numerous templates for different types of projects, many with matching DVD templates, which creates a very polished look for your production. All you need to do is customize the text, replace an image, or do both to create a great-looking title.

1   Select Titles (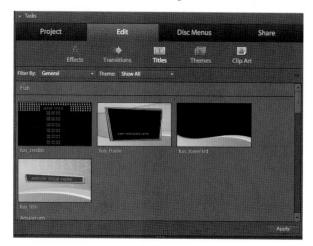) in the Edit tab in the Tasks panel. Choose a category of title templates from the menu on the left, and then choose a template name from the menu on the right. If necessary, scroll down to see all available templates within the chosen theme, such as rolling titles and alternative title graphics.

2   To superimpose a title template over a video clip, select the clip in the Sceneline, and then drag the template from Titles view onto the Monitor panel. If you're working in the Timeline, drag it to a track above the target video clip.

3   Use the Type tool to select the default text and replace it with your own text. Use the Selection tool to reposition or resize text and image frames. Add or delete text and image frames as necessary.

Exploring on Your Own

Experiment with the different templates Premiere Elements provides. Keep in mind that elements like the color of text and the position of graphics can be modified. Here are a few steps to follow as you discover what's available.

1   Replace the custom title you created with a title created from a template.

2   Explore the drawing tools available to you when in title-editing mode.

3   Change the font for the titles that you added to Comic Sans MS to match the opening title.

4   Create an animated title, choosing from the available options under Text Animation in Properties view.

5   Place different transitions between your title clips and your video clips to view the various effects you can achieve.

Congratulations; you have completed the lesson. You've learned how to create a simple still title with text and graphics. You changed the style, size, alignment, and color of text. You've positioned and aligned text and graphic frames in the Monitor panel, and you've used one of the Arrange commands to change the stacking order of overlapping frames. You added black video to your project and applied fade-in and fade-out effects to your title clip. You know how to create rolling credits and how to use and customize title templates. It's time for a well-earned break. But before you stop, review the questions and answers that complete this lesson.

Review Questions

1 How do you create a new title?

2 How do you exit title-editing mode, and how can you reenter it to make adjustments to a title clip?

3 How do you change the color of title text?

4 How do you add a fade-in or fade-out effect to a superimposed title clip?

5 What is a rolling credit, and how do you speed it up or slow it down?

Review Answers

1 With a video clip selected in the My Project panel, choose Title > New Title > Default Still. A title clip will be created and superimposed over the selected video clip.

2 To exit title-editing mode, click Done in the lower-right corner of Properties view, or click to select any clip in the My Project panel. To reenter title-editing mode, click to select the superimposed title text image in the Monitor panel, and then double-click it.

3 Switch to title-editing mode in the Monitor panel. Select the text using the Type tool. Then click the Color Properties button, and pick a new color in the Color Properties dialog.

4 In the Monitor panel, right-click the scene, and then select the title clip from the context menu. Under Opacity in Properties, click the Fade In or Fade Out button.

5 A rolling credit is text that scrolls vertically across your screen. The only way to make a rolling credit change speed is by selecting the clip in the Timeline in the My Project panel and then extending the length of the clip to slow it down or shortening the clip to speed it up.

9 WORKING WITH SOUND

Lesson overview

The sound you use has a big impact on your movies. Adobe Premiere Elements provides you with the tools to narrate clips while previewing them in real time; to create, add, and modify sound tracks; and to control the volume levels within clips. The project in this lesson helps you explore the basics of working with audio. You'll create a background music track, adjust the volume of an audio clip, add sound effects, add a narration clip, and mix the audio for maximum effect. Specifically, you'll learn how to do the following:

- Create a custom-length background music track with SmartSound (Windows only)

- Add narration

- Use SmartMix to automatically optimize the volume of your background music track and narration

- Adjust the volume of an audio track with and without keyframes

- Use the Audio Mixer

- Use audio effects

 This lesson will take approximately 1.5 hours.

Applying SmartMix to your project.

Getting Started

To begin, you'll launch Premiere Elements and open the project used for this lesson. Then you'll review a final version of the project you'll be creating.

1 Before you begin, make sure that you have correctly copied the Lesson09 folder from the DVD in the back of this book onto your computer's hard drive. For more information, see "Copying the Classroom in a Book Files" in the "Getting Started" section at the beginning of this book.

2 Launch Premiere Elements and click the Open Project button in the Welcome screen. If Premiere Elements is already open, choose File > Open Project, and click the Open folder.

3 Navigate to your Lesson09 folder and select the project file Lesson09_Start_Win.prel (Windows) or Lesson09_Start_Mac.prel (Mac OS). Click the Open (Windows) or Choose (Mac OS) button to open your project. If a dialog appears asking for the location of rendered files, click the Skip Previews button. The Premiere Elements work area appears with the Edit workspace selected in the Tasks panel.

4 The project file opens in the Properties view with the Media, Monitor, and My Project panels open. Choose Window > Restore Workspace to ensure that you start the lesson with the default panel layout.

Viewing the Completed Movie for the First Exercise

To see what you'll be creating as your first project in this lesson, a video about a visit to the Georgia Aquarium, you can play the completed movie.

1 In the Project tab in the Tasks panel, click Media (![Media]( )). In Media view, locate the file Lesson09_Movie.mov, and then double-click it to open the video into the Preview window.

2 In the Preview window, click the Play button (![Play]( )) to watch the video that you will build in this lesson.

3 When you're finished watching the completed video, close the Preview window.

Creating Background Music with SmartSound

Adobe has partnered with SmartSound to provide you with a library of musical sound tracks to match your project, as well as easy access to a complete library of background music that you can purchase directly from SmartSound (www.smartsound.com). As you'll learn in this exercise, using SmartSound Quicktracks for Premiere Elements, you can quickly choose and create a custom-length sound track that matches the mood of your production. You can create SmartSound music tracks in either the Sceneline or Timeline of the My Project panel; in this exercise, you'll work in the Timeline.

1 If necessary, switch to the Timeline by clicking the Timeline button in the upper-left corner of the My Project panel.

2 Press the End key to move the current-time indicator to the end of the project. Note the timecode in the bottom left of the Monitor panel, which should be around 00;02;27;16. You'll use this duration in a later step to choose the duration of the background music track.

3 Press the Home key to return the current-time indicator to the start of the project.

4 In the upper-left tool set in the My Project panel, click the Audio Tools drop-down list (![audio tools icon]), and choose SmartSound. If this is the first time you're use Quicktracks, you may have to click through a license agreement, registration window, and search screen, and SmartSound may need to download and install some preview files. If necessary, click SmartSound in the Audio Tools drop-down list again to load Express Track.

5 Elements opens SmartSound Express Track. As you can see in the Find Music column, you can select Owned Titles to search for tracks you already own, or select All to search for music on the SmartSound website. Once you choose the library, you can search by style and intensity to narrow your choices in the Results area.

6 In the Find Music column, choose Owned Titles.

7 In the Style list box, choose World.

8 In the Keyword list box, choose Earthy. In this case, the keyword doesn't impact the tracks that appear in the Title window because you're searching through only the tracks on your computer. If you were searching in the SmartSound Store, which has a much wider selection, your keyword choice would further narrow the selection.

9 In the Title window that displays the tracks your search criteria returned, choose Global Vibes, which is the track you'll add to this project (and likely the only available track). To preview the track, click the Play button on the lower right of SmartSound Express Track.

10 In the Length box, type *02;27;16*. Note that you'll have to enter each two-digit number separately into the Length duration box, starting with those on the left, which is different from other similar numeric fields within Premiere Elements.

11 Note that each song has different variations and moods. You can experiment with these; I like the New shores variation and the Background mood. For this exercise, choose those so your files are identical to the ones I use in this exercise.

12 Click the Send button. SmartSound saves the file, briefly displaying an export window, and inserts it into the Soundtrack track in the project starting at the location of the current-time indicator. If you can't see your Soundtrack track in the Timeline, use the scroll bar on the right to scroll down and view it.

13 Choose File > Save As, name the file *Lesson09_Work.prel* in the Save As dialog, and then save it in your Lesson09 folder.

● **Note:** SmartSound will create a WAV file on Windows and an AIFF file on the Mac. Both files should be named Global Vibes - New shores with either the .wav extension on Windows or .aiff on the Mac.

A. Narration track. **B.** Soundtrack track. **C.** New SmartSound audio track. **D.** End of SmartSound audio track. **E.** Scroll bar to view audio tracks.

You can play the new sound file by pressing the spacebar. If you drag your current-time indicator to a few seconds before the end of the movie, and then press the spacebar again to play the last few bars, you'll note that the sound track ends naturally, not abruptly, demonstrating that SmartSound really does deliver theme-specific, custom-length sound tracks.

Adding Narration

Now let's add narration to the project.

1 Make sure you have the Timeline selected in the My Project panel.

2 Choose File > Get Media from > PC Files and Folders, if necessary, navigate to the Lesson09 folder, select the file narration.wav, and click Open (Windows) or Import (Mac OS).

3 Drag the narration.wav clip from Media view and drop it onto the start of the Narration track in the Timeline.

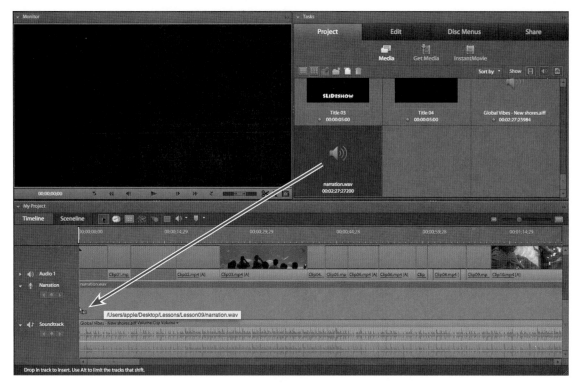

4 Click the Play button (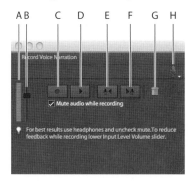) to hear the voice-over added to the project. Between the narration, talking, and other ambient noise in the videos and the background music, you can barely hear the Narration track. Let's fix that.

Record voice narration: **A.** Volume indicator.
B. Input Volume Level slider. **C.** Record.
D. Play. **E.** Go To Previous Narration Clip.
F. Go To Next Narration Clip.
G. Delete Present Narration.
H. Microphone source.

Narrating a Clip

In this exercise, you're working with a narration that I supplied, but at some point, you may want to create your own narration. For best results, confirm that your microphone is working correctly with your computer and Premiere Elements before narrating a clip.

Using your computer's microphone, you can narrate clips while previewing them in the Monitor panel. Your narration is then added to the Narration sound track visible in either the Timeline or Sceneline. Follow these steps to narrate a clip.

1 *Do one of the following*:

   • In the Timeline, drag the current-time indicator to the point where you want the narration to begin.

   • In the Sceneline, select the clip you want to narrate. Then, in the Monitor panel, drag the current-time indicator to the point where you want the narration to begin.

2 In the Timeline or Sceneline, choose Add Narration from the Audio Tools menu.

3 In the Record Voice Narration window, click the Mic Source button, and choose your sound device from the menu.

4 For best results, turn off your computer speakers to prevent feedback. To monitor sound while you narrate, plug headphones into your computer, and deselect Mute Audio While Recording. If your speakers are turned on, move as close to the microphone as possible, and keep the microphone as far away from the speakers as possible to prevent feedback.

5 Speak into the microphone at a conversational volume, and raise or lower the Input Volume Level slider until your loudest words light up the orange part of the meters.

6 Click the Record Narration button.

7 Near the top of the Record Voice Narration window, a timer appears next to Start Recording In. When Start Recording In changes to Recording, speak your narration as the selected clip plays.

8 When you finish narrating, click the Stop button. An audio clip containing your narration is added to the Media panel and to the Narration track in the Timeline or Sceneline (below the selected clip). If you do not click the Stop button, recording automatically stops at the beginning of the next file in the Narration track, or 30 seconds past the end of the last clip in the Timeline or Sceneline.

9 To preview your recording, click the Go To Previous Narration button. Then click the Play Present Narration button.

10 To continue recording from the point at which you stopped, click the Record button again. Clicking Record again overwrites any narrations that are already in the Narration track.

11 Click the Pause button at anytime to stop the preview. In the Sceneline, a microphone icon appears in the top-right corner of the clip you've narrated.

—From Adobe Premiere Elements Help

Adjusting Project Volume with SmartMix

You now have three audio tracks: the one included with the videos, the background music from SmartSound, and the narration that you just added. All these tracks add value to your production. The ambient noise from the aquarium adds valuable context to the video, the background music supplies a nice flow, and the narration provides a colorful commentary. The problem is that the three tracks drown out each other.

Intuitively, when present, the narration takes precedence and needs to be heard over the other two tracks. Fortunately, there's a tool that can do just that: SmartMix, which you'll learn how to apply in this exercise.

1   Make sure you have the Timeline selected in the My Project panel.

2   Click the Backslash (\) key to show the entire project. Adjust the interface so you can see all three audio tracks.

3   In the upper-left tool set in the My Project panel, click the Audio Tools drop-down list, and choose SmartMix > Options. Premiere Elements opens the Mixer Options dialog.

4   Here's where you tell Premiere Elements which audio tracks to prioritize and which to place in the background. Premiere Elements assumes that Audio 1—the audio shot with the video—should be in the foreground—which, in many instances, it should be. Here, however, it should not, so click the Audio 1 list box and choose Background. Then click Apply. Premiere Elements analyzes all audio tracks and applies the SmartMix.

5   Premiere Elements prioritizes the narration by reducing the volume of Audio 1 and the Soundtrack with keyframes in the audio file (which you'll learn to insert and adjust next).

6   Press the spacebar to play the first few moments of the video. Overall, the audio is much better, but the narration is still a bit indistinct, and the ambient noise from the aquarium is still a bit too loud. You'll have to fix that manually by undoing the first application of SmartMix and then applying it again after disabling any adjustment to the Audio 1 track. Then you'll adjust the Audio 1 track and Narration tracks manually as described later in this exercise.

7   Click the Undo key (Undo) on the upper right of the Premiere Elements interface to undo SmartMix.

8   If you closed the Mixer Options dialog, in the upper-left tool set in the My Project panel, click the Audio Tools drop-down list, and choose SmartMix > Options. The Mixer Options dialog opens.

9   Click the Backslash (\) key to show the entire project. Adjust the interface so you can see all three audio tracks.

10 Click the Audio 1 list box and choose Disabled; then click Apply; and then close the Mixer Options dialog. This tells SmartMix to ignore this track during the SmartMix analysis and to leave it untouched. This gives you the result that you want with the Soundtrack, which would be the time-consuming component of the audio mix if you had to correct for this manually.

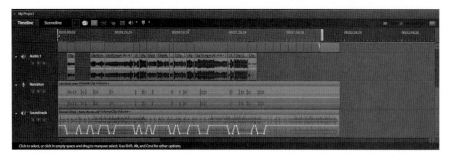

Adjusting the Volume of an Audio Track

The background music track is set; now you need to adjust the volume of the Video 1 and Narration tracks.

Adjusting Clip Volume with Gain Controls

Premiere Elements offers two basic ways to adjust the volume of your audio tracks. You can adjust *gain*, which is the level of volume within a clip, or *volume*, which is the level of audio output of a particular clip within a sequence. The difference is pretty subtle. In most instances, you can use one or the other control to get the desired volume.

There is a key implementation difference, however, when working with multiple clips, as you are here. Specifically, you can adjust the gain levels, but not the volume levels, of multiple clips simultaneously. So, to control the volume of the traffic and other noise in the Video 1 track, you'll apply a group gain adjustment to all clips in the track. Here's how.

1 Drag along the Audio 1 track to select all files in that track.

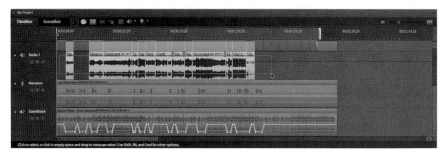

2   Right-click any audio clip in Audio 1 and choose Audio Gain. Premiere Elements opens the Clip Gain panel.

● **Note:** In Premiere Elements, volume is measured in decibels. A level of 0.0 dB is a track's original volume, not silence. Changing the levels to a negative number reduces the volume (but not necessarily to silence). Changing the volume to a positive number increases the volume.

3   Click the Gain level text box to make it active, and type -25. Or, click on the number and drag it to the left to about the same level.

4   Click OK to apply the gain adjustment and close the Clip Gain panel. You'll see the levels in the waveform on the Audio 1 track decrease substantially.

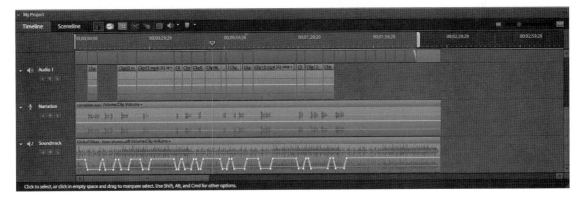

5   Press the spacebar to play the movie again. Although you can still hear the background noise faintly, it's much less prominent, and the complete audio mix is coming together quite nicely. Now let's boost the volume of the narration.

Adjusting Clip Volume with the Volume Graph

In Lesson 6, you learned how to adjust clip opacity on the Timeline by dragging the Opacity connector line upwards and downwards. You can adjust the volume of any audio clip the same way. Let's adjust the volume of the Narration track using this technique.

1   Working with the narration.wav clip on the Narration track, place your pointer over the yellow volume graph line. You can do this at any location in the clip. The pointer changes to a double-arrow icon (⇕).

Note: Adjusting the volume line doesn't change the waveform display. However, as you'll see in the next exercise, adjusting gain directly does change the waveform. Although adjusting the volume line is easier and more accessible than adjusting gain directly, if you overboost volume, you can produce distortion without being able to view the clipping in the waveform. For an explanation of waveform and clipping, see the sidebar "About Waveforms."

2   Drag the volume graph upwards to the limit, which should be about 6.02 dB.

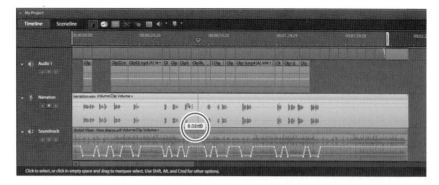

3   Shift the current-time indicator to the start of Clip01.mp4, and press the spacebar to play the movie again. Although you can still hear the ambient noise faintly, it's much less prominent, and the complete audio mix is definitely in great shape. Cut it, print it—let's move on.

4   Choose File > Save to save your work.

Note: If 6.02 dB isn't sufficient to boost your audio to the desired level, you can also adjust the Gain control as detailed in the previous exercise. In fact, try boosting the Gain of the narration.wav clip by about 5 dB, and then preview again and decide if that sounds even better.

About Waveforms

By default, Premiere Elements' audio tracks display the file as a waveform, which is a graphic representation of the volume of audio in the file. When volume is low, the bushy line representing the waveform narrowly surrounds the center line. As volume increases, the bushy line extends farther away from the center line. Volume is optimal when the peaks in the individual waveform approach but just barely touch the outer edges of the graph area. I've reset the gain values of the clips on Audio 1 to illustrate this concept.

The audio on most of the clips on Audio 1 and the Soundtrack are both healthy—just about approaching the outer edges of the graph area but never touching for long. The exceptions are the first and the last video clips, which were shot outside.

On the other hand, in the narration, the peaks don't come close to the edges, indicating that volume could be increased, which is what you accomplished with the volume slider in the previous lesson. In practice, I would likely use the Normalize function to boost volume here. To do this, I would right-click the clip, choose Audio Gain, and then

click the Normalize button in the Clip Gain control. Go ahead and try this on narration.wav in the Narration track.

Premiere Elements will close the dialog immediately after you click Normalize, but you'll notice that the waveform gets a bit bushier, and if you open the Clip Gain dialog again (right-click the audio clip and choose Audio Gain), you'll notice that Premiere Elements inserted the number 4.6 in the dB field, indicating that it boosted the volume of the clip by 4.6 dB. If you try this same exercise with the SmartSound clip, you'll get a -2 dB decrease, indicating that SmartSound produced the background music clip closer to the optimal volume.

Technically, when you click the Normalize button, Premiere Elements analyzes the clip and boosts clip volume as much as possible without introducing distortion into the clip. This makes Normalization a superior option to manual volume adjustments, as you did in the previous lesson, because those can distort your audio. Plus, when you adjust gain, either manually or via the Normalize function, Premiere Elements updates the waveform, so you can see if you've overcooked the audio or boosted volume to the point where it might cause distortion.

As an example, open the Clip Gain dialog for narration.wav again by right-clicking the clip and choosing Audio Gain. Enter *12* in the dB field, and click OK. Your waveform will expand even further with several areas flattened against the top and bottom of the track. This is called *clipping*, and in moderate-to-extreme cases, clipping will distort your audio. If you preview the clip now, you'll hear the distortion that I'm talking about. Closing the loop, this means that on occasion manual volume adjustments may cause distortion. Normalization prevents that, and using the Gain control gives you a visual indicator of clip volume. If you make any of these changes in your own project, be sure to undo them before you continue.

The only problem with Normalization comes when you have a single long clip with extreme low and high volumes. Let's say you were shooting a wedding and didn't get close enough (or mic the bride, groom, or officiant) to capture the vows at sufficient volume. So the levels are very low when the bride and groom are speaking. However, when the crowd starts applauding, the levels are quite high. If you apply Normalization to this clip, Premiere Elements won't boost the volume of the applause beyond the point of causing distortion, which often means that it won't boost the volume of the vows at all. Your best option in this case is to split the clip into low- and high-volume regions—vows in one, applause in another—and apply Normalization separately or only to the vows audio.

The other issue with Gain—as opposed to Volume—adjustments is that you can't vary the adjustment by using keyframes, which you'll learn how to do in the next lesson.

Note that whenever you boost audio volume, either via the Gain or Volume adjustment, you also increase the background noise present in the clip. In these instances, you can try Premiere Elements' DeNoiser filter, but like all noise reduction filters, it isn't a panacea and may not resolve the problem.

Raising and Lowering Volume with Keyframes

You learned about working with keyframes in video in Lesson 6 in a section titled (appropriately enough) "Working with Keyframes." Audio keyframes operate identically to the video-related keyframes discussed in that lesson. To refresh your memory, a keyframe is a point in the Timeline where you specify a value for a specific property—in this case, audio volume. When you set two keyframes, Premiere Elements interpolates the value of that property over all frames between the two keyframes.

For some properties, including opacity for video and volume for audio, you can create keyframes in the Timeline by pressing the Ctrl/Command key and then clicking the associated graph with your pointer. Next, drag the keyframe upwards or downwards to adjust its value, or to the left or right to adjust its location. To delete keyframes in the Timeline, click to select them, right-click, and then choose Delete.

Alternatively, you can create and modify keyframes in Properties view. This exercise will review these procedures and reinforce the relationship between keyframes in the Timeline and keyframes in Properties view. Specifically, in this exercise, you'll add keyframes to fade in the volume of the music track at the beginning of your movie.

1 Using the My Project panel in the Timeline, place the current-time indicator near the start of the project, around the 00;00;01;00 mark.

2 Click to select the Global Vibes - New shores clip in the Timeline's Soundtrack.

3 Select Window > Properties, and then click the Show Keyframes button (▶️⌖) in the upper-left tool set of Properties view.

4 Use the Zoom slider to zoom into the mini-timeline until you can see the 00;00;01;00 timecode in the mini-timeline.

5 Make sure the current-time indicator is at the 00;00;01;00 mark, and then click the Toggle Animation button (⊠) for the Volume effect to activate keyframes. This will set the first keyframe at the current-time indicator. If the Toggle Animation button is already activated, click to disable it (and delete all keyframes), and then click again to activate keyframes.

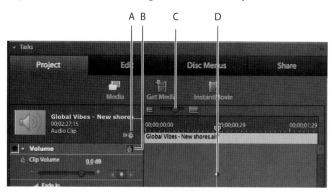

A. Show Keyframes button. **B.** Toggle Animation button. **C.** Zoom slider. **D.** Keyframe.

You'll set the next keyframe in the Timeline.

6 Press the Page Up key to move the current-time indicator to the beginning of the movie. If necessary, use the Zoom slider on top of the Timeline to zoom in for more detail.

7 In the Timeline in the My Project panel, position the pointer over the orange volume graph of the Global Vibes - New shores clip at the current-time indicator. Be sure not to position the pointer too far to the left. The pointer needs to change to a white arrow with double arrows (⇕), not the Trim Out tool (🔲). Press the Ctrl/Command key, and the pointer changes to the insert keyframe pointer (🔲). Click the volume graph to add a second keyframe.

8 Drag the new keyframe all the way down to create the start of the fade-in. You can check Properties view: The Clip Volume reads -oo to resemble the mathematical symbol $-\infty$ for negative infinity.

9 To hear this change, press the Page Up key, and then press the spacebar to play. You'll hear the sound track fade in over the first second of the production rather than starting at full strength.

● **Note:** This exercise was designed to help show the relationship between audio keyframes in the Timeline and Properties view. However, a faster way to produce a fade-in effect is to click the Fade In icon for the audio clip in the Properties view, as shown in the preceding figure. With the Global Vibes - New shores clip selected, click the Fade Out button to insert a fade-out (🔲 Fade Out) at the end of the audio clip. It's not really necessary because the SmartSound clip fades at just the right time, but you'll likely want to insert the fade-out in most projects.

10 Save your project as *Lesson09_Work.prel*.

Working with the Audio Mixer

If, for some reason, SmartMix doesn't produce the result you want, you have an alternative: Premiere Elements' Audio Mixer. Using the Audio Mixer, you can adjust the volume and balance of the different audio tracks as the audio plays, so you can make sure your audience hears what you want it to hear. For example, you can lower the volume for the Soundtrack while people are talking and increase it again when they are silent.

Let's start fresh by reloading Lesson09_Start.prel and then the narration and background music clips.

1 Navigate to your Lesson09 folder and select the project file Lesson09_Start.prel. Click the Open button (Windows) or Choose (Mac OS) to open your project.

2 Choose File > Get Media from > PC Files and Folders, select the file narration. wav, and click Open (Windows) or Import (Mac OS).

3 Press the Home key to move the current-time indicator to the start of the clip. Then drag the narration.wav clip from Media view and drop it onto the start of the Narration track in the Timeline.

4 Choose File > Get Media from > PC Files and Folders, select the file Global Vibes - New shores, and click Open (Windows) or Import (Mac OS).

5 Drag the Global Vibes - New shores clip from Media view and drop it onto the Soundtrack track in the Timeline at the start of the movie.

6 If it isn't there already, press the Home key to place the current-time indicator at the beginning of the movie. Press the spacebar to begin playing your video. You should hear the same familiar mess that we started with.

7 When you're finished previewing the movie, press the Home key again to set the current-time indicator right at the beginning of the video, which is where you want to start mixing audio.

8 In the upper-left tool set of the My Project panel, click the Audio Tools drop-down list, and choose Audio Mix. The Audio Mixer panel opens.

9 Your Audio Mixer panel shows five audio tracks, but only three—Audio 1, Narration, and Soundtrack—contain audio. You can ignore the last two.

10 Press the spacebar to begin playback.

11 Grab the levels handles for Audio 1, Narration, and Soundtrack, and adjust them as desired while the video plays. Good luck. Note that all adjustments made via the Audio Mixer will be reflected as keyframes on the audio track and in its respective Properties view but will become visible only after you stop playback.

Edit to the Beat of Your Favorite Song

You can use Detect Beats in the Sceneline or Timeline to automatically add markers at the beats of your musical sound track. Beat detection makes it easy to synchronize slide shows or video edits to your music.

1 Add an audio clip or a video clip that includes audio to the sound track in the Timeline or Sceneline.

2 In the upper-left tool set of the My Project panel, click the Audio Tools drop-down list, and choose Detect Beats. The Beat Detect Settings panel opens.

Creating a Split Edit

Typically, when you shoot and capture video, your captured files contain both audio and video. By default, with these files, the audio and video are linked together, so when you trim one, you trim the other. This helps ensure that you don't lose audio/video synchronization.

However, sometimes, you may want the audio to begin before the video or to extend after the video into the next clip (or vice versa). These are called split edits because the audio is split from the video. As detailed in the Premiere Elements Help file, there are two kinds of split edits:

- A *J-cut*, or audio lead, in which audio starts before linked video or video continues after the audio.

- An *L-cut*, or video lead, in which video starts before linked audio or audio continues after the video.

To accomplish either, you have to unlink the audio from the associated video. You can do this in two ways. First, if you press the Alt/Option key while trimming on the Timeline, you can trim the audio and video separately. Once you release the pointer, the audio and video are re-linked so that if you drag the video, the audio will go with it.

Second, you can permanently unlink the audio and video by choosing either track on the Timeline and choosing Unlink Audio and Video. This breaks the link between the two clips, so if you drag the video file, the audio file won't move at all. This is useful when you want to delete the audio captured with a video clip, or vice versa.

3 In the Beat Detect Settings dialog, specify settings as desired and click OK.

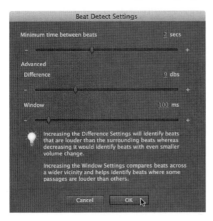

4 Markers appear in the Timeline corresponding to the beats in the sound track.

Working with Sound Effects

In most projects, the primary audio-related variable that you'll adjust is volume, and you've explored a number of techniques to accomplish that here. In addition, Premiere Elements has multiple audio effects to further enhance your projects, including controlling the volumes and frequencies of the different channels in your audio files, detecting and removing tape noise, eliminating background noise, and adding the reverberation of sounds to give ambience and warmth to the audio clip.

You can find the audio effects in Effects view by choosing Audio Effects in the effect type list box. You apply audio effects by dragging them onto the target audio clip. You can then configure them in Properties view. If any of the effects look particularly interesting, you can search Premiere Elements Help for more details.

Exploring on Your Own

Great news: You've finished another lesson and learned the basics of working with sound. Specifically, you learned to create a custom-length sound track with SmartSound, to add narration to your projects, to use SmartMix to adjust audio gain directly, and to create and adjust keyframes in the Timeline and Properties view.

But you're not finished yet. The best way to master the audio tools in Premiere Elements is to continue to explore them.

1 Experiment with different songs available in SmartSound. Think of some upcoming projects (birthdays, holidays, vacations) and try to find the appropriate tracks for those videos.

2 Experiment with various audio effects such as Delay and Dynamics. A description of Premiere Elements audio effects can be found in the "Audio Effects" section of Premiere Elements Help.

3 As you did for the fade-in of the sound track, try to create a fade-out for the end of your project.

Review Questions

1   What is SmartMix, and when should you use it?

2   What is the Audio Mixer, and how do you access it?

3   How would you change the volume of a clip over time using keyframes?

4   How do you change the presets of an audio effect?

5   What is Normalization, and how is it different from adjusting audio volume directly?

Review Answers

1   SmartMix is a feature that lets you identify which audio track(s) you want in the foreground and which ones you want in the background. It automatically adjusts the volume of the background clips to ensure that the foreground clip—usually speech or narration—is clearly audible. You should use SmartMix whenever you're trying to mix two audio tracks, especially when one contains narration or other dialogue.

2   Using the Audio Mixer, you can easily adjust the audio balance and volume for different tracks in your project. You can refine the settings while listening to audio tracks and viewing video tracks. Each track in the Audio Mixer corresponds to an audio track in the Timeline or Sceneline and is named accordingly. You can access the Audio Mixer by clicking the Mix Audio button or by choosing Window > Audio Mixer.

3   Each clip in the Premiere Elements Timeline has a yellow volume graph that controls the keyframes of the clip. To add keyframes, Ctrl-click/Command-click the line. You must have at least two keyframes with different values to automatically change the volume level of an audio clip. You can also use the Audio Mixer to set keyframes to change the volume of your audio clip over time.

4   First, select the clip that contains the effect you want to adjust in the Timeline. Second, in the Effects view, click the Edit Effects button. In Properties view, expand the property by clicking the disclosure triangle next to the property name (if available), and then drag the slider or angle control.

5   Normalization boosts the audio volume of all samples of an audio clip the same amount, stopping when further volume increases would produce distortion in the loudest sections of the clip. When you boost volume manually, you run the risk of causing distortion.

10 WORKING WITH MOVIE THEMES

Lesson overview

In the previous chapters, you learned how to produce a completely customized movie from your source clips. In this chapter, you'll learn how to apply a Movie theme to your source clips to produce an engaging, stylized movie in a matter of moments.

Movie themes are collections of professionally created, theme-specific titles, effects, transitions, and background music. Before applying a theme, Adobe Premiere Elements analyzes your video footage for content and then edits your content to best fit the tone of the theme.

As with InstantMovies, you can apply an entire theme or just parts of it to perfectly fit your creative concept. In this lesson, you'll learn how to do the following:

- Select a Movie theme
- Choose some Movie theme properties and apply them to your clip
- Edit your movie after applying a Movie theme

This lesson will take approximately 30 minutes.

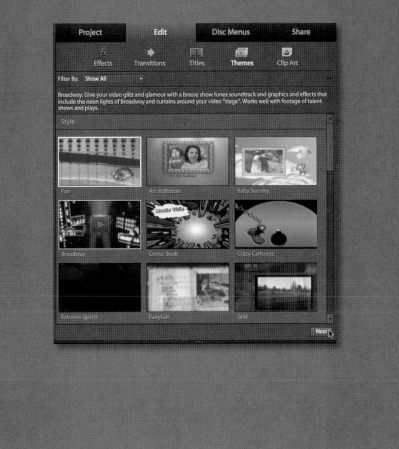

Choosing a Movie theme.

Getting Started

To begin, you'll launch Premiere Elements, open the Lesson10 project, and review a final version of the movie you'll be creating.

1   Before you start the project, make sure that you have correctly copied the Lesson10 folder from the DVD in the back of this book onto your computer's hard drive. See "Copying the Classroom in a Book Files" in the "Getting Started" section at the beginning of this book.

2   Launch Premiere Elements.

3   In the Welcome screen, click the Open Project button. If necessary, click Open in the pop-up menu. The Open Project dialog opens.

4   Navigate to your Lesson10 folder and select the project file Lesson10_Start_Win.prel (Windows) or Lesson10_Start_Mac.prel (Mac OS). If a dialog appears asking for the location of rendered files, click the Skip Previews button.

   Your project file opens with the Monitor, Tasks, and My Project panels open.

5   Choose Window > Restore Workspace to ensure that you start the lesson with the default panel layout.

Viewing the Completed Movie Before You Start

To see what you'll be creating in this lesson, take a look at the completed movie.

1   In the Project tab in the Tasks panel, click Media (![Media]). In Media view, locate the file Lesson10_Movie.mov, and then double-click it to open the video into the Preview window.

2   In the Preview window, click the Play button (![Play]) to watch the video about a visit to the Georgia Aquarium, which you'll build in this lesson.

3   When you're finished watching the completed video, close the Preview window.

About Movie Themes

You first had a glimpse of Movie themes back in Lesson 4 when you learned how to create an InstantMovie from the Organizer. Recall that an InstantMovie is a Movie theme applied to clips in the Organizer. In this lesson, you'll learn how to apply a Movie theme to clips in the Timeline.

When should you use each approach? When you create an InstantMovie, you can choose your content via tagging and apply Smart Tagging to your source clips, which is fast and effective when attempting to identify the best three or four minutes of video from a mass of source clips.

Note that creating an InstantMovie in the Organizer differs from working in the Timeline in one fundamental way: You can't edit source clips before applying an InstantMovie. This makes applying Movie themes in the Timeline a better option if there's source footage that you don't want included in the final movie.

Movie themes enable you to quickly create videos with a specific look and feel. The Outdoor Wedding theme, for example, adds an elegant, animated introduction, wedding background music, multiple custom picture-in-picture and other animations, and closing credits for a wedding video. In contrast, the Comic Book theme provides more funky effects and fonts along with Picture-in-Picture overlays that might be more appropriate for a kids' party video.

You can apply all the properties in a theme, choose to add only a subset, or even just modify some parts. Likewise, you can add a theme to an entire movie or to only a single clip.

You access Movie themes via the Themes button () in the Edit tab in the Tasks panel. The various themes use animated thumbnails that give you a good idea of the overall feel of the theme.

Applying a Movie Theme

In the exercises that follow, you'll apply a Movie theme to the aquarium clips that you've edited throughout the book. You'll apply the theme to clips in the My Project panel using the Timeline, so you should edit out any undesired scenes before applying a theme.

However, don't spend a lot of time ordering the clips on the Timeline: If you choose, Premiere Elements will either arrange the clips to best fit the Movie theme or display them in chronological order. In addition, don't correct brightness, contrast, or stabilization issues before applying a theme, because in order for Premiere Elements to apply the theme-specific effects, it will have to remove all the effects you've previously applied. Don't worry; as with InstantMovies, you can edit your movie after applying the Movie theme and correct any color, brightness, or stabilization issues then.

When you have all the desired clips in the Timeline, follow this procedure to apply a Movie theme.

Note: The Auto-Analyzer check box is active only when you're applying an InstantMovie in the Organize panel.

1   Click the Themes button ( ) in the Edit tab in the Tasks panel.

2   Click the Fun Theme to select it, and then click Next.

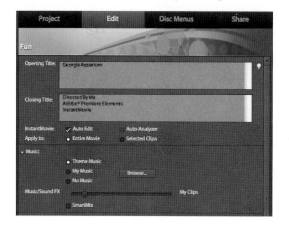

3   To customize the theme, *do the following*:

- Customize the Opening and Closing Titles. Keep the Opening Title relatively short, or your text may not fit in the title box used by many themes.

- Select the Auto Edit check box to have Premiere Elements analyze your clips and edit them to fit the selected theme. If you don't select Auto Edit, Premiere Elements uses the clips as is and doesn't edit them.

- Select the Entire Movie radio button to apply the theme to all clips on the Timeline.

- In the Music box, select Theme Music.

- Drag the Music/Sound FX slider to the left, as shown in the previous figure, to prioritize background audio over the ambient noise in the original clips.

- If you have dialogue in your project (which this clip doesn't), select the SmartMix check box, and Premiere Elements will reduce the volume of the music track when it detects dialogue.

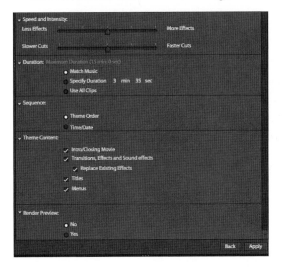

- In the Speed and Intensity dialog, adjust the Effects and Cuts sliders as desired. I'll use the default values.

- In the Duration box, select Match Music, which produces a movie that matches the duration of the selected music. This is the approach I recommend in most instances. Or, you can specify a duration or select Use All Clips, which uses all your clips at their original duration with no background music.

- In the Sequence box, select Theme Order, which allows Premiere Elements to use clips as they best match the theme. Your other option, Time/Date, uses the clips in the order that they were shot.

- In the Theme Content box, leave all check boxes selected.

- In the Render Preview box, leave No selected.

4 After selecting your options, click Apply to create the InstantMovie. Click No when the InstantMovie dialog asks if you want to add more clips. Click Yes when another dialog warns that user-applied effects will be replaced.

5 Premiere Elements creates the InstantMovie and inserts it into the My Project panel.

6   Use the playback controls in the Monitor panel to preview the InstantMovie. If a dialog appears that asks if you want to render before previewing, click No. In general, you probably would want to render for smoother playback, but it could take a while with this source footage, and you can preview with sufficient quality for our purposes without rendering.

7   Premiere Elements adds the InstantMovie to the My Project panel in consolidated form. To break apart the InstantMovie into its components to edit them, click to select the new InstantMovie, right-click, and choose Break Apart InstantMovie.

8   Choose File > Save As, name the file *Lesson10_End.prel* in the Save As dialog, and then save it in your Lesson10 folder.

Exploring on Your Own

Experiment with the different Movie themes provided with your copy of Premiere Elements. Keep in mind that you can apply an entire theme or pick and choose parts of it.

Apply a Movie theme to selected clips in the My Project panel to become familiar with this option.

Well done—you've completed this lesson. You've learned how to apply a Movie theme and how to customize its properties.

Review Questions

1 What is a Movie theme?

2 How is a Movie theme different from an InstantMovie?

3 When are InstantMovies a better option than applying Movie themes to clips in the Timeline?

4 How do you edit a movie after applying a Movie theme?

Review Answers

1 Movie themes are templates that enable you to quickly turn your clips into a professional-looking movie. You can choose from event-based themes like Birthday or more style-based themes like Silent Film. A Movie theme includes coordinated transitions, effects, and music, as well as layouts for titles and credits. You can apply an entire theme or choose to select only parts of it.

2 InstantMovies are Movie themes applied to clips in the Organizer.

3 InstantMovies are a better option when you'd like to use tagging and Smart Tagging to help choose videos included in the movie. Applying Movie themes in the My Project panel is preferred when you have to edit content before applying the Movie theme.

4 Right-click the finished movie and choose Break Apart InstantMovie.

11 CREATING MENUS

Lesson overview

In this lesson, you'll create a menu for a movie to be recorded on a DVD or Blu-ray Disc. You can follow along with most of this lesson even if your system does not have a DVD or Blu-ray Disc burner, although it will be helpful if it does. You'll learn how to add menu markers that allow your viewers direct access to scenes in your movies and how to create and customize disc menus. You'll also learn how to preview a menu and then burn a DVD or Blu-ray Disc for playback on a standard DVD or Blu-ray Disc player. Specifically, you'll learn how to do the following:

- Add menu markers to your movie

- Create an auto-play disc

- Use templates to create disc menus

- Customize the look of the menus

- Preview a disc menu

- Record a DVD, Blu-ray, or AVCHD disc

- Create a Web DVD

This lesson will take approximately two hours.

Creating a DVD with menus.

Getting Started

To begin, you'll launch Adobe Premiere Elements, open the Lesson11 project, and review a final version of that project.

1   Before you begin, make sure that you have correctly copied the Lesson11 folder from the DVD in the back of this book onto your computer's hard drive. See "Copying the Classroom in a Book Files" in the "Getting Started" section at the beginning of this book.

2   Launch Premiere Elements.

3   In the Welcome screen, click the Open Project button, and then click Open in the pop-up menu. In the Open Project dialog, navigate to the Lesson11 folder, select the file Lesson11_End_Win.prel (Windows) or Lesson11_End_Mac.prel (Mac OS), and then click Open (Windows) or Choose (Mac OS). If a dialog appears asking for the location of rendered files, click the Skip Previews button.

A finished version of the project file you will create in this lesson opens with the Monitor, Tasks, and My Project panels open. You may review it now or at any point during the lesson to get a sense of what your project should look like.

4   Select Disc Menus in the Tasks panel to switch to the Disc Menus workspace. In the Disc Layout panel, click Preview to open the Preview Disc window.

The Preview Disc window allows you to view and test your menus as they will appear when played on a DVD or Blu-ray player.

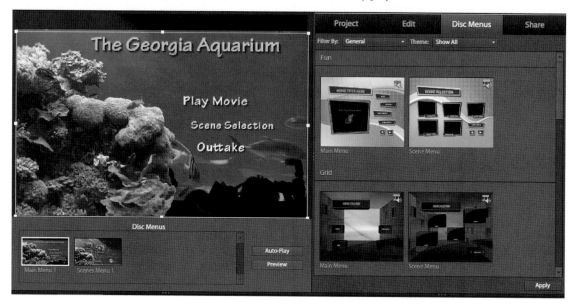

5   In the Preview Disc window, click the Scene Selection button in the main menu to switch to the Scene Selection menu. Click the Videos button to begin playing this selection.

6   Press the spacebar to stop the playback, and then close the Preview Disc window by clicking the Exit button (⊠ EXIT) in the lower-right corner of the window.

7   After reviewing the finished file, choose File > Close. In the dialog, click No so that you do not save any changes made to the project. Then choose File > Open Project, select the file Lesson11_Start_Win.prel (Windows) or Lesson11_Start_Mac.prel (Mac OS), and click Open (Windows) or Choose (Mac OS). If a dialog appears asking for the location of rendered files, click the Skip Previews button.

8   Choose Window > Restore Workspace to ensure that you start the lesson with the default panel layout.

● **Note:** If you don't have the Aquarium template installed on your system, you're not going to see the DVD as shown in the previous figure. You can drag a different template into the "To add menu drag Template here" window to approximate the experience, but it won't look precisely the same.

Understanding DVD, Blu-ray, and AVCHD Discs

DVD is a generic term that encompasses a few different formats. The format you'll work with in Premiere Elements is commonly referred to as DVD-Video. In terms of disc content and playability, this is the same type of DVD that you can purchase or rent and play on a DVD player connected to your TV set or on a computer fitted with the appropriate drive. Premiere Elements can burn both single-layer (4.7 GB) and dual-layer (8.5 GB) DVD media.

A Blu-ray Disc—often abbreviated as BD—is an optical disc format that can store 25 gigabytes (GB) on a single-layer disc or 50 GB on a dual-layer disc. It gets its name from the blue-violet laser a Blu-ray player uses to read it (as opposed to the red laser used by CD and DVD players and drives).

An AVCHD disc is a traditional DVD that contains HD video in AVCHD format, but not the menus you can create for standard DVDs or standard Blu-ray Discs. AVCHD discs are playable on Blu-ray players and some computers but not traditional DVD players. The key benefit of the AVCHD disc is that it enables you to burn HD content to inexpensive DVD media without purchasing a Blu-ray Disc recorder. The limitations are the inability to add menus and the lower capacity of standard DVD-Recordable media (4.7 GB or 8.5 GB) as compared to Blu-ray media (25 GB). Overall, though, for many projects, AVCHD discs provide a wonderfully convenient way to affordably view and share your HD content on Blu-ray players.

To make a DVD, Blu-ray, or AVCHD disc in Premiere Elements, you must have a compatible DVD or Blu-ray Disc burner. It's important to note that although your system may have a DVD or Blu-ray Disc player, it may not be a recordable drive, also known as a DVD or Blu-ray Disc writer or burner. A computer drive that's described as DVD-ROM or BD-ROM will only play DVDs or Blu-ray Discs, not record them. (But a BD-ROM/DVD-R/CD-R drive will play Blu-ray Discs, play and record DVDs, and play and record CDs.) Check your computer's system specifications to see which drive (if any) you have. Drives capable of recording DVDs and Blu-ray Discs are also available as external hardware. Often, such external recordable drives are connected through your system's IEEE 1394 port, although some drives connect through the USB port.

Note that the process of authoring your projects, or creating menus and menu markers, is identical for Blu-ray Discs and DVDs. You'll designate which type of disc to record just before you burn the disc in the final exercise of this lesson.

Physical Media

The type of disc onto which you'll record your video is important. You should be aware of two basic formats: Recordable (DVD-R and DVD+R for DVD and AVCHD discs, BD-R for Blu-ray Discs) and Rewritable (DVD-RW and DVD+RW for DVDs and AVCHD discs, BD-RE for Blu-ray Discs). Recordable discs are single-use discs; once you record data onto a recordable disc, you cannot erase the data. Rewritable discs can be used multiple times, much like the floppy disks of old.

Also available are dual-layer DVD-Recordable discs (DVD-R DL and DVD+R DL) that offer 8.5 GB of storage space instead of the 4.7 GB of standard DVD-R, DVD+R, DVD-RW, and DVD+RW discs. Dual-layer BD-R discs, featuring 50 GB of storage space, are also available.

So which format should you choose? The first thing to note is that DVD-R and DVD+R discs are 100 percent interchangeable. Any drive that records one will record the other, and the same players and drives that play one will almost certainly play the other, at least with single-layer media. It's the same with DVD-RW and DVD+RW. In the very early days of DVD, there was a meaningful distinction between the – and + formats, but it's been irrelevant for more than a decade now.

Compatibility is one of the major issues with recordable disc formats. On the DVD side, many older DVD players may not recognize some rewritable discs created on a newer DVD burner, for example. Compatibility is also more of a concern with dual-layer media than with single-layer discs. Another issue is that, as of this writing, the media for recordable discs is less expensive than the media for rewritable discs (usually much less than $1 per disc). However, if you make a mistake with a recordable disc, you must use another disc, whereas with a rewritable disc you can erase the content and use the disc again. For this reason, I suggest using rewritable discs for making your test discs, and then using recordable discs for final or extra copies.

On the Blu-ray Disc side, the technology is still fairly new and playback compatibility is at least a minor issue with all media. But because the BD-R and BD-RE formats were developed at the same time, BD-RE discs are just as likely to play in a given player as their BD-R counterparts. That said, BD-R discs have come down in price to under a dollar in quantities of 25+, whereas BD-RE discs remain quite a bit more expensive, so you'll probably find BD-R discs more cost-effective, even though they can't be erased and reused. Dual- or Double-Layer BD-R Discs sell online for around $4/disc.

Manually Adding Scene Markers

When watching a DVD or Blu-ray Disc movie, you normally have the option to jump to the beginning of the next chapter by clicking a button on the remote control. To specify the start of chapters or sections in your project, you must add scene markers.

● **Note:** This project is only about two minutes long due to necessary limitations on the file size. Most projects would likely be longer, but the basic principles remain the same.

1 Click the Edit tab to return to the Edit workspace. Then scroll through the entire movie in the Timeline in the My Project panel.

   This project consists of two main sections, the videos and the slide show. You will place scene markers at the beginning of each section so your viewers can access these sections more easily during playback. You'll start by adding the marker for the videos.

2 Press the Home key to move the current-time indicator to the start of the movie. Then press the Page Down key to move to the start of Clip01.mp4.

3 On the top left of the My Project panel, click the Markers drop-down list box ( ), and choose Menu Marker > Set Menu Marker. The Menu Marker panel opens.

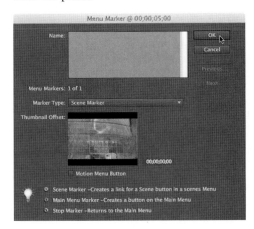

4 You'll work more with this panel later in this lesson; for now, just click OK to close the panel.

Note: You may have to move the current-time indicator to better see the green scene marker beneath.

5 Notice the green scene marker icon added on the time ruler.

6 In the My Project panel, click the Sceneline button to switch to Sceneline. If necessary, scroll to the right to view Clip01.mp4. Notice the faint scene marker icon added to the upper-right corner of the clip in the Sceneline.

7 Click the Timeline button in the My Project panel to return to the Timeline.

8 Drag the current-time indicator to the start of the slide show, which should be around 00;01;44;13.

9 Right-click the time ruler at the current-time indicator and choose Set Menu Marker. Click OK to close the Menu Marker panel.

10 You should now have two markers in your project, one for each section of this short movie.

Creating an Auto-play Disc

Most professional DVDs and Blu-ray Discs have menus to help viewers navigate through the disc content. You will work with menus shortly, but there is a quick and easy way to produce a disc without menus: creating an auto-play disc. An auto-play disc is similar to videotape: When you place the disc into a player, it will begin playing automatically. There is no navigation, although viewers can jump from scene to scene—defined by the markers you just added—using a remote control.

Note: The Auto-Play button should be dimmed and no template selected. Click the Auto-Play button if your Disc Layout panel looks different from the one shown in the next figure.

Auto-play discs are convenient for short projects that don't require a menu or as a mechanism to share unfinished projects for review. For most longer or finished projects, you'll probably prefer to create a menu.

1   Select Disc Menus in the Tasks panel to switch to the Disc Menus workspace. The Disc Layout panel replaces the Monitor panel, and Templates view opens in the Disc Menus tab in the Tasks panel. If you want to see the panel names, choose Window > Show Docking Headers.

2   In the Disc Layout panel, click the Preview button to open the Preview Disc window. The Preview Disc window allows you to view and test your disc as it will appear when viewed on a DVD or Blu-ray Disc player.

3   In the Preview Disc window, click the Play button (▶) to begin playing your project. Once the first video clip begins playing, click the Next Scene button (▶▌), and the video will jump to the next scene. The scenes are defined by the scene markers you added to your project. When viewing this disc on a TV set, viewers can use a remote control to advance through the scenes.

4   Click the Exit button (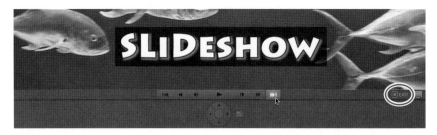) on the bottom right of the Preview Disc window to close it.

5   Choose File > Save As and save this project file into your Lesson11 folder as *Lesson11_Work.prel*.

Automatically Generating Scene Markers

Manually placing markers in the Timeline gives you ultimate control over the placement of your markers. For long videos, however, you may not want to place all the markers by hand. To make the process of placing markers easy, Premiere Elements can create markers automatically based on several configurable parameters.

1   Choose File > Save As and save this project file into your Lesson11 folder as *Lesson11_Markers.prel*. You'll return to the original project file after you finish exploring the automatic generation of scene markers.

2   Right-click in the preview area of the Disc Layout panel, and then choose Auto-Generate Menu Markers.

3   The Automatically Set Menu Scene Marker dialog appears. Keep the default option selected to set a scene marker At Each Scene, or to be more specific, at the beginning of every clip on the Video 1 track. The Clear Existing Menu Markers check box should remain deselected unless you want to erase existing markers. Click OK to close the dialog. Scene markers appear at the beginning of every clip.

4   If you're not in the Timeline already, switch to the Timeline in the My Project panel to review the position of all the markers in your project.

5   Click the Preview button in the Disc Layout panel.

6   In the Preview Disc window, click the Play button (   ) to begin playing your project. Once the first video clip begins playing, click the Next Scene button (   ) repeatedly and notice how the video jumps from scene to scene.

7   Click the Exit button (   ) on the bottom right of the Preview Disc window to close it.

8   Right-click in the preview area in the Disc Layout panel, and then choose Auto-Generate Menu Markers to again open the Automatically Set Menu Scene Marker dialog.

● **Note:** You can reposition markers in the Timeline by dragging them to the left or right.

9   Select the Clear Existing Menu Markers check box. Choose the Total Markers
    option, type *4* into the number field, and then click OK.

Four markers are now evenly spread out across the Timeline.

Using the Total Markers option may be preferable to creating a marker for every
clip to reduce the number of scenes in your movie. As you'll see in the next
exercise, when creating a disc with menus, Premiere Elements automatically
creates buttons and menus based on the markers in your project. Too many
markers might result in too many navigation buttons and screens for your movie.

10 Choose File > Save. Then choose File > Open Recent Project > Lesson11_Work.
    prel to return to the project file from the previous exercise.

Creating a Disc with Menus

Building an auto-play disc as you did in the previous exercise is the quickest way
to go from a Premiere Elements project to an optical disc you can watch in your
living room. However, auto-play discs lack the ability to jump directly to different
scenes, as well as other navigational features that most users expect when watching
a DVD or Blu-ray Disc. You can quickly create such navigation menus in Premiere
Elements using a variety of templates designed for this purpose.

1   If you're not currently in the Disc Menus workspace, select Disc Menus in the
    Tasks panel to switch to it now.

2   Premiere Elements ships with many distinctive menu templates—predesigned and customizable menus that come in a variety of themes and styles. Select General from the category menu, and then select the template called Aquarium from the menu next to it. If you don't have this category or template, choose another.

3   To apply the Aquarium template to your project, click to select the template in Templates view, and then click the Apply button (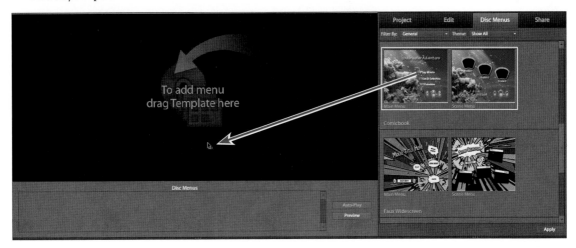) in the lower-right corner of Templates view. Or, drop the template from Templates view onto the Disc Layout panel.

Each template contains a Main menu and a Scenes menu. The Main menu is the first screen that the viewer sees when the disc is played. The Scenes menu is a secondary panel accessed when the viewer clicks the Scene Selection button in the Main menu.

4   Under Disc Menus at the bottom of the Disc Layout panel, click to select Main Menu 1.

Two text links are currently visible in this menu: Play Movie and Scene Selection. Additionally, there is a generic text box called Movie Title Here. You'll now change the text of this generic button to something more appropriate for your project.

5   In the preview area of the Disc Layout panel, click the Movie Title Here text once. A thin, white rectangle appears around the button indicating that it is selected.

6   Double-click the Movie Title Here text to open the Change Text dialog. If the text under Change Text is not already highlighted, select it now, and then type *The Georgia Aquarium*. Click the OK button to close the Change Text dialog and to commit the change.

● **Note:** To replace the selected template, click another to select it, and then click Apply to apply it to the project, or drop it onto the Disc Layout panel. To delete all menus, choose Disc > Change to Auto-Play in the Premiere Elements menu.

7   Let's make the text *The Georgia Aquarium* stand out a bit more. Click the text to make it active, and then on the right in the Properties view, click the Font drop-down list box and choose 48 pt. Note that you could also change the font and font size, and unbold, italicize, or underline the text.

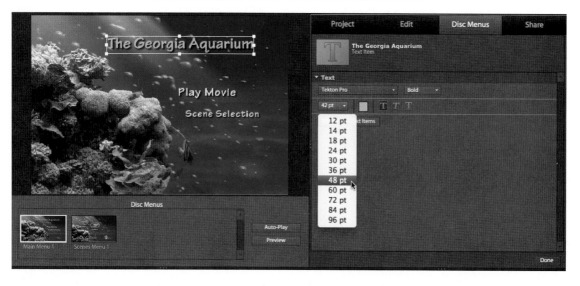

● **Note:** Rollover effects like the wavy lines in this example vary from template to template.

8   Click the Preview button to preview the main menu. Place your pointer over the Play Movie and Scene Selection buttons, but don't click them yet. Notice the wavy lines that appear in the text box when the pointer passes over the text. This rollover effect is part of the menu template and shows viewers which button they're selecting. Click the Play Movie button and the movie begins to play.

The preview feature shows how your DVD will look after recording the project to disc. Note, however, that the quality of the previewed video may not be indicative of the final video. Because of the differences between computer monitors and TV sets, you may see noticeable horizontal lines as the video is playing on the computer monitor. These lines are referred to as *interlacing* and will not be visible in the final movie when played on a TV.

9   As the movie is playing, click the Main Menu button (▦) at the bottom of the Preview Disc window. Clicking this button at any point during playback returns you to the main menu, so you don't have to watch the entire movie if you're just testing your menus.

10 Click the Exit button (▧EXIT) on the bottom right of the Preview Disc window to close it.

11 Choose File > Save to save your project file.

Modifying Scene Marker Buttons

One of the benefits of DVDs and Blu-ray Discs is the ability to jump quickly to specific scenes in a movie. For each scene marker you add in the Timeline, Premiere Elements automatically generates a Scene Marker button on the Scenes menu. If the template has image thumbnails on the Scenes menu, as the menu you're working with does, Premiere Elements automatically assigns an image thumbnail to it. You can customize the appearance of a Scene Marker button by providing a name for the label and changing the image thumbnail used to identify the scene. Note that if you have more scene markers than scenes on a Scenes menu, Premiere Elements creates additional Scenes menu pages and navigational buttons to jump back and forth between the pages.

Changing Button Labels and Image Thumbnails

Let's begin by opening the Scenes menu.

1   Click the Scenes Menu 1 thumbnail under Disc Menus in the Disc Layout panel to view the Scenes menu.

Premiere Elements has generated the two Scene Marker buttons and their image thumbnails based on the scene markers you added in the first exercise. By default, Premiere Elements named the Scene Marker buttons Scene 1 and Scene 2. You'll customize these for your content shortly.

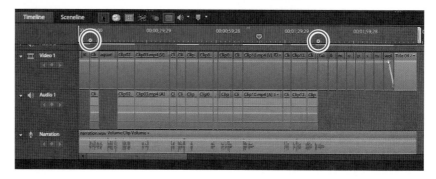

In addition, by default, the thumbnail in the Scene Marker button is the first frame of the clip the button links to. This doesn't work well in this case because the thumbnail is obscured either by the animated pastel sketch effect or is in the midst of a Fade to Black transition, so viewers can't easily discern the content of the scene. Let's change these thumbnails to more appropriate frames.

Note: When using menu templates, one- or two-word titles fit best into the text boxes.

2 Double-click the first marker to open the Menu Marker panel for the first marker. In the Name field, type *Videos*.

3 In the Thumbnail Offset section, notice that the time counter is set to 00:00;00;00. Place your pointer over the time counter, drag to the right about 00;00;03;25, and then release the pointer to freeze the movie at that location.

Or, click the time counter and enter the timecode directly. Click OK, and Premiere Elements updates the button name and image thumbnail in the Scenes menu.

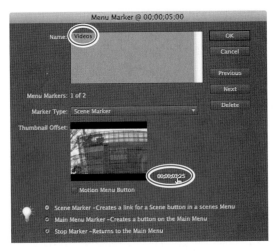

Next, you'll change the name of the remaining button and its image thumbnail.

4 Double-click the second marker, type *Slideshow* into the name field, and drag the time counter to about 00;00;30;00. Click OK. Premiere Elements updates the button name and image thumbnail in the Scenes menu.

5 When you're finished, click the Preview button to open the Preview Disc window. Click the Scene Selection button to navigate to the Scenes menu. Notice that Premiere Elements has updated button names and thumbnails.

6 At the bottom of the Preview Disc window you can see a group of navigation buttons, which simulate the controls on a DVD remote control. Click any of the arrows to advance through the Scene Menu buttons, and click the center circle (the Enter button) to play that scene. Premiere Elements automatically controls the navigation of all menu buttons, so you should preview all scenes on the disc to ensure that you placed your markers logically. When you're done, close the Preview Disc window.

A. Up. **B.** Right. **C.** Main Menu button.
D. Left. **E.** Down. **F.** Enter.

7 Choose File > Save to save your project file.

Working with Submenus

Before you start customizing menu appearance, you should be aware of some other navigation and button placement options. For example, many Hollywood movies have a link on the main menu to bonus or deleted clips sections. Premiere Elements lets you create a submenu button on your main menu by adding a special menu marker.

In addition, by default, once a viewer starts watching any portion of the movie, the video will continue on to the end, even if there are intervening scene markers. In the project you've been working on, this isn't a problem, but with other projects, you may want to stop playback after a scene completes and return the viewer to the menu. You can accomplish this by using the stop marker discussed here.

In this exercise, you will add a button on the main menu linking to a bonus video clip.

1 Under Disc Menus in the Disc Layout panel, click to select Main Menu 1. Currently, two buttons are in this menu: the Play Movie and Scenes Selection buttons. The template design leaves space for more buttons below these two buttons, if needed.

2 Select the Timeline in the My Project panel. Press the End key to move the current-time indicator to the end of the last clip.

You will now add a special marker to the end of your movie.

3 Right-click the time ruler at the current-time indicator and choose Set Menu Marker. The Menu Marker panel opens.

4 Choose Stop Marker from the Marker Type menu. When a stop marker is reached during playback, the viewer will return to the main menu.

5 Click OK to add the stop marker. In the Timeline, stop markers are colored red to help you differentiate them from the green scene markers and the blue main menu markers. You will learn more about main menu markers later in this lesson.

Next, you'll add an additional clip named Outtake.mp4 to the end of the Timeline. This clip will be a bonus clip that users can access from the main menu but is not part of the main movie.

6 Select the Project tab in the Tasks panel, and then click Media. In Media view, drag the Outtake.mp4 clip into the Video 1 track after the credit title sequence at the end of your Timeline. Be sure to place the clip a few seconds from the last clip, leaving a gap between the clips.

7 Press the Page Down key to advance the current-time indicator to the beginning of the added Outtake.mp4 clip, and then right-click and choose Set Menu Marker to open the Menu Marker dialog.

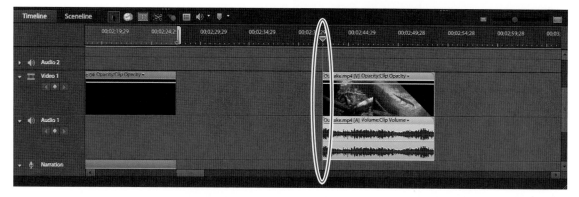

Note: You don't have to add a stop marker at the end of the Outtake. mp4 clip. When Premiere Elements reaches the end of the Timeline, it will automatically return the viewer to the main menu.

8 In the Menu Marker dialog, choose Main Menu Marker from the Marker Type menu. In the name field, type *Outtake*, and then click OK to close the Menu Marker dialog.

Premiere Elements adds a button named Outtake to the Main Menu 1 in the Disc Layout panel.

9 Click the Disc Menus tab and then the Preview button, and then click the Outtake button to play the video associated with it. When the clip has finished playing, the main menu appears. If you play the main movie from start to finish, you will not see the Outtake.mp4 clip because of the stop marker you added at the end of the last clip in the main movie.

10 Close the Preview Disc window.

11 Choose File > Save to save your project file.

Three Types of Menu Markers

Scene markers ( ): Adding a scene marker to your Timeline automatically adds a scene button to the scene menu of your disc. Scenes menus are secondary to the main menu, and there should be a Scenes button on the main menu that links to the Scenes menu.

Main menu markers ( ): Adding a main menu marker to your Timeline automatically adds a button to the main menu of your disc. Most templates have space for either three or four buttons on the first menu page. The Play Movie button and the Scenes button are present by default. This will leave you with space for one or two more buttons, depending on the template you have chosen. If you add additional main menu markers to your movie, Premiere Elements will create a secondary main menu.

Stop markers ( ): Adding a stop marker to your Timeline forces Premiere Elements to stop playback of your Timeline and return the viewer to the main menu. Use stop markers to control the viewer's flow through the movie. For example, if you want the viewer to return to the main menu after each scene, insert a stop marker at the end of each scene. You can also use stop markers to add bonus or deleted scenes after the main movie, linking to this content using either scene or main menu markers.

Customizing Menus in Properties View

When you produce a disc in Premiere Elements, you have multiple customization options for your menu, including the ability to change fonts and font colors, to add a still image or video background, to add background music to the menu, and to animate the button thumbnails on your menus. You accomplish all these tasks in Properties view, which displays different options depending on the object you select. Let's take a quick tour.

1 Make sure you are in the Disc Menus workspace, and then choose Window > Restore Workspace to reset the location of your panels. If necessary, click Disc Menus to reenter that workspace.

2 Under Disc Menus in the Disc Layout panel, click the Scenes Menu 1 thumbnail to make sure the Scenes Menu 1 menu is loaded.

3 Click in the Scenes Menu 1 menu near the bottom of the menu, being careful not to select any navigational or thumbnail buttons.

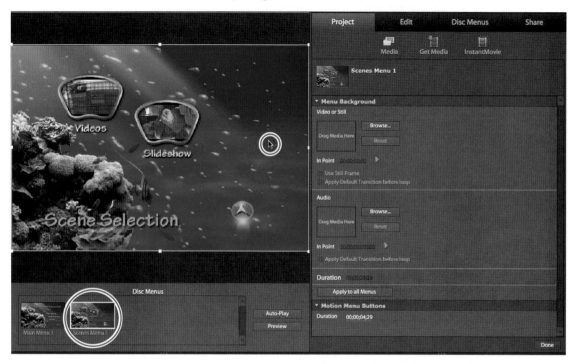

Properties view displays two sections: Menu Background and Motion Menu Buttons. You can expand and collapse these two sections by clicking the arrows to the left of the section title. In the Menu Background section are subsections for Video or Still backgrounds and Audio backgrounds.

4 In the Disc Layout panel, click the Slideshow marker button. Premiere Elements displays a rectangle, referred to as a *bounding box*, around the button. There are eight selection points around the box that you'll work with in a moment.

Note that Properties view now displays two sections: Menu options on top and Text options on the bottom. The Menu options are very similar to those selected in the Menu Marker panel. Some, such as the Poster Frame In Point, you can change directly in Properties view; others, such as the Button Type, you have to return to the Menu Marker panel to modify.

5   Click the Scene Selection title in Scenes Menu 1. Premiere Elements displays a bounding box around the title and displays only the Text options in Properties view.

Those are the different control sets of Properties view. Fortunately, you don't have to remember what they are and what they do. Just click the menu component you'd like to edit, and Premiere Elements automatically opens the necessary controls.

● **Note:** As always, in addition to clicking the menu to open Properties view, you can also choose Window > Properties from the Premiere Elements main menu to open Properties view.

Customizing Menus with Video, Still Images, and Audio

You can customize your menus in Premiere Elements by adding a still image, video, or audio to the menu. You can also combine multiple items, such as a still photo and an audio clip. Alternatively, you can add a video clip and replace the audio track with a separate audio clip.

Note that your customization options differ based on the menu template you select. If the menu has a drop zone, still images or video inserted into the menu will display in the drop zone. Otherwise, with templates that don't have drop zones, such as the template you're working with in this lesson, the inserted still image or video will appear full screen in the menu background.

Although Premiere Elements allows you to customize a disc menu, keep in mind that changes made will not be saved back to the template; they apply only to the current project. If you'd like to create custom templates to be used in multiple projects, you can create one in Adobe Photoshop Elements, and then add the template to Premiere Elements.

Adding a Still Image or Video Clip to Your Menu

Whether you want to add a still image or a video clip to your menu, you'll use the same procedure in either case. In this exercise, you'll insert a video clip into a menu. By default, when you insert a video, the audio plays with the video as well, although you can change this by inserting a separate audio file, as you will do later.

Follow this procedure to add a video clip to your menu.

1   Under Disc Menus in the Disc Layout panel, click to select Main Menu 1. Click in the main menu, being careful not to click one of the active buttons.

● **Note:** You'd follow this same procedure to select a still image either to fit into the drop zone or to use as a full-screen background image.

2 In Properties view, in the Menu Background box, click the Browse button, navigate to the Lesson11 folder, and choose Clip03.mp4. Click Open (Windows) or Choose (Mac OS) to close the dialog and insert the clip into the menu.

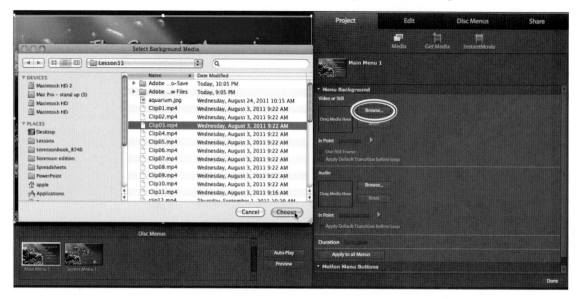

3 Note the options available in the Menu Background box in Properties view. Specifically, you can do the following:

- Play the video by clicking the green play triangle (▶).

- Choose an In point for the video to start, either by dragging the time counter or by typing in the timecode for the desired starting point.

- After choosing an In point, you can select the Use Still Frame check box to use the current frame as the background or within the drop zone.

- Apply the default transition to the video clip before the menu starts to loop by selecting the Apply Default Transition before loop check box. Note that the maximum duration for video menus is 30 seconds, and that the menu will loop indefinitely after that time.

For this exercise, leave the options at their default settings, and click Preview to preview the menu. When you're finished, close the Preview window and return to the Disc Layout panel. Because the graphic of the coral reef stays in front, ideally you would find a clip with the action on the right, where it's completely visible. The flipping manta ray will definitely do for this project, though.

4   Choose File > Save to save your project file.

As mentioned, when you add a video to a menu with a drop zone, the video plays within that drop zone. When you add a video to a menu without a drop zone, the video plays in the background of the menu.

Accordingly, to create a menu with your own full-screen still image or video in the background, choose a template without a drop zone. If you opt to customize a menu with a full-screen background image or video, you'll have to manually insert it into each menu created by Premiere Elements. Note that you can insert a different still image or video clip as a background in each menu, or use the background image that came with the menu template.

Adding an Audio Clip to the Background

Let's substitute a separate audio clip for the audio included with the Clip01.mp4 video clip. Use this same procedure to add audio to any menu template, whether modified with a still image background or used as is.

1   Click Main Menu 1 in the Disc Layout panel to open its Properties view. If necessary, scroll down the Properties view to locate the Audio section.

2   Click the Browse button, select the Global Vibes - New shores clip in the Lesson11 folder, and then click Open (Windows) or Choose (Mac OS).

3   If you'd like to add a fade-out so the audio loops nicely, select the Apply Default Transition before loop check box.

4   In the Disc Layout panel, click the Preview button. You can see the video or video frame and hear the audio track you selected for the main menu background.

5 Close the Preview window.

6 If you'd like to remove the audio portion from the menu background, click the Reset button next to the speaker icon in the Audio section of Properties view (but, for the purposes of this task, don't actually do this).

7 To insert the same video and audio file combination as background for your other menu, click the Apply to All Menus button in the Properties view.

8 Save your project.

Animating Buttons

If the menu template that you select uses thumbnail scene buttons, you can elect to animate the buttons. With an animated button, a designated duration of video from the linked scene will play within the thumbnail while the menu displays. The main menu for this project does not include any buttons with image thumbnails. However, the Scenes menu does have image thumbnails. Let's animate these thumbnails.

1 Select the Scenes Menu 1 thumbnail under Disc Menus in the Disc Layout panel.

2 Click the Videos button to select it. Currently, this button displays a still frame extracted from the video clip at the 00;00;03;25 mark.

● **Note:** You can't set the Out point or the end of clips in Properties view, but you can set all your motion menu buttons to be the same duration, as explained in the following steps.

3 In Properties view, in the Menu box, scroll down if necessary to see all of the Poster Frame section, and then select the Motion Menu Button check box. Click the Apply to all Marker Buttons button to animate all Marker buttons.

4 If you'd like to change the In point of the video clip and play a different segment in the animated thumbnail, drag the time counter (which currently reads 00;00;03;25) to the desired spot.

5 Click an empty area of your background menu. This deselects the current scene button, and Properties view switches to the Menu Background properties. Scroll down to the bottom of Properties view, if necessary, to locate the Motion Menu Buttons box.

6 Note that the default duration for the Motion Menu Buttons is 00;00;04;29, which is the length of Clip01.mp4, the first clip after the scene marker. You can shorten this duration but not lengthen it. Note that the default duration will be as long as the first clip after the scene marker, up to 00;00;29;29, or just under 30 seconds.

7 Click the Preview button in the Disc Layout panel. In the main menu, click the Scene Selection button to access the Scenes menu. All the buttons should now be animated, which is definitely a bad idea for the Slideshow, because the animation immediately goes into the closing credits. If you decide to use motion menus, make sure the footage in the video works in the context of the motion menu.

8 Close the Preview Disc window.

Overlapping Buttons

Buttons on a disc menu should not overlap each other. If two or more buttons overlap, there is a potential for confusion. Someone who is using a pointer to navigate and click the menu may not be able to access the correct button if another one is overlapping it. This can easily happen if button text is too long or if two buttons are placed too close to each other.

Overlapping buttons can sometimes be fixed by shortening the button name or simply by moving the buttons so that there's more space between them. By default, overlapping buttons in Premiere Elements are outlined in red in the Disc Layout panel. This feature can be turned off or on by right-clicking in the Disc Layout panel and choosing Show Overlapping Menu Buttons from the menu.

9 If you'd like to pick a different In point for your thumbnail video, select the Motion Menu Button option and choose suitable In points for the two other scene buttons. If you didn't click the Apply to all Marker Buttons button in step 3, you must individually activate scene buttons to animate them. All animated buttons share the same duration.

10 Let's deselect Motion Menus for this project by clicking each button and unchecking the Motion Menu Button for each.

11 Save your project.

Customizing Button Size, Location, and Text Attributes

Beyond adding still images, video, and audio to your menu, you can also change the size, appearance, and location of buttons and text on your menus. In this exercise, you will make changes to your menu appearance and buttons.

1 Make sure you are in the Disc Menus workspace, and then choose Window > Restore Workspace to reset the location of your panels.

2   Under Disc Menus in the Disc Layout panel, click the Main Menu 1 thumbnail to make sure the main menu is loaded.

3   Click "The Georgia Aquarium" title text to select it. The eight-point bounding box opens. Place your pointer on the lower-right corner, and then drag downward and outward to enlarge the text box.

4   Press Ctrl+Z/Command+Z to undo the changes. Premiere Elements allows you to undo multiple steps, so you can backtrack through your changes.

5   Click the Scenes Selection button in the Disc Layout panel to select it, and then press the Left Arrow key on your keyboard to move it (Windows only). Pressing the arrow keys allows you to move a button one pixel at a time in the direction of the arrow. Press the Right Arrow key to move the button back to its original location.

6 Save your project.

● **Note:** All buttons and titles within Premiere Elements templates are within the title-safe zone. If you plan to resize or move buttons or text on the menu, you should enable Show Safe Margins in the Disc Layout panel menu at the right side of the docking header menu, as shown in the following figure, and make sure that all content is within the title-safe zone before recording your disc.

Changing Menu Button Text Properties

Properties view lets you modify the font, size, color, and style of your menu buttons, and you can automatically apply changes made to one button to similar buttons.

You can modify the text attributes of five types of objects: Menu Titles, which are text-only objects that aren't linked to clips or movies; Play buttons, which link to the beginning of your main movie; Scene Marker buttons, which link to the Scenes menu; Marker buttons, which directly link to a menu marker on the Timeline; and Navigational buttons, such as the link back to the main menu in the Scenes menu.

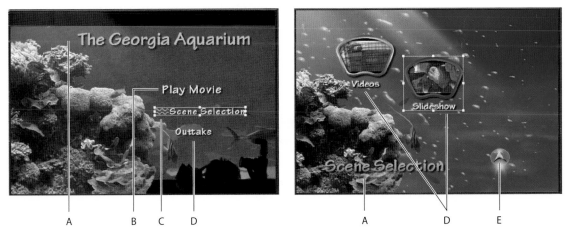

A. Menu title. **B.** Play button. **C.** Scene button. **D.** Marker button. **E.** Navigational button.

1 Under Disc Menus in the Disc Layout panel, click the Scenes Menu 1 thumbnail.

2 Click the Videos marker button. Properties view updates automatically and shows that this is a marker button—specifically, a Scene Marker button. The Text subsection allows you to change the properties of the text. If necessary, scroll down in Properties view to see all of the Text subsection.

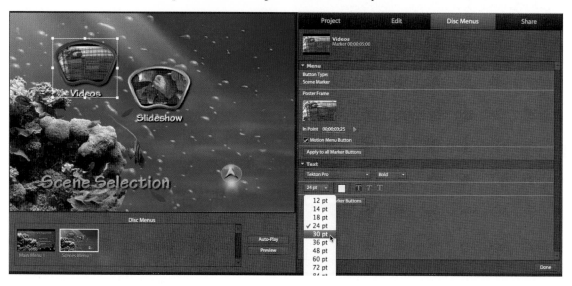

3 In the Text subsection, click the font menu, and note that you can change the font of this or any text in the menu. The Tekton Pro font looks best here, so let's leave that selected.

4 The next menu, the Text Size menu, allows you to change the text size to any of the preset sizes. Change the text size to 30 pt.

5   Next, let's change the color of the text to orange to match the color of the tiny
    goldfish in front of the coral reef. To begin, click the white color swatch next to
    the Text Size menu to open the Color Picker dialog. Click once in the vertical
    color spectrum in the general range of red. Then click in the lower-right corner
    of the large color field to choose a bright red. The parameters of the color I
    selected are R: *250*, G: *136*, and B: *20*. Click OK to apply the color.

A   B

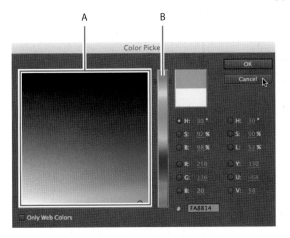

A. Click here to pick the
specific shade within the
selected range of colors.
B. Click here to change the
general range of colors.

    Notice that the other Scene Marker buttons have retained their original
    formatting. Normally, changes affect only the selected object. But Premiere
    Elements also gives you the option to change the text attributes of all buttons
    of the same type simultaneously.

6   In the Text subsection of Properties view, click the Apply to all Marker Buttons
    button. This applies the same text attributes to both Scene Marker buttons.

7   Under Disc Menus in the Disc Layout panel, click the Main Menu 1 thumbnail.
    Notice that the Outtakes marker has also changed its appearance. This is
    because the Marker Button category encompasses both Scene Marker and Main
    Menu Marker buttons. To fix this, you could change the Outtake button back to
    30 point white, or change the Play and Scene buttons to match the look. I'll do
    the former to restore symmetry to Main Menu 1.

8   Choose File > Save As and save this project file to your Lesson11 folder as
    Lesson11_Final.prel.

Creating Web DVDs

Web DVDs create the DVD experience within a web page, complete with menus, links, and very high-quality video. If you have your own website, you can create files to upload and present from there. If you don't, you can upload your presentations to Photoshop.com and invite friends and family to watch it from there. This lesson will take you through the second workflow.

1   Select the Share workspace by clicking the Share tab in the Tasks panel.

2   Save your current project. It's always a good idea to save your Premiere Elements project file before rendering your project.

3   Click the Web DVD Disc button () in the Share workspace.

4   In the "web DVD: Choose location and settings" workspace, choose Upload to Photoshop. To create files for uploading to a different website outside of Premiere Elements, choose Save to folder on Computer, and type the Project Name and Save In location.

Note: You can create SD Web-DVDs from HD content, but you shouldn't try to create HD Web DVDs from SD content, because the video will likely look pixelated and/or blurry.

Note: Once you choose a preset, Premiere Elements will display its parameters below the Presets list box. The HD PAL preset uses a frame size of 1280x720, at 25 frames per second, and will produce a file about 82.6 MB in size.

5   Choose the appropriate preset in the Presets list box, choosing first the video standard (NTSC for the United States and Japan; PAL otherwise) and then the quality level. When choosing, try to select the quality level that best matches the connection speed of your intended viewers. Although HD provides the best overall quality, only viewers with very fast connection speeds will be able to play the videos without stopping. SD High Quality is the best-quality, highest-bandwidth option in SD mode, and SD Medium Quality will create an experience that can be viewed most smoothly by the broadest range of viewers. Click Build to continue.

6 Complete the information on the next screen, including the Movie Title and Email Message, and identify the invitees you want to email about the video. Click Share to continue.

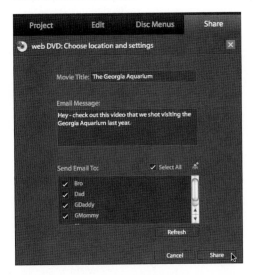

7 Premiere Elements will render and upload your project to Photoshop.com with status messages informing you of its progress. Once complete, you'll see the following screen.

8 You can click the "Click here to view your web DVD online" text to watch the Web DVD, and your invitees will receive emails with similar links. As shown in the next figure, the experience is identical to a DVD except that you don't have to burn and send one to your friends and family for them to enjoy the movie.

9 Click Done to close the Web DVD window and return to Premiere Elements.

Burning DVD, Blu-ray, or AVCHD Discs

After you've previewed your disc and have checked the menus and button names, you're ready to record the project to a DVD or Blu-ray Disc. Of course, if you're producing an AVCHD disc, you don't have to add menus, which aren't available in the AVCHD format. As noted at the beginning of the chapter, you must have a DVD recorder to produce a DVD or AVCHD disc, or a Blu-ray Disc writer to record a Blu-ray Disc.

When making any of these discs, Premiere Elements converts your video and audio files into a compressed format. Briefly, compression shrinks your original video and audio files to fit them on a disc. For example, a 60-minute video in DV or HDV format requires approximately 13 GB of hard disk space. However, a DVD-Video holds only 4.7 GB of space. So how do you fit a 13 GB video onto a 4.7 GB disc? Through compression!

The process of compression can be quite lengthy. In essence, Premiere Elements evaluates every frame of video in your project and attempts to find redundancies in the visual information within them that will allow it to reduce the file size without sacrificing the image quality. You should allow quite a bit of time for this process. For example, 60 minutes of video may take 4–6 hours to compress and record onto a DVD, and compressing and recording HD video onto a Blu-ray Disc can take even longer. For this reason, it may be a good idea to initiate the disc-burning process (which begins with compressing the video) at a time when you will not need your computer.

To maintain maximum quality, Premiere Elements compresses the movie only as much as is necessary to fit it on the disc. The shorter your movie, the less compression required, and the higher the quality of the video on the disc.

1 Select the Share workspace by clicking the Share tab in the Tasks panel.

2 Save your current project. It's always a good idea to save your Premiere Elements project file before burning a disc.

3 Click the Disc button (🔘) in the Start a new Share workspace. Choose DVD from the list at the top of the view. To burn a Blu-ray Disc, select Blu-ray from that list, or select AVCHD to burn an AVCHD disc.

4 Make sure Disc is selected in the "Burn to" menu. Select the option to burn to a folder on your hard drive if you prefer to use an alternative program to burn your discs.

5 In the Disc Name field, type *Georgia Aquarium*. Software playing DVDs or Blu-ray Discs on a personal computer may display this disc name.

● **Note:** This exercise ends with the burning of a DVD. If you don't want to create a DVD, follow the steps of the exercise only up to the point of writing the disc. If you will be creating a DVD, I suggest using a DVD-RW or DVD+RW (Rewritable) disc, if you have one available, so that you can reuse the disc later.

6 Select the desired DVD or Blu-ray Disc burner from the Burner Location menu. If you don't have a compatible disc burner connected to your computer, the Burner Location menu is disabled and the Status line reads "No burner detected."

7 If you want to create a DVD, AVCHD, or Blu-ray Disc, ensure that you've inserted a compatible blank or rewritable disc in the disc burner. If you insert a disc after you start this process, click Rescan to have Premiere Elements recheck all connected burners for valid media.

8 Next to Copies, select the number of discs you want to burn during this session. For this exercise, choose 1. When you select multiple copies, Premiere Elements asks you to insert another disc after the writing of each disc is completed until all the discs you specified have been burned.

9 Select the "Fit Contents to available space" check box to ensure that Premiere Elements maximizes the quality of your video based on disc capacity.

10 From the Presets menu, select the NTSC_Widescreen_Dolby DVD option. Premiere Elements is also capable of burning a project to the PAL standard (used in Europe, parts of Africa, South America, the Middle East, Australia, New Zealand, some Pacific Islands, and certain Asian countries) in both normal or widescreen format.

11 If you want to burn a disc at this point, click the Burn button. If you don't want to burn a disc, click the Back button.

Congratulations! You've successfully completed this lesson. You learned how to manually and automatically add scene markers to your movie, create an auto-play disc, and—by applying a menu template—create a disc with menus. You added a submenu for an outtake clip and learned about stop and main menu makers. You customized the disc menus by changing text attributes, background images, button labels, and image thumbnails. You added sound and video clips to the menu background, and activated (and then deactivated) motion menu buttons. You created and uploaded a Web DVD to Photoshop.com to share with the world, and you learned how to burn your movie onto a DVD, Blu-ray, or AVCHD disc.

Choosing Blu-ray and AVCHD Disc Quality Options

When burning to a Blu-ray or AVCHD disc, you have multiple resolution and video standard options. If you're producing your video for playback in the United States or Japan, choose NTSC; otherwise, choose PAL.

When choosing a target resolution, use the native resolution of your source footage. For example, HDV has a native resolution of 1440x1080, so if you recorded in HDV, you should produce your disc at that resolution. If you're shooting in AVCHD, you may be recording in native 1920x1080, so use that resolution for your disc. If you're not sure what resolution you're recording in, check the documentation that came with your camcorder. Ditto if you're shooting with a DSLR or other recording device.

Review Questions

1   What is an auto-play disc? What are one advantage and one disadvantage of creating such a disc?

2   How do you identify separate scenes for use in your disc menu?

3   What is a submenu, and how would you add one to your disc menu?

4   Which menu button text properties can you change, and how are these properties modified?

5   Which type of menu template should you choose if you want to insert a still image or video file as a full-screen background for your disc menus?

6   What is a Web DVD, and when should you use one?

7   What are the key benefits of an AVCHD disc?

Review Answers

1   An auto-play disc allows you to create a DVD or Blu-ray Disc quickly from the main movie of your project. The advantage of an auto-play disc is that it can be quickly and easily created; the disadvantage is that it doesn't have a menu for navigation during playback.

2   Separate scenes can be defined by placing a scene marker on a specific frame in the Timeline. Scene markers are set in the Timeline using the Add Menu Marker button.

3   A submenu is a button on your main disc menu that points to a specific section of your project, such as a credit sequence or a bonus clip. Submenus are created by adding a main menu marker to your Timeline.

4   You can change the font, size, color, and style of your text buttons. Changing the properties of your text is done in Properties view for objects selected in the Disc Layout panel.

5   You should choose a template that does not include a drop zone. If you insert a still image or video into a menu template with a drop zone, Premiere Elements will display that content within the drop zone.

6   A Web DVD presents a DVD-like experience on the web, complete with menus, themes, and high-quality video. Use Web DVDs to share your productions with friends and family without having to burn and send them a physical DVD.

7   The key benefits of an AVCHD disc are the ability to record HD video onto a standard DVD recordable disc using a standard DVD recorder. The resulting disc will have no menus, however, and will play only on a Blu-ray player.

12 SHARING MOVIES

Lesson overview

This lesson is based on a project that you finished in a previous chapter, which you'll now share using multiple techniques. In this lesson, you'll learn how to send your completed video project to your digital media site or device of choice—for example, to YouTube or an iPod. You'll also learn the different ways you can export movies to view online or on a personal computer. Specifically, you'll learn how to do the following:

- Upload a video file to YouTube, Photoshop.com, and Facebook

- Export a video file for subsequent viewing from a hard drive

- Export a video file for viewing on an iPod or other mobile device

- Export a single frame as a still image

- Create a custom preset to save and reuse your favorite encoding parameters

 This lesson will take approximately 1.5 hours.

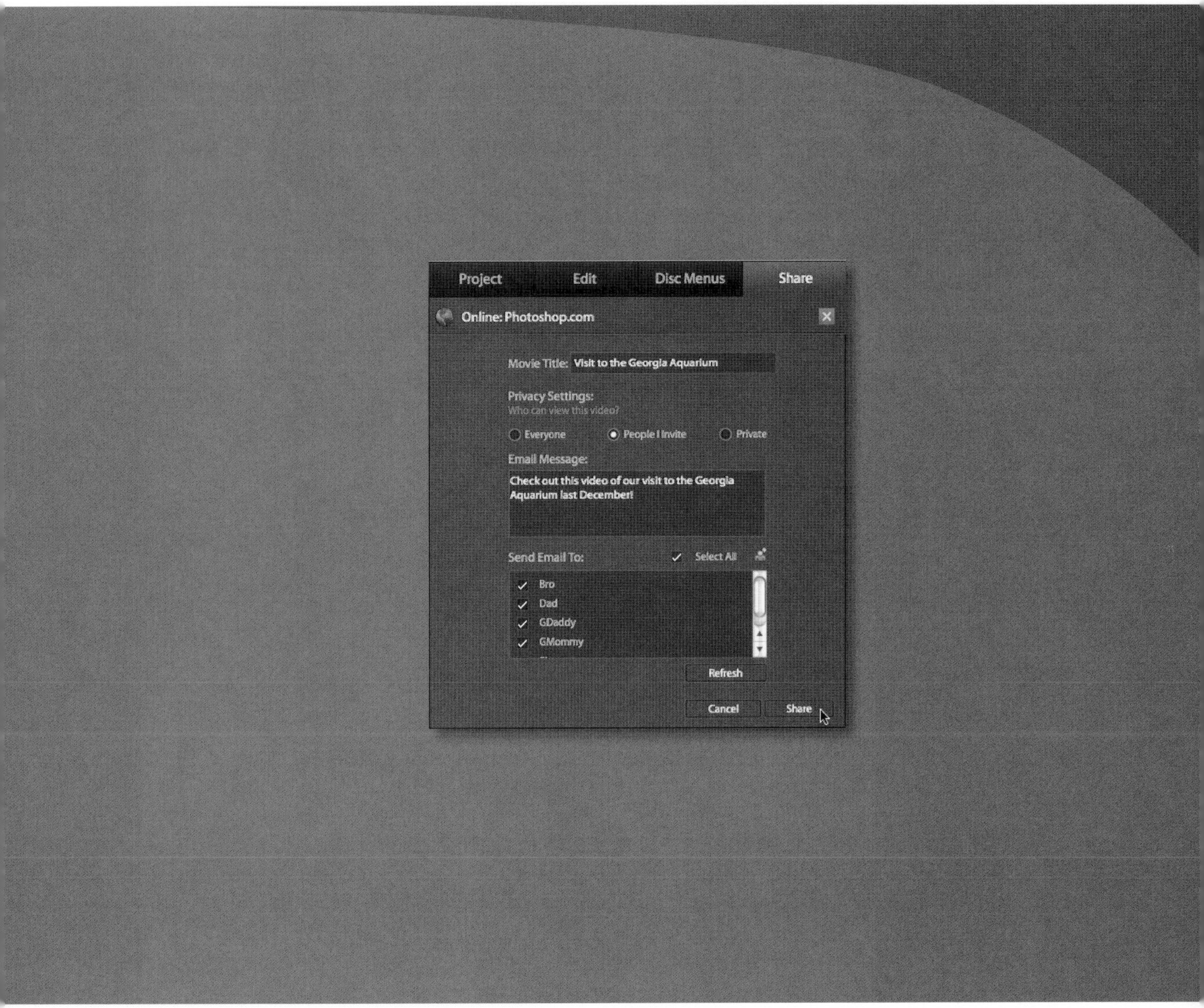

Sharing a video on Photoshop.com.

Sharing and Exporting Video

Apart from creating Web DVDs, DVDs, or Blu-ray Discs, you can export and share movies, still images, and audio in a variety of file types for the web, computer playback, mobile devices, and even videotape. The Share workspace in the Tasks panel is your starting point for exporting your finished project. Here you choose your target and configuration options.

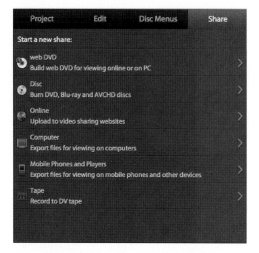

Selecting any of the options listed under "Start a new share:" opens a view in the Tasks panel that provides output-specific options and settings. Share view simplifies sharing and exporting by providing presets of the most commonly used formats and settings. If you want to specify unique settings for any format, you can click Advanced options and make changes.

The first step for all sharing is choosing your desired target. The exercises in this chapter walk you through examples of the available targets in the Share workspace.

Getting Started

To begin, you'll launch Premiere Elements and open the project used for this lesson. Then you'll review a final version of the project you'll be creating.

1 Before you begin, make sure that you have correctly copied the Lesson12 folder from the DVD in the back of this book onto your computer's hard drive. See "Copying the Classroom in a Book Files" in the "Getting Started" section of this book.

2 Start Premiere Elements, click the Open Project button in the Welcome screen, and then click Open. If Premiere Elements is already open, choose File > Open Project.

3 Navigate to the Lesson12 folder and select the project file Lesson12_Start_Win.prel (Windows) or Lesson12_Start_Mac.prel (Mac OS). Click the Open button to open your project. The Premiere Elements work area appears with the Edit workspace selected in the Tasks panel.

4 The project file opens with the Media, Monitor, and My Project panels visible. Choose Window > Restore Workspace to ensure that you start the lesson with the default panel layout.

Viewing the Completed Movie for the First Exercise

To see what you'll be exporting in this lesson, play the completed movie.

1 In the Project tab in the Tasks panel, click Media ( ). In Media view, locate the file Lesson12_Movie.mov, and then double-click it to open the video into the Preview window.

2 In the Preview window, click the Play button ( ) to watch the video about a visit to the Georgia Aquarium, which you'll render in this lesson.

3 When you're done, close the Preview window.

If the movie looks familiar, that's because it's the project you finished back in Lesson 9 after adding a sound track and narration. Now it's time to share the fruits of your hard work with the world!

Rather than duplicating the project file and content from Lesson 9 to Lesson 12, I inserted the rendered file that you just played onto the Timeline in the project you just opened, because it simulates the Lesson 9 project completely and saves a few hundred megabytes on the DVD that accompanies this book. The experience will be *exactly* the same as if you were working with the original content and project file.

Still, if you'd like to work with the original assets, you can load the Lesson09_Work.prel file that you created in Lesson 9, or load Lesson09_Work.prel (if you didn't make it to the end) and follow the instructions in this chapter to render those contents. Obviously, those projects would be in the Lesson09 folder, not the Lesson12 folder. In your shoes, I would simply use the project file you currently have loaded, but feel free to work with the original content if that's your preference.

Uploading to YouTube

Premiere Elements provides presets for three online destinations—YouTube, Photoshop.com, and Podbean. The workflow is very similar for all with a simple wizard guiding your efforts. Here, I'll work through the first two, starting with YouTube. It's faster if you already have an account with YouTube, but if not, you can sign up as part of the process. Follow these steps to upload your project to YouTube.

1   Click Share in the Tasks panel, and then click Online ().

2   Choose YouTube from the list at the top. Premiere Elements uses the Flash preset for YouTube for all files produced to upload to YouTube.

● **Note:** What if you shot in 720p resolution with your AVCHD or DSLR camera? Your results on YouTube will depend on your footage and the quality that you choose for viewing on YouTube. I recommend that you try uploading using both Flash Video for YouTube (widescreen) and High Definition Video for YouTube 1920x1080, and retaining the video that looks the best.

3   Choose a preset. Use Flash Video for YouTube for standard definition (SD) 4:3 projects and Flash Video for YouTube (widescreen) for (SD) 16:9 projects. To upload high-definition (HD) video to YouTube, choose the preset that matches your source footage, which will be High Definition Video for YouTube (1440x1080) for HDV and older AVCHD camcorders, and High Definition Video for YouTube 1920x1080 for most newer AVCHD camcorders and most DSLR cameras.

4   If desired, click the Share WorkArea Bar Only to upload only the work area bar. It's not shown in the immediately preceding figure because it's hidden behind the Preset drop-down list box, but you'll see it after selecting your preset.

5   Click Next.

6　Log in to YouTube. If this is your first time uploading to YouTube, click Sign Up Now and register. Then log in.

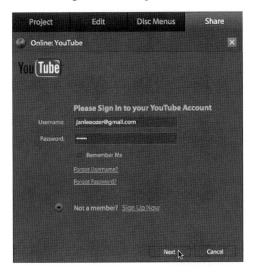

7　Click Next.

8　Enter the required information about your project: Title, Description, Tags, and Category, and then click Next.

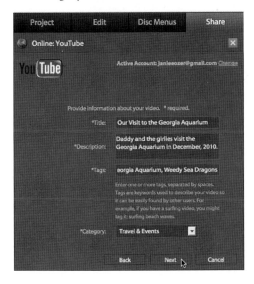

9　Choose whether you want to allow the public to view your project or to keep it private, and then click Share. Premiere Elements renders the project and starts uploading to YouTube, with status messages advising you of the progress during each step.

Note: I'm pretty sure that there will be (at least) dozens if not hundreds of copies of this video on YouTube by sometime in early 2012. It might be a better idea if you follow the latter steps to upload your own video to YouTube, or if you do upload this sample movie, that you later delete it.

10 When the share is complete, the URL appears in the Share workspace. You can choose View My Shared Video to open YouTube and watch your video, or choose Send an E-mail to alert friends to your new posting.

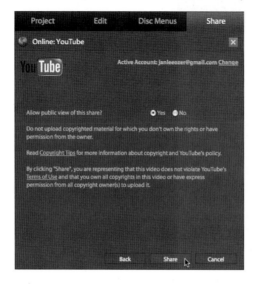

11 Click Done to return to the main Share workspace.

Uploading to Photoshop.com

YouTube is a great place to upload your video for it to be seen by the multitudes, but video quality ranges from very good to poor, and some of the comments can be, well, rude. If you'd like to upload a video primarily for friends and family at very good quality, your Photoshop.com account is ideal, and the workflow is exceptionally simple. Here's how.

1 Click Share in the Tasks panel, and then click Online ().

2 Choose Photoshop.com from the list at the top. There's currently only a single preset for Photoshop.com, so there are no options available. If desired, click the Share WorkArea Bar Only to upload only the work area bar.

3 Click Next.

4 If you're not already logged into Photoshop.com, you'll see the login screen. Log in to Photoshop.com. If you don't have a Photoshop.com account, click Create New Adobe ID and sign up. Then enter your account name and password, and click Sign In. Click OK to close the Success dialog.

5 Enter the required information about your project: Movie Title, Privacy Settings, Email Message, and Send Email To addresses, and then click Share.

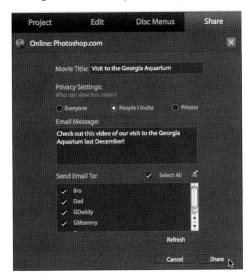

6 When the share is complete, Premiere Elements will display a hyperlink that you can click to view your online video.

7 Click Done to return to the main Share workspace.

Uploading to Facebook

Lots of folks are sharing their videos via their Facebook accounts, and here's a very simple way to upload your videos from Premiere Elements to Facebook. This will be smoother if you log into your Facebook account before starting the upload process.

1 Click Share in the Tasks panel, and then click Online (▦).

2 Choose Facebook from the list at the top. In the Presets drop-down list, choose Facebook HD if your video is HD source or SD video for SD source. If desired, click the Share WorkArea Bar Only to upload only the work area bar.

> ▶ **Tip:** You can also upload a Web DVD to Photoshop.com, which provides the same menus and navigation as a DVD. It's a great alternative that you can learn about in Chapter 11 (if you haven't already read that chapter).

3 Click Next.

4 Premiere Elements requires your authorization to upload content to your Facebook account. Click Authorize to start this process. A browser window will open, and if you're not logged into Facebook, you should be directed to log in now.

5 In the browser window, click Allow in the Facebook Request for Permission Screen, and then close the browser window (if desired).

6 Back in Premiere Elements, click the Complete Authorization button.

7   Enter the required information about your project: Name, Description, and who can see the video, and then click Upload.

8   When the share is complete, Premiere Elements will display a hyperlink that you can click to view your online video and a link to send emails to invite friends and family to view the video.

9   Click Done to return to the main Share workspace.

Sharing on Your Personal Computer

In the previous exercises, you exported a Premiere Elements project to YouTube, Facebook, and Photoshop.com. In this exercise, you'll export your project as a stand-alone video file to play on your own system, upload to a website, email to friends or family, or archive on DVD or an external hard drive.

As you'll see in a moment, Premiere Elements lets you output in multiple formats for all these activities. Each file format comes with its own set of presets available from the Presets menu. You can also customize a preset and save it for later reuse, which you'll do in this lesson.

See the sidebar "Choosing Output Formats" for more information on which preset to choose. In this exercise, you'll customize a preset and output a file using the QuickTime format.

1   In Share view, click the Computer button (■).

2   In the list at the top of Share view, choose QuickTime.

3 In the Presets list box, choose NTSC DV 16:9. After you complete the lesson, the custom preset that you create will be available via this list box.

4 Enter *Lesson12_SharePC* in the File Name field, and then click Browse to select the Lesson12 folder as the Save in folder.

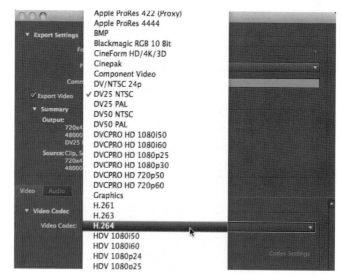

5 Click the Advanced button (Advanced...) beneath the Save in: text box. Premiere Elements opens the Export Settings dialog.

The NTSC DV 16:9 preset is great if you want to edit the file further in a Mac-based program, but the files are too large to easily email to friends and family. You'll create a custom preset that creates more compact files.

6 To start, click the Video Codec list box and choose the H.264 codec.

7 In the Basic Settings box, if necessary, uncheck the box to the right of the Width and Height values, and then click and insert *640* in the Width text box and *360* in the Height text box. Otherwise:

- Leave the Frame Rate at 29.97.

- Click the Field Type list box, and choose Progressive.

- Click the Aspect: list box and choose Square Pixels (1.0).

8 Click the disclosure triangle next to Advanced Settings (if necessary) to reveal those controls.

9 Select the Frame Reordering check box.

10 Click the disclosure triangle next to Bitrate Settings (if necessary) to reveal that control. Select the "Limit data rate to" check box and type *3000* into the text field.

11 Click the Audio tab to open those controls. In the Audio Codec list box, choose AAC, and conform the other settings to those shown in the next figure.

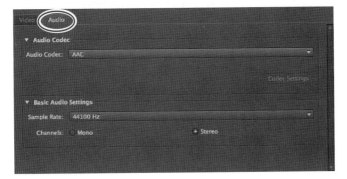

● **Note:** Note the circled box in the figure next to Width and Height. When a link (⊞) appears in the box, Premiere Elements links the width and height to maintain the aspect ratio of the source footage. Most of the time, that's the right decision, but sometimes you'll want to change the aspect ratio, and if the link appears, Premiere Elements will automatically adjust the values in the height and width fields to maintain the aspect ratio, preventing you from entering the desired values. In these cases, simply click the link to disable this option. The box should not be selected when using the preset that you selected, but if it is, click the box to deselect it.

12 Click OK to close the Export Settings dialog; the Choose Name dialog opens. Type the title *H.264 640x360 3 Mbps preset* into the name field, and click OK to close the dialog.

13 Back in the Share workspace, note that Premiere Elements inserted the preset that you just created into the Presets list box. The next time you click that list box, the new preset will be available with the other custom presets.

14 If desired, select the Share WorkArea Bar Only check box.

15 To start exporting your movie, click Save.

Premiere Elements begins rendering the video and displays a progress bar in Share view and an estimated time to complete each phase of the rendering process. Click Cancel at any time to stop the exporting process. Otherwise, you'll see a Save Complete! message in Share view when the rendering is complete.

16 Click Done to return to the main Share workspace.

⬤ **Note:** Many Windows Media Premiere Elements standard definition (SD) presets are for 4:3 projects. When producing a 16:9 project, you'll have to change the preset to a 16:9 output resolution. Do this by clicking the Advanced button shown in the preceding screen to open the Export Settings dialog as shown earlier. Click the Video tab to reveal those settings, and then adjust the Frame Width and Frame Height text boxes to a 16:9 output resolution. For your reference, the most common 16:9 SD output resolutions are 640x360, 480x270, and 320x180. Make sure that Field Type is set to Progressive and Pixel Aspect Ratio is set to Square Pixels (1.0). Click OK to close the Export Settings dialog. You'll be prompted to save the preset, and then you'll return to the Share screen.

Choosing Output Formats

- **Adobe Flash Video:** Adobe Flash Video is a very high-quality format that's used by the majority of sites on the Internet for playback via the ubiquitous Adobe Flash Player. Use this format if you're producing files to be distributed from a website. However, the FLV files produced by this format require a stand-alone player to play back from a hard drive outside of the browser environment, which many viewers don't have. Accordingly, the format is not appropriate for creating files to view on other computers outside the browser environment, whether by email, file transfer protocol (FTP), or via a Universal Serial Bus (USB) drive.

- **MPEG:** MPEG is a widely supported playback format, although it is used almost exclusively for desktop or disc-based playback rather than for streaming. Use MPEG to create files for inserting into Blu-ray or DVD projects produced in other programs. For most casual hard drive-based playback, however, either QuickTime or Windows Media offers better quality at lower data rates, making each a better option for files shared via email or FTP.

- **AVCHD:** AVCHD is a high-definition format that you can burn to a DVD to play on a Blu-ray player (as you learned in Chapter 11). AVCHD is also a good choice for archiving a high-quality version of your edited video for long-term storage or for playing back on a computer that has software that can play AVCHD files. Though very high quality, AVCHD is not a good medium for sharing video files because the files are quite large and difficult to transfer.

- **DV AVI:** This is the format used by DV camcorders on the Windows platform. DV AVI is an excellent archival format for standard-definition (SD) productions and is a good choice for producing files to be further edited in other programs. However, DV AVI files are too large for casually distributing via email or FTP, and although many Mac OS programs can import AVI files, QuickTime is a better choice when planning to edit your projects further on the Mac platform.

- **Windows Media (Windows only—not available on the Mac version of Premiere Elements):** Windows Media files—whether distributed via a website, email, or FTP—can be played by virtually all Windows computers via the Windows Media Player. Quality is good at low bit rates, making Windows Media a good choice for producing files to be distributed via email to other Windows users. However, Macintosh compatibility may be a problem because Microsoft hasn't released a Windows Media Player for OS X, forcing users to download a third-party solution from Flip4Mac. When producing files for viewing on Macintosh computers, use the QuickTime format.

- **QuickTime:** QuickTime is the best choice for files intended for viewing on both Macintosh and Windows computers, whether distributed via the web, email, or other technique. All presets use the H.264 codec, which offers very good quality but can take a long time to render.

- **Image:** Use for exporting images from your project.

- **Audio:** Use for exporting audio from your project.

When producing a file for uploading to a website like Yahoo Video, Vimeo, or Blip.tv, check the required file specifications published by each site before producing your file. Typically, a QuickTime file using the H.264 codec offers the best blend of high quality at modest data rates and near universal compatibility.

Exporting to Mobile Phones and Players

Premiere Elements also includes an option for producing files for mobile phones and players, such as the Apple iPod or iPhone, the Creative Zen, and the Microsoft Zune. Note that most of these devices have very specific and inflexible file and format requirements, so you shouldn't change any parameters in the Export Settings window, because you may produce a file that's unplayable on the target device.

In this exercise, you'll learn how to create a file for the iPod; if you're producing a file for a different device, just choose that device and preset in the appropriate steps.

1 In Share view, click the Mobile Phones and Players button (▣).

2 In the list at the top of Share view, choose Apple iPod, iPad, and iPhone.

3 In the Presets list box, choose an Apple iPhone, Apple iPod preset to produce a high-quality file compatible with iPods, iPhones, the iPod touch, the iPad (1 or 2), and similar, newer portable media players, keeping in mind that this file won't play on some older portable players. Use a Widescreen preset for 16:9 content and a Standard preset for 4:3 content. Choose an Apple iPad Widescreen or Standard preset to produce a file that will play on Apple iPads and newer iPhones and iPod touch devices but may not play on many older iPods or other portable players. For the purposes of this exercise, choose Apple iPad Widescreen High Quality.

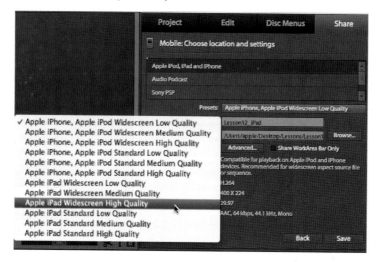

4 Next to File Name, enter *Lesson12_iPad*, and then click Browse to select your Lesson12 folder as the Save in folder.

5 If desired, select the Share WorkArea Bar Only check box.

6 To start exporting your movie, click Save.

Premiere Elements starts rendering the video and displays a progress bar in Share view and an estimated time to complete each phase of the rendering process. Click Cancel at any time to stop the exporting process. Otherwise, you will see a Save Complete! message in Share view when the rendering is complete.

7 Click Done to return to the Share workspace.

After producing the file, transfer it to your device in the appropriate manner. For example, use iTunes to upload the file to your iPod or iPhone.

● **Note:** If you produced your movie using video captured from DV or HDV tape, you may want to archive your project back to tape. For instruction regarding this process, search the Premiere Elements Help file for Sharing to Videotape.

Exporting a Frame of Video as a Still Image

Occasionally, you may want to grab frames from your video footage to email to friends and family, include in a slide show, or use for other purposes. In this exercise, you'll learn to export and save a frame from the project. To perform this exercise, reload Lesson12_Start_Win.prel (Windows) or Lesson12_Start_Mac.prel (Mac OS) as detailed in the "Getting Started" section near the start of this chapter.

1 In the Timeline, drag the current-time indicator to timecode 00;00;26;15, or click the current timecode box at the lower left of the Monitor panel, type *2615*, and press Enter/Return.

2 Click the Freeze Frame button (▣) in the lower-right corner of the Monitor panel. You might have to enlarge the Monitor panel to see the Freeze Frame button. Premiere Elements opens the Freeze Frame dialog.

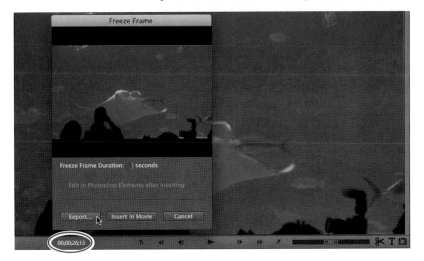

3 In the Freeze Frame dialog, click Export to create a separate still image, which is what we want to do here. Note the Insert in Movie option which you'll use to insert the frame into the movie. You can also select the check box to edit the captured frame in Adobe Photoshop Elements if you choose the Import in Movie option.

Tip: You can also export Audio only from the Personal Computer output group.

Tip: The snapshot export function is very quick and easy but outputs only BMP files at the resolution of your current project. For more control over export size and formats, click Share, then Computer, and choose Image, which exposes multiple presets that you can customize by clicking the Advanced button.

4 In the Export Frame dialog, locate the Lesson12 folder and name your file *manta.bmp*. Click Save to save the still image onto your hard drive and close the Freeze Frame dialog.

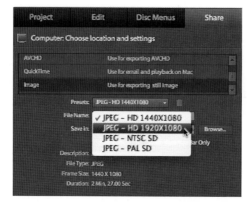

Review Questions

1 What's the best format to use for creating files to view on Windows computers or to share with other viewers with Windows computers?

2 Why shouldn't you change any encoding parameters for files produced for iPods or other devices?

3 What's the easiest way to write a project to an analog tape format, such as VHS?

4 What's the easiest way to upload your movie to a website, such as YouTube, Facebook, or Photoshop.com?

5 When might you want to export a file into AVCHD format?

Review Answers

1 Windows Media is the best format for Windows because it combines small file size with high quality. Although virtually all computers can play MPEG-1 or MPEG-2 files, the files are usually too large for easy transport. QuickTime files may pose a problem because not all Windows computers support QuickTime, and Adobe Flash Video files with a .flv extension require a stand-alone player, which not all computers have installed.

2 Devices have very specific playback requirements, and if you change a file parameter and deviate from these requirements, the file may not load or play on the target device.

3 Connect a VHS recorder to your DV camcorder via composite or S-Video connectors plus audio while writing your project to DV tape. Most DV camcorders will display the recorded signal out the analog ports while recording, which you can record on the VHS deck by pressing the Record button on the deck.

4 Switch to Share view, and then click the Online button. Choose YouTube, Facebook, or Photoshop.com, and then follow the instructions in Share view to render and upload your movie.

5 You might want to export a file into AVCHD format for subsequent burning to a Blu-ray Disc or as a high-quality archive of the project.

13 WORKING WITH PHOTOSHOP ELEMENTS

Lesson overview

Adobe Photoshop Elements and Adobe Premiere Elements are designed to work together and let you seamlessly combine digital photography and video editing. You can spice up your video projects with title images or customized menu templates created in Photoshop Elements, or build slide show presentations in Photoshop Elements, and then use parts of them in Premiere Elements for further editing.

To work on the following exercises, you must have Photoshop Elements installed on your system. In this lesson, you will learn several techniques for using Photoshop Elements together with Premiere Elements. Specifically, you will learn how to do the following:

- Add single and multiple images from the Elements Organizer to a Premiere Elements project

- Create a Photoshop file optimized for video

- Edit a Photoshop image from within Premiere Elements

 This lesson will take approximately 1.5 hours.

A cool text title created in Photoshop Elements for use
in Premiere Elements.

Viewing the Completed Movie Before You Start

To see what you'll be creating, let's take a look at the completed movie.

1   Before you begin, make sure that you have correctly copied the Lesson13 folder from the DVD in the back of this book onto your computer's hard drive. See "Copying the Classroom in a Book Files" in the "Getting Started" section of this book.

2   Navigate to the Lesson13 folder, and double-click Lesson13_Movie.mov to play the movie in your default application for watching QuickTime files.

Getting Started

You'll now open Photoshop Elements 10 and import the files needed for the Lesson13 project.

1   Launch Photoshop Elements.

2   In the Welcome screen, click the Organize button to open the Photoshop Elements Organizer.

3　If you've previously used Photoshop Elements, your Organizer may be displaying the photos in your current catalog. If this is the first time you've launched Photoshop Elements, you may receive a message asking if you would like to designate a location to look for your image files. Click No to work with an empty Organizer panel.

4　Choose File > Get Photos and Videos > From Files and Folders. Navigate to your Lesson13 folder and select—but do not open—the images subfolder. Then click Get Media. Photoshop Elements will import the photos.

5　If a message appears telling you that only the newly imported files will appear, click OK. In the Organizer, you should see nine images from the aquarium. Thumbnail images are small versions of the full-size photos. You'll be working with the full-size photos later in this lesson.

6　Under Albums in the Tagging window, click the Create new album or album group button (⊞), and choose New Album. Premiere Elements opens the Album Details dialog.

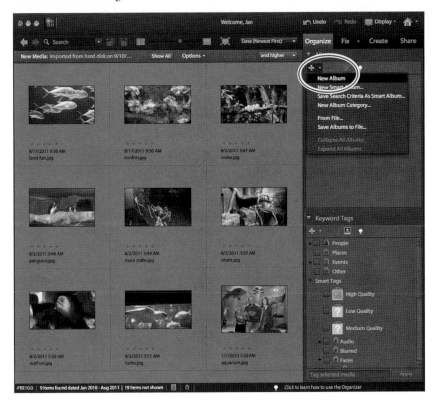

7 In the Photoshop Elements menu, choose Edit > Select All to select the nine new images. Then click on any one image, drag all the images into the Items window on the right, and release the pointer.

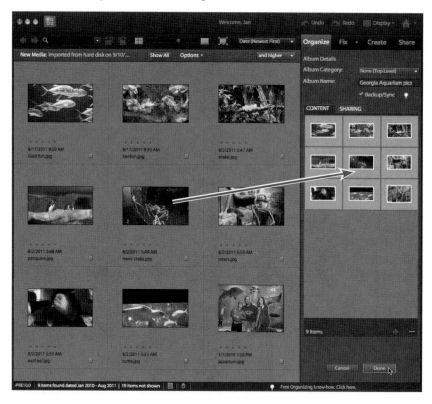

8 In the Album Name field in the Album Details dialog, type *Georgia Aquarium pics.*

9 On the lower right of the Album Details dialog, click Done to save the album.

As you may recall from Lesson 4, Premiere Elements and Photoshop Elements use the same Organizer, which Premiere Elements can access from the Media view in the Edit workspace. You'll review how to access the newly created Georgia Aquarium pics album from Premiere Elements in a later exercise.

Using the Edit Videos Command
in Photoshop Elements

You learned back in Lesson 1 that you can create a project in Premiere Elements after selecting video files in the Organizer. Similarly, you can create a Premiere Elements project from images using the same technique. Let's review that quickly in this exercise.

Briefly, if you have a project open in Premiere Elements when you use this technique, the Organizer will add the selected files to the current project at the end of the current Sceneline or Timeline. If no project is open, the Organizer will create a new project, which is the workflow you will follow in this exercise. Accordingly, if you have a project open in Premiere Elements, please close it (after saving if necessary) before starting this exercise.

To sort images in the Organizer, Photoshop Elements uses the date and time information embedded in the image file by the digital camera. In the Organizer menu, choosing to show the oldest files first by selecting Date (Newest First) enables you to create a slide show in chronological order when transferring the photos to Premiere Elements.

● **Note:** Before performing the first step, make sure you do not have a project open in Premiere Elements. Otherwise, the images will be placed in the open file.

1 Press and hold the Ctrl/Command key, and then in the Photo Browser click the top six images to select them (gold fish.jpg, lionfish.jpg, snake.jpg, penguins.jpg, more crabs.jpg, and otters.jpg). The Organizer highlights the gray area around the thumbnail to indicate a selected image. In the next step, Photoshop Elements will process only the selected images.

2 In the Fix panel, click the downward triangle on the top right of the Fix tab, and choose Edit Videos. A dialog may appear informing you that the files will be inserted at the end of your Timeline and that the Premiere Elements defaults will be used. Click OK. If Premiere Elements is not already open, it will launch automatically.

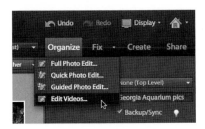

3 In the Premiere Elements New Project dialog, type *Lesson13_Start* in the name field. Click the Browse button. In the Browse For Folder dialog, navigate to the Lesson13 folder located on your hard drive and select it. Click OK (Windows) or Choose (Mac OS) to close the Browse For Folder dialog.

4 If necessary, click the Change Settings button and change the preset to NTSC-DV-Widescreen 48kHz. Click OK to close the Setup dialog, and then click OK to close the New Project dialog.

A Premiere Elements project is created, and the images you selected in Photoshop Elements are now visible in the Organize view in the Tasks panel. They have also been added to Media view and placed in the Sceneline (or Timeline) of the My Project panel. The first image is displayed in the Monitor panel. In the Sceneline of the My Project panel, you'll see all images as individual scenes.

5   With all scenes selected in the Sceneline, choose Clip > Group to place the entire group onto one target that can be moved as a single clip. Then choose Clip > Ungroup to treat each still image as its own scene in the Sceneline.

6   Press the spacebar to play your project. Premiere Elements uses the default duration of five seconds for each still image and applies a cross-dissolve as the default transition between each clip.

7   Return to the Organizer by clicking the Organizer button on the upper right of Premiere Elements or by holding down the Alt/Command key and pressing Tab until you see the icon for the Elements Organizer. Release the Alt/Command key and the Elements Organizer opens. If all nine images aren't shown, click the Georgia Aquarium pics album at the upper right to display the contents of that album.

8   Click to select only one image, the one named Aquarium.jpg, and then choose Edit > Edit with Premiere Elements Editor. Click OK to close the Edit with Premiere Elements dialog if it appears. Your open application should switch to Premiere Elements, and the image will be placed at the end of your Sceneline or Timeline.

9   Choose File > Save As and save this project file in your Lesson13 folder as *Lesson13_Work.prel*.

● **Note:** Because you're sending only a single image from Photoshop Elements to Premiere Elements, no transition has been placed on the image. In this case, if you wanted to add a transition, you would have to do so manually, but do not add one at this time. See Lesson 7 for more information about adding transitions.

● **Note:** Although you might assume that the total length of the slide show is equal to the number of images multiplied by the default duration for still images, it's actually less than that. The is reason is that Premiere Elements inserts the transition effect between the images by overlapping the clips by the default length of the transition effect. Note that you can change the default still image duration and transition duration in the Premiere Elements Preferences panel. See the section "Working with Project Preferences" in Lesson 2 for more details.

Creating a New Photoshop
File Optimized for Video

The first part of this lesson focused on importing image files from the Organizer into Premiere Elements. In this exercise, you'll create a new still image, modify it in Photoshop Elements, and then use it in your Premiere Elements project.

One of the more common workflows between the two programs is to create a project title in Premiere Elements, edit it in Photoshop Elements, and then deploy the title in Premiere Elements. That's what you'll do in this and the following exercise.

1 Make sure you're in Photoshop Elements. Choose File > New > Blank File. In the New file dialog, type *title*. Then click the Preset list box and choose Film & Video.

2 Click the Size list box and choose NTSC DV, which matches the project you should have open in Premiere Elements. If you're working on a different project, choose the size that matches the resolution of your Premiere Elements project. If you don't know or have forgotten, click Edit > Project Settings > General in Premiere Elements to view your project settings.

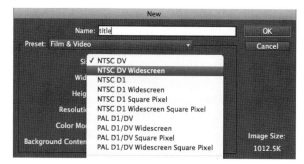

3   Click OK to create the file, and then click OK to close the dialog regarding using a video monitor.

4   Now let's save the file in the Lesson13 folder. Choose File > Save As, and in the Save As dialog, check to make sure that you named the file *Title.psd*; then navigate to your Lesson13 folder and click Save.

Customizing a Title in Photoshop Elements

Now you have your Photoshop file. Next, you'll add the background that you captured in the previous lesson, customize the background, and then add some text.

1   In the Editor, make sure Full mode is selected on the extreme upper-right corner of the interface. If necessary, click the Full button to choose that mode.

2   If necessary, in the top menu, choose View > Guides to hide the title and action safe guides, which you don't need because you're not producing a DVD with this project or otherwise producing a file that will be viewed on a television set.

3   In Photoshop Elements, choose File > Open. The Open dialog opens. Navigate to the Lesson13 folder on your hard drive, choose manta.bmp, and click Open to load the image into Photoshop Elements.

4   In the Photoshop Elements menu, choose Select > All to select the image, and then choose Edit > Copy to copy the image to the clipboard.

5   Click Title.psd to make it active, and choose Edit > Paste to paste the copied manta.bmp image into Title.psd. If you see an error message about the background of the image being locked, click OK to enable the paste.

6 You may need to adjust the size of the pasted image to fit Title.psd, which you accomplish by clicking and dragging any of the eight small squares on the edges and sides of the bounding box. Position the image so that it fills the white area. Then click the Commit Current Operation check mark on the lower right to set the adjustment.

7 On the upper-right side of the Photoshop Elements interface, in the EFFECTS tab, click the first icon from the left, which is Filters (■). Make sure that Artistic is selected in the drop-down list.

8 Drag the Smudge Stick effect onto Title.psd and release. Photoshop Elements applies the effect to the image.

9 Let's add a text title to Title.psd. Click the Horizontal Type Text (T) tool in the Tools panel.

10 In the Text tool options bar, choose the Postino Std style at 72 pt, center text alignment, and set the font color to Pure Blue. If you don't have that font on your system, choose a different font that delivers the same *je ne sais quoi*.

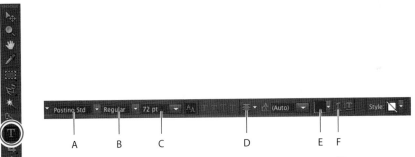

A. Font. **B.** Style. **C.** Font Size. **D.** Alignment. **E.** Color. **F.** Create Warped Text.

11 Click the image about halfway between the manta ray and the top of the image, around the horizontal center of the image, and type *The Georgia* (carriage return) *Aquarium*.

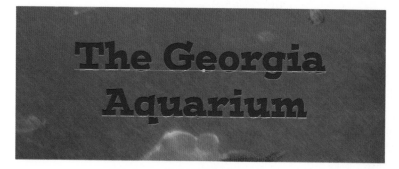

12 Click the Move tool () in the toolbox to return to the selection arrow. Position the text to approximately where it's shown in the figure (if necessary). Now let's make the text more legible. To do this, right-click the text box and choose Edit Layer Style.

13 Let's make several adjustments in the Style Settings dialog:

- Click the Drop Shadow box to add a drop shadow.

- Add an inner glow by clicking the Glow check box, then clicking the Inner check boxes, and then conforming their settings to the figure.

- Add a bevel by clicking the Bevel check box, and otherwise make sure that your settings match those in the figure.

- Add a stroke by clicking the Stroke check box, and otherwise make sure that your settings match those in the figure.

- Click OK to close the dialog.

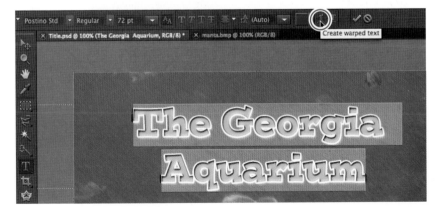

14 The text is much more legible and distinctive. Now let's warp the text to make it look like a fish. Double-click the text box to select all text, and then click the Create Warped Text icon on the text tools option bar.

15 In the Warp Text dialog, click the Style drop-down list and choose Fish. Then Click OK to close the dialog.

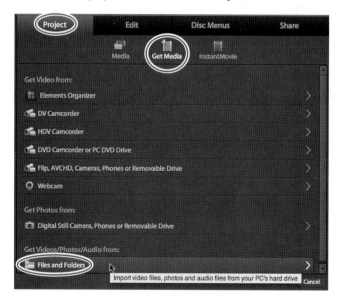

16 Choose File > Save to save Title.psd.

17 Switch to Premiere Elements by holding down the Alt/Command key and pressing Tab until you see the icon for Premiere Elements. Release the Alt/Command key and Premiere Elements opens.

18 Now let's import the file into Premiere Elements. Click the Project Tab, then the Get Media icon, and then Get Videos/Photos/Audio from Files and folders. The Add Media dialog opens. Navigate to the Lesson13 folder, click to select Title.psd, and click Open (Windows)/Import (Mac OS). Premiere Elements imports the file and displays it in the Media workspace.

19 In the Timeline, drag Title.psd to the beginning of the movie, waiting for about two seconds for the other images to shift to the right. Then release the pointer. If Premiere Elements opens the SmartFix dialog, click No.

Premiere Elements inserts Title.psd at the start of the movie and shifts all other content to the right.

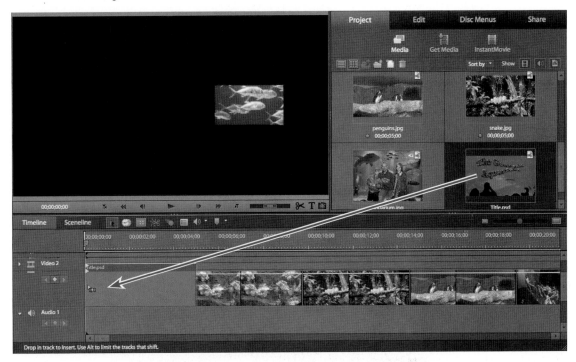

20 Save your work. Your title should look like the one shown in the Monitor panel in the next figure.

Editing a Photoshop Image in Premiere Elements

Tip: When in the Timeline, pressing the equals sign (=) on your keyboard is a quick way to zoom in to better view the clips.

You can edit a Photoshop Elements image (or any image for that matter) while you're working in Premiere Elements by using the Edit in Photoshop Elements command. Changes you make to the image will be updated automatically, even if the clip is already placed in your Sceneline or Timeline. Let's add a bit of color to the currently drab title.

1 Right-click the Title.psd clip in the Timeline and choose Edit in Adobe Photoshop Elements. The Title.psd file opens in Photoshop Elements. Click OK if the dialog discussing the video monitor opens.

2 If necessary, click the Move tool () in the toolbox to choose the selection arrow. Then right-click the text box and choose Edit Layer Style.

3 In the Style Settings dialog, click the Stroke check box to deselect that style setting. Click OK to close the dialog.

4 Choose File > Save As. In the Save As dialog, deselect the Save in Version Set with Original check box. Click Save and then Replace to overwrite Title.psd. Then switch to Premiere Elements.

The changes made to the Title.psd file in Photoshop Elements have automatically been updated in the Premiere Elements project. This is very useful because it eliminates the need to re-import an image file every time a change is made.

5 Click the top of the Timeline to select it, and then press the Home key to place the current-time indicator at the beginning of the Timeline. Press the spacebar to play your project. When you're finished reviewing, save your work.

Congratulations! You've finished the lesson on working with Photoshop Elements. You've discovered how to get photos from the Organizer and how to enhance them using the Editor. You've also learned how to create a title in Photoshop Elements for use in Premiere Elements.

This is the last lesson in this book. We hope that you have gained confidence in using Premiere Elements 10, developed some new skills, and increased your knowledge of the product and the many creative things you can accomplish with it.

But this book is just the beginning. You can learn more by studying the Premiere Elements 10 Help system that is built into the application. Simply choose Help > Adobe Premiere Elements Help and browse or use the search functionality to find what you need. Also, don't forget to look for tutorials, tips, and expert advice on the Adobe Systems website at www.adobe.com.

Review Questions

1   What's the best way to make sure that an image you create in Photoshop Elements matches the video that you'll be adding it to?

2   How can you edit an image included in a Premiere Elements project in Photoshop Elements?

3   What are the advantages of editing your images in Photoshop Elements?

Review Answers

1   Make sure that you create the file using the same size as your video project.

2   Right-click the image in the Premiere Elements Timeline and choose Edit in Photoshop Elements.

3   Photoshop Elements has many more still image effects and several more advanced text-related adjustments.

INDEX

B

background color, 62, 142, 143
background music, 199–201, 223, 245
background noise, 207, 209, 215
background rendering, 86
backlighting, 126–128
backups, 21, 74–77
Balance effect, 112
beat detection, 214–215
bevels, 292
black balance, 122
black video clips, 173–174
Blu-ray Discs. *See also* DVDs
    adding scene markers, 231–232
    auto-play, 233–234
    burning, 229–230, 258–260
    overview, 229–231
    quality settings, 260
Blu-ray format, 229–231, 275
BMP files, 278
bonus clips, 242–244, 245
bounding box, 246, 247, 290
Browser pane, 10
burning DVDs, 229–230, 258–260
buttons
    animating, 250–253
    changing text properties for, 253–255
    customizing, 251–253
    modifying scene markers, 239–242
    navigation, 239, 242, 253
    overlapping, 251
    playback, 233, 253
    text, 251–255
    thumbnail scene, 250–255

C

camcorders. *See also* video devices
    AVCHD, 16, 30, 47–52, 266
    capturing video from, 37, 38–47
    capturing video without device control, 45
    connecting to computer, 40–42
    device control for, 44–45
    DSLR, 30, 260
    DV, 10, 16, 48–49, 83
    HDV, 10, 16, 26, 48–49. *See also* camcorders
    importing video from AVCHD, 16, 30, 47–52
    inputting video footage from, 10
    previewing video on TV monitor, 83
    tape-based, 10
    troubleshooting problems, 47, 48–49
    types of, 10, 16
cameras, digital, 10, 16, 38, 52
Capture panel, 39, 40–47

capturing video, 38–47
    Auto Analyzer and, 47
    from camcorders, 37, 38–47
    capture interfaces, 39–40
    Capture to Timeline option, 43
    capturing without audio, 43
    capturing without device control, 45
    capturing/splitting into scenes, 43–44
    device control, 44–45, 52
    options for, 43–44
    overview, 38
    saving imported files, 50–51
    Scene Detect and, 43–44
    stop-motion video, 51
    stopping capture, 46, 47
    from tape-based devices, 10, 40–47
    time-lapse video, 51
    troubleshooting problems, 47, 48–49
    from webcams, 16, 40, 42, 44, 45
Cartoonr Plus effect, 112, 147–148
cell phones. *See* mobile phones
clipping, 209
clips. *See also* content; video footage
    adding in Sceneline, 86–89
    adding to menus, 247–249
    black, 173–174
    bonus, 242–244, 245
    compositing with Videomerge, 142–144
    correcting shakiness of, 130–131
    deleting, 90
    editing. *See* editing
    effects. *See* effects
    enhancing, 115–123
    finding in Media view, 60–62
    importing. *See* importing
    keywords. *See* keyword tags
    layering, 93, 95
    moving, 89
    playing. *See* playback
    previewing, 58–59
    reframing, 128–130
    rendering, 118–120
    reversing, 112
    running Auto Analyzer on, 63, 67–70
    sharpening, 130
    SmartFix adjustments, 114–115
    speed of, 112, 131, 144–145
    splitting, 92–93, 99–103
    superimposed, 141–142
    superimposing titles over video, 185, 186–189
    synchronizing, 76–77
    tagging, 63–78
    transitions in. *See* transitions
    trimming. *See* trimming clips
    working with multiple, 127
    zoom controls. *See* zoom controls

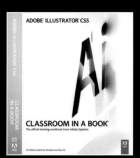
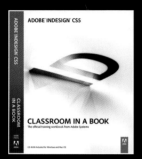

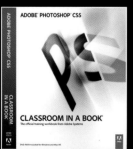

The fastest, easiest, most comprehensive way to learn
Adobe® Creative Suite® 5

Classroom in a Book®, the best-selling series of hands-on software training books, helps you learn the features of Adobe software quickly and easily.

The **Classroom in a Book** series offers what no other book or training program does—an official training series from Adobe Systems, developed with the support of Adobe product experts.

To see a complete list of our Adobe® Creative Suite® 5 titles go to www.peachpit.com/adobecs5

Adobe**Press**